LOVE

— AND —

HEALING

A GUIDE TO EMOTIONAL WELLNESS

DR. RUSSELL CLAYTON

BALBOA.PRESS
A DIVISION OF HAY HOUSE

Balboa Press books may be ordered through booksellers or by contacting:

Balboa Press
A Division of Hay House
1663 Liberty Drive
Bloomington, IN 47403
www.balboapress.com
844-682-1282

Because of the dynamic nature of the Internet, any web addresses or links contained in this book may have changed since publication and may no longer be valid. The views expressed in this work are solely those of the author and do not necessarily reflect the views of the publisher, and the publisher hereby disclaims any responsibility for them.

The author of this book does not dispense medical advice or prescribe the use of any technique as a form of treatment for physical, emotional, or medical problems without the advice of a physician, either directly or indirectly. The intent of the author is only to offer information of a general nature to help you in your quest for emotional and spiritual well-being. In the event you use any of the information in this book for yourself, which is your constitutional right, the author and the publisher assume no responsibility for your actions.

Any people depicted in stock imagery provided by Getty Images are models, and such images are being used for illustrative purposes only.
Certain stock imagery © Getty Images.

Print information available on the last page.

ISBN: 978-1-9822-6200-6 (sc)
ISBN: 978-1-9822-6198-6 (hc)
ISBN: 978-1-9822-6199-3 (e)

Library of Congress Control Number: 2021900834

Balboa Press rev. date: 05/27/2021

CONTENTS

PREFACE

Love And Healing is a spiritual guidebook designed to assist in the healing of your past emotional trauma. I seek to shed light and attention on ancient honored healing techniques. It is my intention to further open the spiritual eyes of the seekers of truth, and to offer keys, mantras, and exercises to reach and expand your sacred heart. I have endeavored to make every word of this manuscript as simple, familiar, and inspirational as possible. I have poured life and divine energy into each word so that this book is forever energetically charged and capable of opening your heart and touching your soul. This book is a map inward to your inner space. This inward journey to connect with your soul can only be undertaken by you. These seventy exercises are virtual checkpoints to help guide you on your journey. Some lessons are purposefully repetitive and appear in multiple chapters. This is to highlight their importance and significance. This manuscript serves to remind you of the many rivers of consciousness that you must cross to get to abundant self-love and deep spiritual healing.

Your Invitation to Healing

*Welcome! I invite you to open the door to your sacred heart and start your restorative healing journey. Now is the time to turn your awareness inward towards healing your past trauma and blocked energy. On these pages I have outlined how negative emotions and subconscious beliefs can lead to disease. Take this opportunity to learn how to control your thoughts and become the master of your mind. This manuscript puts an intense magnifying glass on healing and emphasizes the rich library of healing methods within your grasp. Everything that you need to heal is already available to you. Many of these ancient secrets and healing traditions have been buried by time. My aim is to bring these beautiful elements of natural healing to light for all to see and to use. Inside this book are useful exercises and life lessons to help bring you into wellness. Don't procrastinate anymore, kickstart your healing journey today. Use your soul as a compass to follow your magnetic true north. **Love And Healing** is a reliable tool for your toolbelt on your journey of deep healing and self-restoration. Along the way, you will awaken to remember the light from which you have come. It is my intention to guide you into alignment with your mind, heart, body, and soul. I offer you these ancient practices, mindsets, hacks, techniques, and exercises to assist you in your times of need on your magnificent journey.*

~ Namaste ~

INTRODUCTION

Transformational healing takes place in the space in which you take a step back and add forgiveness, compassion, gratitude, and unconditional love to your daily life. In the dimension where true healing takes place, it doesn't matter what you are doing or what transgressions you have committed. Radically forgive yourself, replenish yourself, and love yourself. Healing represents the end of conflict inside your mind. Start your healing journey today. Start wherever and however you find yourself right now. Be aware that deep healing takes place at the level of your spirit and it's energy impact radiates and shines outwardly. Once your healing arrives it brightens your aura, which results in a deeper penetration of your energetic power and potential impact on the world. When you are finally able to overcome the addiction to your emotions, you break the cycle of suffering and find freedom. Once your body-mind is free, you can look at your scars from past trauma with understanding and forgiveness. This spiritual healing happens by keeping your full attention in the present moment, the space where nothing else matters. May love be your light and may grace be upon you. Let the healing begin. Ten years ago, I set the intention to live each day of my life as a better version of myself. This manuscript is the reflection and manifestation of my brightest dreams for humanity as living and loving emanations of the Divine.

What's your special talent?
Make service to others your priority.
The world needs your unique gift.
Share your blessings with those that need it the most.
Heal yourself. Help a friend.
Love deeper. Heal the planet.

CHAPTER 1

THE HUMAN CONDITION AND THE JOURNEY OF ALL SOULS

HUMAN CONSCIOUSNESS TODAY

We are aware that all generations of our ancestors and future generations are present inside us. We are one as human beings, we are all on a continuous journey of never-ending change and advancement into greater forms of ourselves. What you make of yourself in this life is what you will be upon your death. If you are full of love and compassion at the time of your death, you will be born again into love and compassion in your next life. Conversely, if you choose to fill your spirit with anger and hatred in this life, it will be your starting point in your next life. Everything you are at the point of your death is what you bring forward into your next life. With this in mind, you will come to realize that every moment of life matters. As more human beings awaken, the entire universe becomes more evolved. There is only one life form in the entire universe that is capable of awakening and we are that, this is humanity.

THE INFORMATION AGE OF TECHNOLOGY

Science and technology have advanced more rapidly than ever. Since the year 2000, we as human beings are sicker and more depressed than ever. We are an aging society that is living longer lives than ever before. Ironically, our aging population is placing increasing strain on our current healthcare system. The entire nation is overwhelmed with older patients, yet our healthcare networks fail to adequately reach our most rural areas. Access and affordability to basic healthcare is simply unavailable to millions of people worldwide. The soaring costs of prescription drugs is leading many to abandon their much needed medications. Increasingly, Westerners have been practicing more ancient Eastern healing techniques to fill in the current void and need. Indeed the world is in need of healing.

This is the age of information and technology. There are new groundbreaking discoveries and innovations happening every single day. New discoveries in quantum physics and epigenetics have increased our understanding of the role of our thoughts and emotions in our overall health. The age of technology and the internet have made unimaginable amounts of information available to us at our fingertips. This volume of information has contributed to the onset of a greater sense of awareness about spirituality amongst the world's population. As a society, we are constantly evolving into a higher state of consciousness. The global pandemic of 2020 has unleashed massive global suffering never seen before. We must remember that suffering, while painful, also opens the door to spiritual transformation. The volatile political climate of today is also pushing our spiritual consciousness at a higher rate of speed. Thousands of souls are awakening to their higher selves everyday. The current world population is roughly two trillion souls, can you imagine the positive effect on humanity of a world with millions of awakened souls?

THE CURRENT HEALTHCARE CRISIS

Due to recent worldwide events of social unrest and the COVID-19 pandemic, there has been a surge in the rates of anxiety, depression, and suicide. Many people are suffering from symptoms of PTSD. It's common knowledge that there are psychological, emotional, and environmental components to every disease of the body. For example, it is proven that chronic worrying leads to disorders of the stomach. The majority of doctor visits today deal with stress-related illnesses. Unprocessed emotions are the cause of many of today's physical illnesses. Whenever and wherever you bury your pain, it eventually becomes an energy blockage and causes you to suffer. Chronic stress and trauma impairs our immune system's ability to fight against dangerous viral and bacterial infections. Remember, the accumulation of dis-ease in your spirit most definitely leads to disease inside your body-mind.

The Energetic Significance of 2020

1. **Shift**: This year we are all experiencing an epic shift of human consciousness. New higher frequencies of awareness are presenting themselves and are available to you.
2. **Calling**: The current worldwide crisis is a calling for your individual transformation and evolution into a realized soul.
3. **Reset**: Today's world events present an opportunity to make upgrades and advancements in understanding your dynamic relationship between you and the power of the universe.

4. **Realign**: The end goal is remembrance and realignment with Source by recentering yourself in love.

WHAT LIES BEYOND CONVENTIONAL MEDICINE? THE FUTURE OF HOLISTIC MEDICINE

Our bodies are intricately connected micro-systems run by natural intelligence. The term "holistic" simply means that we're looking to treat and heal the complete system rather than the individual parts. Holistic medicine accounts for both the mind and the entire body, as opposed to specialized or compartmentalized medicine, which just treats one organ system or just a part of it without taking into account the whole organism. Holistic medicine therefore considers a person's mental, emotional, and social factors— not just their physical symptoms. This is why many people are finding alternative medicine more and more compelling. This is because they feel less like a patient and more like a human being.

People who have the same DNA, who have the same
susceptibility to illness, one can become ill and the other can stay well.
One can heal and the other can't. All because they optimize
the environmental factors that control gene activity and
that's what the field of epigenetics is all about.
~ Joan Borysenko, PhD

BIOENERGETICS AND EPIGENETICS

The science of epigenetics, which literally means "control above genetics," profoundly changes our understanding of how life is controlled. The idea is that a past trauma can leave a chemical tag or mark on a person's genes, which is then passed down to subsequent generations. The mark doesn't directly damage the gene itself, there's no mutation. The alteration isn't genetic. This is epigenetics; where the expression of genes are modified without changing the DNA code itself. Current studies suggest that we inherit a trace of our parents' and grandparents' experience, particularly their suffering. This negatively impacts our health and perhaps the health of our children's children as well. The idea is that we carry some biological trace of our ancestors' pain. This concept resonates with the feelings that arise whenever anyone views images of famine, war, or slavery. It seems to support current psychodynamic narratives about ancestral trauma. Suffering travels through time, reverberates through generations, and has the potential to go up and down your family tree.

The human body is made up of a vast intelligent community of cells inside a larger microbiome which is constantly adapting, self-regulating, and healing itself. Your amazing body miraculously creates new cells everyday. If you start to add and integrate new age belief practices of wellness and vitality, those same beliefs and practices will influence your newborn cells to function at a higher level.

In the last decade, epigenetic research has established that
DNA blueprints passed down through genes are not set in concrete at birth.
Genes are not destiny! Environmental influences, including nutrition,
stress and emotions can modify those genes without
changing their basic blueprint.
And those modifications, epigeneticists have discovered,
can be passed onto future generations as surely as DNA
blueprints are passed on via the double helix.
~ Dr. Bruce Lipton

QUANTUM PHYSICS

Quantum physics is essentially the space where math and science meet consciousness and spirituality. Quantum physics proves our intimate connection with the majestic universe that surrounds us. In 1984, quantum physicists discovered that the atom was not the smallest particle in the universe. It was discovered that atoms are made up of even smaller subatomic elements. A human body is made up of over a trillion cells. Each cell contains over one hundred million molecules. Each single molecule contains over a billion atoms. Quantum physicists have discovered that physical atoms are made up of tiny tornado-like vortices of energy, that are constantly spinning and vibrating, each one radiating its own unique energy signature. These elements are what make up the structure of an atom. If you focus in closer on the structure of the atom, you would see empty space, a literal void.

This phenomenon is similar to the relationship between the stars and the universe. The universe is composed of mostly empty space. The stars are the physical matter of the universe but represent less than one percent of the vast universe itself. By this light, human beings are also mostly empty energetic space, we are more invisible than we are solid. Einstein's work revealed that we do not live in a universe with discrete, physical objects separated by dead space. The universe is alive in one indivisible dynamic whole. A space in which energy and matter are so deeply entangled that it's impossible to consider them as independent.

> *The atoms of our bodies are traceable to the stars that manufactured*
> *them in their cores and exploded these enriched ingredients across*
> *our galaxy, billions of years ago. For this reason, we are*
> *biologically connected to every other living thing in the world.*
> *We are chemically connected to all molecules on earth.*
> *And we are atomically connected to all atoms in the universe.*
> *We are not figuratively, but literally stardust.*
> *~ Neil deGrasse Tyson*

IMAGINE YOURSELF AS LIGHT AND ENERGY

The body and mind is constantly changing, but the soul is eternal. Your soul is composed of subatomic particles of pure consciousness with no beginning or end. Your most powerful state is that of knowing; the realization and acceptance of your truth. You can always become more aware of who you really are. You accomplish this by learning how to remain as pure awareness. The more you practice being the witness of your thought patterns and energy fields, the more adept you will become at closing the distance between you and your higher self. In your highest energy state, there is no separation between you and your God Essence. Alignment with your soul may only take place in the present moment, that's why it's so crucial to reside in the Now.

Being caught up in your emotions is to be trapped in the chemical residue of the past. Most people can't find their soul because their identity is chained to their body. To upgrade your identity to the level of your higher self, you must transcend your body-mind and come into alignment with your soul.

THE HEALING POWER OF ENERGY

If the Chi, the "Prana", or life force energy gets stuck somewhere inside you from an emotional and spiritual level and it is not addressed, then over time that blockage will lead to an actual physical blockage in your body. The idea is to release your emotional blockages before they cause you bodily harm. There are countless ways to release your negative stored emotions. Emotions can only get stuck in your body after you develop an attachment to them. The key to releasing your emotional attachments is to raise your energy. Higher frequency vibrations bring peace and calm. In order to elevate, some people do yoga, zumba, pilates, meditation, exercise, or hire a therapist. Others travel to distant lands for spiritual interventions. Some people take Ayahuasca. Others simply start their healing journey and find peace in knowing that their spiritual awakening is tied to the overall wellness of their bodies.

RAISING YOUR VIBRATION, VIBRATIONAL DNA

The simple way for you to raise your vibrational energy is by shifting your awareness to the present moment. Your DNA is being created every single day and is stamped with the history of your emotions. The DNA that you create today can be no greater than the power of its source.

The most beautiful experience we can have is the mysterious.
It is the fundamental emotion that stands at the
cradle of true art and true science.
~ Albert Einstein

Tips to Remain in Present Moment Awareness

- **Find a moment to be alone with yourself.**
- **Let your mind become soft, receptive, and permeable.**
- **Get silent and still.**
- **Imagine seeing yourself as energy: "light as a feather'"**
- **Feel yourself floating freely in the universal field.**
- **Take three conscious breaths and open up to your deeper dimension.**

- **Activate your five senses.**
- **Slow down time by becoming the witness of your experience.**
- **Experience timelessness.**
- **Access your power of intuition in your sacred heart.**
- **Be at peace with yourself.**

MULTI-SENSORY HUMANS

We are evolving from our five senses as humans into multi-sensory beings. Author Gary Zukov says, "The perceptions of a multi-system sensory being, extend beyond physical reality to the larger dynamic system, of which our physical reality is a part. The multi-sensory being is able to perceive and appreciate the role that our physical reality plays in a larger picture of evolution and the dynamics by which our physical reality is created and sustained. This realm is invisible to the five-sensory human." There are two notions that should be kept at the forefront of your mind; the first is that everyone is moving towards becoming a more spiritual being. The second is that the process must be experienced and tested by each and every person in their own way and at their own pace. The journey of awakening has many roads, but they all lead to the same place, oneness with Source.

DIVINE ENERGY PERSONIFIED

All beings are divine in the sense that all living entities are sparks of God. As humans, our light is encased in our body-mind temples. As each person is born into the physical world we instantly become love temporarily hidden from itself with no awareness of our true nature. The most important part of our spiritual journey is the remembering of who you really are. The divine essence of you awaits your readiness and willingness to receive it. Once you decide to let go of your old useless mindsets your divine energy flows, until then it won't. You are divine when you finally believe that you are. Nothing needed, nothing conceded. Coming into alignment with your divine nature clears karmic baggage. It's like an electric current that runs through your body. Spiritual transformation brings your inner light forward so that your physical self can merge into you, the light vessel. It's transformational in that it empowers a person to go far beyond their believed physical limitations. It transforms a normal human into a divine human. Ultimately, when we remember our true nature, soul consciousness expands and our inner light shines forth for all to see.

The definition of divine means God-like. You are a piece of God-like energy created in the image of God. Divine nature can be seen as a cup overflowing with infinite wisdom and intelligence as it's foundation. It is by increased awareness of this ever-expanding quality whereby miracles are performed and wholeness is restored. This is why we are here on earth, to remember and display our true selves. Each human being is divine love personified. Blessed with the gift of life and the treasure of heart intelligence. Certain genes have a timer on them and get expressed in divine moments in your life. We are each born into this world to leave our positive, unique, and historical imprint on humanity. To the extent that God lives within you, you are immortal.

AWAKENING IS THE CALLING OF ALL SOULS

The soul is a seed of immortal spirit placed inside each of us by God. The philosopher Ralph Waldo Emerson likened the soul to the sun, too bright to be gazed upon directly, yet by it we see all things. He also pictured it as a vast ocean, with our individual souls seen as waves, emerging for a time and then returning to the whole. There are no such things as "lost souls," in Emerson's view, there are only people who have forgotten their connection to soul. That connection can be rediscovered and nurtured by looking within.

Your spiritual awakening is not a choice, it's a calling. Awakening is the calling of all souls to realize the interrelatedness of life. It's happening for you right now, whether you realize it or not. What's stopping you from alignment with your higher self is nothing but your ego and multiple old layers of trauma. Use each day to practice your spiritual alignment. The more you connect with your inner essence, the more you become one with God. Once you reclaim your divine power you will no longer see yourself or believe yourself to be a poor helpless victim.

Everyday you are literally rewriting your biological programs and signaling the formation of new genes in your body thereby creating a new genetic destiny. The more emotionally balanced you feel, the more chemically and physically balanced you will become. If healing is your objective then you must develop a healing mindset. To be completely healed you must change the way you think, feel, talk, and walk through your experiences.

CHAPTER 2

INNER RESTORATIVE HEALING

THE HEALING JOURNEY

The healing journey is different for everyone. The journey requires self-analysis and self-discovery to uncover the hidden sources of your pain. Somehow we all must get better at processing the stress and strain that life inherently brings. Our tech driven society is moving at a rapid pace. As technology continues to push mankind towards greater innovations, the need to "keep up" brings additional wellness concerns and burdens to the table. Those who don't keep abreast of the latest technology risk being separated by the digital divide. In today's world, stress is now the main cause of most diseases. The impact of the medical sequelae of stress and its costs are having a profound impact on billions of people's health. The way to healing is always just around the corner. You must look for it to find it, and when do, you must uncover it, love it, and embrace it. The healing journey is the way broken hearts mend and the way tattered spirits become whole again.

INNER RESTORATIVE HEALING: THE NEED FOR A GLOBAL HEALING OF ALL HUMANITY

Rising rates of obesity, morbidity, anxiety, depression, chronic diseases, cancer, and suicide all point to a looming devastating worldwide health crisis. The world is truly in desperate need of healing and global healing starts with each and every one of us. There is no superhero coming to save the world. It's up to you to intentionally heal your inner world which assists in the healing of your outer world. The world needs you to be your most magnificent self. You are a manifestation of the Divine. Your connection with Source is the key component to healing yourself. Inner Restorative Healing (IRH) is an integrated healthcare program that I developed which establishes a three way connection between you the patient, you the healer, and Source Energy. Once this amazing 3-way divine connection is made, true transformative healing takes place. Restorative healing recharges your life and restores proper rhythm to your mind, body, heart, and soul.

To tap into the force of the universe itself,
we must see ourselves as part of it, rather than separate from it.
~ Gregg Braden

BECOME A RECEIVER TO THE UNIVERSE AND INVITE HEALING INTO YOUR LIFE

The universe is full of energy and you can harness it to reduce your stress, tension, body aches, diseases, pains, and suffering. The key to activation is to become a better receiver of Source energy. Say yes to your healing and start your journey, it's time to change your fortune. Your decision to invite healing into your life is a win-win situation. The more you state your intention to heal and master your emotions, your healing accelerates. Every time you visualize your healing all the way to completion, you attract it closer to you. Visualization increases the likelihood that your dreams will one day manifest. Healing is like planting. Declaring the deliberate intention to heal yourself plants a seed and initiates a creative action plan which eventually produces a plant. Use this intuitive guidebook to choose your own healing methods.

PLACEBO VS. NOCEBO AND THE SPONTANEOUS HEALING OF BELIEF

If you don't believe in your own healing, it can't happen for you. Sometimes the power of faith is the only belief that's required to heal. Indeed positive thinking has been proven to have a strong healing effect. In the scientific world, this is known as the placebo effect. As a physician, I define placebo as a pill which has no pharmacological effect, but satisfies a patient who supposes it to be a medicine. Sometimes anything presented as a medicine will work. In my office practice, the placebo effect is a commonly seen phenomenon where people get relief from their physical symptoms simply from taking a sugar pill. The placebo effect is extraordinarily powerful because it demonstrates that positive beliefs are capable of shifting biology. The hidden question is: "Do we heal from the medicines physicians prescribe, or do we innately heal from our own divine energy?" Current research points to the mind-body connection as the biggest contributor to healing. Strong beliefs are capable of influencing and shifting our body's healing potential. We don't perceive truth, we perceive what we believe to be true. Restoring belief in oneself has been proven to have a profound effect on a person's mood, circumstances, and outcomes. Without a doubt, the power of belief is the most powerful agent of change in our lives.

> *Whether you think you can or*
> *think you can't, you're right.*
> *~ Henry Ford*

It's important to mention that in addition to the placebo effect of positive thinking, there is an equal and opposite effect that negative thinking has on healing. What can heal can also harm. The "nocebo effect" is an adverse reaction to negative ideas in the mind. It's a negative effect which worsens a patient's current symptoms, due to the onset of new adverse symptoms. The nocebo effect is triggered by disbelief in the effectiveness of a therapy or a belief that a particular therapy is harmful. Researchers have proven that women who believed they were prone to heart disease were four times more likely to develop heart problems than women who are at the same risk factors, but lacked a negative mindset. Similarly, the nocebo effect sometimes causes bad side effects from a medicine because the patient was already expecting side effects. It could also mean that there will be no effect at all from a medicine containing an active ingredient, because the patient expects there to be no effect. In conclusion, both placebo and nocebo effects are presumably psychogenic, but they can both induce measurable changes in the body. This all illustrates the importance of maintaining a high quality of thoughts during any recovery period. A positive attitude attracts positive results.

APPLYING THE LAW OF ATTRACTION TO YOUR ADVANTAGE

The universe sends you situations that have the same energy of your vibration. Based on the universes' law of attraction, whatever vibration you hold, it is mirrored in your life. If you are happy, then happiness will follow you. If you are anxious, then anxiety will find you. Sadness will create more sad situations to feel sad about. Remember that your emotions are in fact a guidance system which is designed to guide you through life. Take note of your emotions throughout the day and remind yourself that you are not your circumstances. Surround yourself with the people and connections that bring you happiness. Whenever you experience negative vibrations in your life, redirect yourself. Keep your positive energy flowing. Always align with love and trust your higher self to make the difficult choices in your life. Every journey is powered by the energy of momentum. In life, the law of attraction turns your thoughts into energetic creations and divine manifestations. LOA activation requires you to send your desires into the universe without the illusion of controlling your outcomes. The one that surrenders their healing to God will know inner peace. Visualize yourself being healed, act as if you are fully healed and you shall be healed in the Mind of God, now and forever.

The longer you focus upon something, the more powerful it becomes; the stronger that your point of attraction is to it, the more evidence of it appears in your life experience. Whether you are focusing upon things you want or things you do not want, the evidence of your thoughts continually flows toward you. If something you want is slow to come to you, it can be for only one reason: You are spending more time focused upon its absence than you are about its presence.
~ Esther Hicks

EXERCISE #1
Law of Attraction Exercise

State Three Clear Objectives of Your Healing Journey:

1. _____
2. _____
3. _____

VISUALIZATION AND HEALING

Paint a mental picture of yourself in your fully desired healed state. Keep this image of yourself in your mind's eye at all times. Once you state your intentions to the universe, the universe hears you and responds appropriately. Always reach for your highest possible outcomes in life. Try to live everyday as the healed version of yourself. Let go of the false notion that you are in control of your healing process. Surrender is the process of releasing control, letting go, and trusting the universe to deliver your healing in divine time. The universe is abundant and there's more than enough of everything to go around. When you live in true abundance, you remember that you came from Source— unlimited inner power and potential in human form.

In treatment, go beyond the disease and apply a spiritual consciousness.
The treatment is not complete without a great realization of life and love,
of God and Perfection, of truth and wisdom, and power and reality.
Sense the divine presence in and through the patient at all times.
~ Dr. Ernest Holmes

GOD'S ROLE; IT IS IN GOD'S PRESENCE THAT ALL HEALING TAKES PLACE

The more you welcome the idea of healing into your life, the easier healing becomes. The more connected you become with Source Energy, the greater the depth of penetration of healing you'll receive. Alignment with Source reduces negative resistance from your mind by reducing mind chatter. The moment you let go of your incessant thinking is the very moment you will see immediate improvement in your wellness. Healing includes how you feel. You can't claim healing without an improvement in your happiness quotient. Also, the more you let go of the idea of how healing will come to you, the sooner it comes. Leave every detail to the Mind of God. It is in God's presence that all healing takes place. Surrender to presence, surrender to love, surrender to grace, and surrender to God. God's wealth is currency and is always circulating in your life. This full surrender and release lessens all negative noise from your mind and opens up your heart and soul to receive its divine healing in whatever form it takes. Everything happens in your life after you invite it, so invite divine healing into your life.

If your body is screaming in pain, whether the pain is muscular contractions, anxiety, depression, asthma or arthritis, a first step in releasing the pain may be making the connection between your body pain and the cause. Beliefs are physical. A thought held long enough and repeated enough becomes a belief. The belief then becomes biology.

~ Marilyn Van M. Derbur

CHAPTER 3

YOU ARE A HEALER, START BY HEALING YOURSELF

YOU ARE A HEALER. YOUR HEALING POWERS HAVE ALWAYS BEEN WITH YOU

You come from a long lineage of healers, that lineage is humanity. For centuries, mankind has always given compassionate aid and support to those in need. Indeed kindness, compassion, empathy, and love are essential ingredients of being human. We are all healers, your healing powers have always been with you. You have all the medicine that you need to heal yourself and others as well. As proof, you often bring joy and happiness to people with a simple smile or pat on their back. Every act or word of encouragement that you have ever spoken travels deep into the universe. In some way, each one of us has touched another so deeply that it literally changed their life's trajectory. You will never truly know how many people's lives you've changed, but rest assured, you have changed many and blessed thousands of people with your smile and presence along the way.

ENERGETIC HEALING

We are now entering the era of energetic medicine. Everything in the universe has an energetic nature, a specific frequency. All you have to do in order to influence a certain vibration is tune into or create a matching frequency. That's how easy it is for you to change anything in your life; whether it be your state of mind, emotional issues, or the behavior of the cells in your body. This mindfulness of your energetic self is the new essential in mind-body healing.

Energetic or spiritual healing begins with the realization that everything is energy. All thoughts, words, dreams, memories, smells, colors, and every movement, has a unique frequency and flow of energy. Your body is a living, active, and diverse energy vortex whose epicenter is a radiant energetic soul. In your healing journey you will regain your ability to detect, feel, and move energy fields. It sounds complicated, but it isn't. You already have everything that you need to modulate your own frequency. You have the innate ability to assess your current vibrational energy and consciously get rid of any negativity you're holding onto. In your highest energetic state you will be able to monitor your thoughts, honor your emotions, trust your intuition, open your sacred heart, and heal your mind and body.

SET THE INTENTION TO HEAL YOURSELF AND BECOME THE CATALYST OF YOUR OWN ACTIVATION

You have the divine inner power to heal yourself, indeed every single organ in your body has the power to heal itself. What every great healer starts with is the intention to heal. Spiritual healing can only take place in the realm of belief. Your intention is the powerful catalyst needed to kickstart healing. Intention is the precursor to manifestation. What's needed to activate your healing is a spark. The catalyst in your equation is you. Your mind-body connection is the "inner environment" that author Greg Braden speaks of. When it comes to healing, perhaps the most important factor is knowing that you have the power to change your mindset and to redirect the emotions in your heart to serve yourself. In the end, the rest is up to you. You are the one with the keys to your own liberation. Alas, healing is not an event, it's a process wrapped in time. In the end, your healing is the greatest comeback you can dream of. The major ingredient for a successful and productive spiritual recovery is unwavering devotion. Be devoted to your healing practices everyday and you will soon see positive results beyond your imagination.

ENERGY BLOCKS

Past pain and suffering have caused some energetic blockages in your body. The best way to clear an energy block is to cleanse, meditate, and pray on it. These blockages accumulate along fascial planes and create blocks at your chakra zones. For example: a common blockage occurs at the heart chakra. Heart blockages are the invisible walls built in your heart by your ego meaning to protect you from further heartbreak. In reality, these heart blockages prevent you from fully opening up emotionally in your relationships, which limits your potential. Clearing these energetic blockages enhances your energetic flow.

HEAL YOURSELF BY DELIBERATE INTENTION

Take your healing into your own hands. Your most powerful tool is your ability to change your mind and body. The first priority is to set your intention to heal. Verbalize your intentions daily to become a better version of yourself. Remember to create and set your intentions only when you are in your highest vibrational state. When you get creative and set your intentions from a high frequency, they have more power and penetrate deeper into the universal field. This is more desirable as opposed to setting your intentions when you are sad. Creating while you're in a state of lack always yields inferior outcomes. Make healing your primary mission and be focused and determined about getting it done. The power of healing is always boosted by your belief in it. No matter what you are suffering from, begin to see yourself as already healed mentally, physically, emotionally, and spiritually. Store mental images of your future self in your mind's eye. You have never been incomplete. You have simply lost the awareness that you are whole. Step into your divine light and begin healing yourself by deliberate intention. Start to imagine the process of your transformation coming to light. Visualize yourself cleared of your dis-ease and living in a state of wellness. Look at your healing as a return to wholeness and shift your attention towards reaching your greatest potential.

Do not be dismayed at the brokenness of the world.
All things break and all things can be mended.
Not with time as they say, but by intention, so go.
Love intentionally, extravagantly and unconditionally.
The whole world is waiting in darkness
for the light that is you.
~ L. R. Knost

WHERE AND HOW TO START YOUR HEALING

First, start by showing love and compassion to yourself. Extend the power of forgiveness to those around you. Be grateful for your existence and your ability to heal. Your mindset is the very key to unlocking the chains that are still holding you back. You have the ability to free yourself. Stop being your own worst enemy and get out of your own way. You were not created to live a mediocre life. Your healing is a choice that only you can make. The key to healing is to pray for acceptance of your divine truth. All that happened to you in your past was for a reason. The past is not your burden to carry your whole life, your struggles point you to what truths you must accept about yourself and what you need to heal and transcend.

Now is always the perfect time for change, get started in your healing journey today. If you don't like what you are seeing in your life, change the type of seed you are planting. An uncommon seed makes an uncommon harvest. Seeds are merely intentions in your life. Invite gratitude, patience, integrity, faith, courage, surrender, and love into your future. When you plant seeds in your life, expect your intentions to manifest. You are a miracle maker. Open your hand and release your seeds into the fertile universe. You won't be losing your seeds, you will be gaining a harvest. The opportunity for personal freedom is here now. You can't heal if you don't try. Once you decide to heal your past suffering, you literally activate and initiate your healing process. The doors you need to open will open, the people you need will appear, and your healing will come.

EXERCISE #2
Create a Vision Board

Make a vision board for your healing journey.
Paste quotes and photos, activities, practices,
therapies, mantras, and goals that reflect
and inspire you to complete your journey. Make
a timeline to accomplish your goals.
Picture yourself already healed and keep
that image in your mind's eye.
Hold yourself accountable for your effort, consistency always pays off.
Dedication, commitment, and persistence makes any journey easier.
See yourself completing your journey and
living a healthy, vigorous, and abundant life.

HEALING HACK

Recognize the repetitive patterns in your life. When life sequences are repetitive, it suggests that you are not advancing your consciousness fast enough. The easiest way to fast track your life is to start making vastly different choices. Veer away from safe but old mindsets and habits that've never served you. Choose wisely and behave differently than in the past. Make sure that you make your important decisions from the platitude of your higher self. You are the first one capable of doing what no one else in your lineage has ever done. You have the power to heal the trauma of generations before and after you.

IN ORDER TO HEAL YOUR TRAUMA YOU'VE GOT TO FEEL YOUR FEEL YOUR EMOTIONS

Emotional trauma results in disruption of connectivity with your higher self. Now is the time to heal and love the aspects of you that have left you feeling uneasy, inadequate, and unworthy. Honesty, truth, authenticity, and power are characteristics of your true self. Learn to become comfortable residing as the greater you. Higher consciousness is scary because it's perceived by the ego to be risky. Your ego will have you to believe that such a journey is unnecessary and potentially harmful. In fact, the only risk to taking on your spiritual journey is the loss of unawareness.

When you open your heart to access your deepest emotions, your feelings can be used as a guidance system to deliver your brightest possible outcomes. Stop believing that you are a prisoner of your past. Stop worrying about a future that you do not control. Immerse yourself in the present moment and live love now! Walk towards your inner fire and sit with your soul. When you step into your divine light, you are not only transformed, you are reborn.

You have long had the power to create worlds, you also have the ability to summon the exact experiences you need to elevate your consciousness. You are of the Most High. Life has you believing the illusion that you are merely flesh and blood, when who you really are is a spirit wrapped in earthly experiences. The real you is matterless, shapeless, formless, and unlimited. Turn your pain into presence. When we see ourselves as spirit, we unveil the true power of our species, which is belief. Once you believe that you are mostly non-physical, your greatest story begins to unfold.

THE ESSENTIAL QUESTIONNAIRE FOR HEALING

- Are you happy with your life right now?
- Are you still suffering from an experience long ago in your emotional past?
- Is your past identity your present view of yourself?
- Are you seeing yourself as flexible and ever-changing, or rigid and fixed?
- How are you participating in and contributing to your current problems?
- What have you learned about yourself from your past mistakes?
- Can you imagine a different, more powerful version of yourself in the future?
- What character traits, tools, or resources can you use to level up, go inside, and make the necessary changes?
- What does your support team look like? Who is in, and who is out?
- Are you willing to accept professional help in order to heal?
- New solutions call for a new mindset which includes New Age healing techniques like: meditation, mindfulness, self-hypnosis, natural diet, exercise, and behavioral therapy. What is your plan for healing?

DEVELOP YOUR HEALING MENTALITY
SEE YOURSELF AS ALREADY HEALED

A healing mentality is essential for anyone on a spiritual journey. You are not complete yet, see your life as a work in progress. Visualize your endgame everyday and work your plan. There are no limitations to what you can manifest, if you can see it, you can do it. Align with your higher self starting in the early morning at sunrise. This action alone, puts you in the mindset of creation and deliberate manifestation. As you continue your way forward, you will begin to attract others who live in higher consciousness. Don't let haters or energy vampires distract you from your higher purpose. It's very important to surround yourself with people that you admire, inspire you, and those who you can learn from. This action alone elevates your consciousness and advances your spiritual healing.

The Four Layers of Healing:

1. **Keep a positive mindset.**
2. **Seek and identify your triggers, don't try to avoid them. Your triggers merely point to aspects of yourself that are in need of love and healing.**
3. **Surround yourself with other conscious people, positive thoughts, and uplifting activities.**
4. **Avoid relapses into any past unconscious behaviors or habits.**

CLAIM YOUR HEALING

You are blessed with divine intelligence, self-awareness, and unimaginable powers of energy and recovery. However, many people don't fully manifest their intentions because they truly don't believe that it's possible to happen for them, thus they remain suspended in the spell of disbelief. What is true is that we are all suffering our experience. Everyone is suffering their own shame, blame, guilt, trauma, thoughts, emotions, fears, and pains of the past and present. Now is the time to claim your healing. It is important to see your healing as already done. All things are possible in the Mind of God.

A deep healing cleanse of your spirit creates a simultaneous upshift in your perception of reality. This also includes an acceptance and embrace of a new mindset, the one of the healer. You are a natural born healer, but in order to master the art of healing, you must first remember how to heal yourself. The journey of healing lies in the remembering that you are a spark of divine love. From that altitude, you can use the power of love to work for yourself and also for others. Don't be confused by the unpredictable events happening in the world. Stay clear in your mission and remain focused on your dreams. The path of least resistance is the way and the answer is always love.

How can you become what you want to become?
You can do it only when you feel that you alone can never make
yourself what you want to become. No human power can do it.
Only by the Grace that comes from above can you do
what you want to do and become what you want to become.
~ Sri Chinmoy

The Ten Principles of Emotional Healing

1. Your healing is activated and powered by your intention to heal.
2. You are responsible for your own healing. Make healing your mission.
3. The purpose of healing is to remove all energetic blockages from your mind, body, heart, and spirit.
4. The roots of emotional trauma are deep and unseen, it is essential that you discover, uncover, and overcome them.
5. Emotional trauma is formed and stored in your long term memory, and then manifests as unease and disease in your body-mind.
6. Fully identifying, feeling, and processing your buried childhood pain is critical to your recovery.
7. No matter what you are suffering from, begin to see yourself as already healed mentally, physically, emotionally, and spiritually.
8. Complete energetic healing is a reflection of total freedom from your body-mind.
9. Until you heal yourself, you will continue to pass your suffering onto future generations.
10. Once you heal yourself, help others to do the same.

WHAT IT MEANS TO BE HEALED

To be healed is not to be free of struggle. To be healed is to live through your pain and allow it to pass through you. You don't need medicine to heal, you just have to connect with the energy of healing. In healing you shed old energies that are not a part of your destiny. Healing results in the emergence of your authentic true self. At your core you are one with the wind, your soul is as free as a bird in flight.

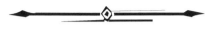

Healing Session

**Emotional Release Exercise: Laugh, Cry, and Scream Therapy
Take a moment to express your sadness and discomfort in
whatever way feels most appropriate to generate a positive
healing session for you. Laugh, cry or scream at the top of
your lungs. Allow yourself to feel the roots of your pain and
allow it to move through you, out of your body, and into
the universe. You may not be strong enough to carry
the burden of your problems, but fortunately the universe is
more than capable of carrying your load for you. Speak your
truth aloud in whatever way that you can. Be thankful.
Ask for forgiveness. Pray for strength, courage,
and patience. Ask to be healed.
Aim to be at peace with yourself. When you find
inner peace, you will find God there.**

HEALING IS POWERED BY INTENTION, MAKE AN ACTION PLAN

Emotional healing starts with you. You are wise enough to recognize the importance of the task before you, and you can do it! In emotional healing, it's necessary to reestablish your true identity as your higher self. Adjust your current mindset to incorporate the belief that you can be healed of your worst affliction. You will never heal your emotional self without activating and implementing a plan of action. Your journey is not about learning how to become a healer, your journey is about remembering, recognizing, and believing yourself to be, a natural born healer since the day that you were born.

DIVINE HEALING, ALL HEALING IS POSSIBLE

Some healing cannot be explained. The only rationalization is that some healings are true miracles of God. As a boy I suffered two serious accidents. At age eleven, I was the victim of a careless act of a classmate in a science lab. I was accidentally splashed in the face with a concentrated solution of hydrochloric acid. As a result, I suffered third degree burns to fifty percent of my face. I can remember it like it happened yesterday. The second it happened, I could feel the acid burning through my skin. It was my instinct to immediately run to the sink and run cold water on my face. I was rushed to the emergency room of the nearest hospital where my wounds were treated. Upon my discharge, I was prescribed a salve of sulfasalazine to put on my face every day. Despite my burns, I never believed that my scars would be long lasting. Every day I was responsible for placing the salve on my wounds. I ceremoniously did so, every hour, every day, for one year. As the months went by, new skin began to grow underneath the dense scars of my wounds. Armed with the powers of belief and devotion, my skin eventually returned to normal. I can tell you that my transformation was truly a miracle to behold and I am grateful to God that I was healed.

EXERCISE #3
The Miracle Question by Ryan Howes

**"Suppose tonight, while you slept, a miracle occurred.
When you awake tomorrow, what would be some of the things
you would notice that would tell you life had suddenly gotten better?
What is the miracle that you wish for?"**

EMOTIONAL HEALING TAKES TIME; BE PATIENT WITH YOURSELF

It doesn't matter how long it takes or how ugly it gets, healing is unpleasant, that's how it works. Your discomfort points out areas of your persona that need your attention and love. Remember to be easy on yourself, emotional healing requires patience and persistence. You are healing thousands of years of outdated conditioning in a relatively short amount of time. Healing your fears, shame, and guilt is a process. Take the time to heal your past and allow love to design your future.

Whatever's missing in your life, you haven't truly valued it enough. What you value and respect is attracted to your life. If deep healing is your top priority, then carve out the space, time, and commitment to do the inner work. There is nothing more important than getting to the root cause of your suffering. Turn your attention towards your wellness and wholeness, then commit to the process. You can do anything you set your mind to. Healing doesn't take place overnight, so along the way, be patient with yourself. Many rewards come to you at the end of your journey. Deep healing brings greater insight and a better understanding of your own complex personality issues. Take time for self-expression during your healing journey. Make sure to take time for a good laugh, cry, scream or yell to get the hurt out of your system. Don't allow your pain to linger and suppress your emotions. You heal by releasing your feelings, not by suppressing them.

It's okay to seek support from healthcare professionals to talk about your troublesome issues. For others who shy away from psychiatrists and therapists consider confiding in a friend that you trust and feel comfortable with. Choose this confidant wisely, everyone won't be empathetic to your story. As you evolve into a greater version of yourself, you may lose some friends and that's okay. Remember that the people who truly love and support you will always be there for you. The ones that stick with you through thick and thin are your angels. Your earth angels give your all the time you need to heal, grow, and evolve into the greater you.

Let your example be the way to change others lives.
Reform yourself and you will reform thousands.
~ Paramahansa Yogananda

BE A CATALYST FOR THE HEALING OF OTHERS

The extent to which you heal yourself is the extent to which you will be able to heal all of your relationships. Once you have healed yourself, prepare yourself to be a healer of others. Identify and reach out to those in your life who need emotional healing. Your primary goal as a healer is to create a safe space around them in the absence of judgement. Listen to them with empathy without the impulse to say something in return. The compassionate action of healing someone starts a chain of reciprocation that comes right back to you. In this way, you and the subject are each touched and blessed by the very same light of love and healing.

Healer heal thyself first, subsequently you will consciously and subconsciously influence others by shining the light of transformation for all to see. Healers heal broken spirits and usher in inspiration and faith. Realized souls don't attempt to match other people's energy, they hold space for them in higher consciousness and raise the frequency of everyone present. We heal one another through shared high vibrational consciousness. It's that way so that every human being can have a taste of pure light which raises the consciousness of the entire collective.

Before you heal someone,
ask them are they willing to
give up what made them sick.
~ Hippocrates

EXERCISE #4
Energy Work by Queen Afua

"The first step in working on someone is to do a body scan.
Use your palm chakras as your eyes to read their energy field.
Have them lie down and breathe quietly, so they are calm and relaxed.
Very slowly move your hands along their
body, get a sense of their energy.

**Stop whenever you come upon an unusual
feeling, a hotspot, a cold spot,
or a void. When you feel a release, a letting go, a sigh, or a deep
breath from a person— your work on that spot is complete.
You will sense that their energy balance has been restored."**

*We must all learn to listen to one another
with understanding and compassion,
to hear what is being felt by the other.
~ Thich Nhat Hanh*

THE POWER OF LISTENING

The most powerful instrument of healing others is your ability to listen. The question is, "Are you going to speak from your judgements and opinions or are you willing to allow love to do the listening?" True listening is an act of love. When love is doing the listening, you connect heart-to-heart with the speaker and they can feel your presence without you saying any words. When your ego is listening, you are only gathering information. Your ability to heal others is a gift. When you come to the aid of someone in need of spiritual healing, it doesn't involve instructing them on what they're doing wrong, but rather supporting them for what they are saying and doing right. Experience the speaker's words from their position by stepping inside his or her shoes. Give them your full attention and put aside your own worries and judgements. Support them with love, kindness, and compassion. Your attention may be the very medicine which heals them and makes them feel whole again. As a healer you don't have to be perfect, you just have to be timely, listen well, and show deep empathy.

EXERCISE #5
Listening With Empathy

Ask someone that you are intending to heal:
"What can I do to support you right now?"
Listen to them without interruption and
respond to them with love, concern, and empathy.

MEET PEOPLE WHERE THEY ARE

Active listening is the healing practice of meeting people where they are, it also promotes positive emotions and trust. It's the process of listening attentively while someone else speaks, paraphrasing and reflecting back on what is said, while withholding judgment and advice. Open and guide the conversation to a meaningful depth. Drill down to the details. Listen for the meaning behind what they are saying. Be empathetic. Try to maintain eye contact, it's important to show your attentiveness. When you sprinkle in positive feedback it indicates that you both hear and understand what they are saying. Use your gestures and body language to show them that you're fully engaged. The aim is to leave the person feeling better about themselves having spoken to you. If appropriate, you can close the impromptu active listening healing session with a hug.

CHAPTER 4

MULTI-SENSORY HEALING THERAPY

Part 1

Source Energy Healing

Silence Therapy

Stillness Therapy

Sleep Therapy

Sound Therapy

Voice Therapy

Music Therapy

Dance Therapy

Play Therapy

Exercise Therapy

MULTI-SENSORY HEALING THERAPY

Multi-Sensory Healing Therapy is a term that I coined to describe the collective healing power of various healing therapies that engage and stimulate each one of your five senses. I have tested my program on thousands of my patients and have a 90% success rate of reducing overthinking, fear, anxiety, emotional turbulence, depression, and pain. Multi-Sensory Healing Therapy is all about opening up your rural pathways to becoming a better receiver to Source Energy. No one is healed by anyone until you are healed by Source.

Each of the therapies mentioned here are ways to lift your mood set-point and raise your vibration. See your entire healing journey in terms of energy. Start by seeing your emotions as tiny outbursts of energy. Become the witness of your rising emotions. If you can self-diagnose your negative emotions, then you can also heal them. Keep one goal in mind, keep raising your personal frequency every single day. The more energy you put into raising your vibration, the better your results will be. In this manuscript, I have gathered together ancient healing practices that are proven to have wellness benefits. Make spiritual healing a daily practice for yourself. An unstable emotional self results in dis-ease in the body. The cure lies in becoming less emotional, yet more spiritual. Emotional release practices are important to apply to your healing journey. Choose a different therapy from the book everyday, or combine several therapies that suit your needs today. Multi-sensory healing therapies are like keys on a piano. Each therapy plays a different note in your healing. When all the notes are playing together, the beautiful music that is created is your healing. The healing song that plays out in the universe is both powerful and invisible. The frequency of the healing song is in the key of love. The power of each of these therapies will help you to attain universal alignment of your mind, body, heart, and soul.

My specialty is working with the mind and helping people see where they're stuck within beliefs of inadequacy. That, for me, is usually a precursor to their suffering. Suffering then stimulates the chemical storm that goes on in their body, but then degenerates their tissues, etc. Until you shift your mindset and beliefs about life, until you find a true inner peace, you can bombard any

kind of disorder that you have and chances are, you may get rid of it for
a sort of transitory period, but it's most likely going to come back.
~ Peter Krohn

SOURCE ENERGY HEALING

For one minute, think of a beautiful waterfall. These amazing wonders of nature have many healing elements to them. The falling water from above creates a symphony of hypnotic sounds as it strikes the rocks and water below. The immense power and glory of nature's waterfalls are a reminder of the absolute magnificence of our planet. To be present here is to simply be in awe of the Creator, and all of creation. The more you connect with your natural intelligence, the more light you receive. Source Energy lifts and uplifts. We awaken ourselves by becoming more aware of our true selves. Becoming and being aware is simply sitting and being one with God. God's energy is soul energy and that aspect of you is pure awareness. In pure awareness, there are no thoughts, emotions, struggles, ambitions, or pain— just the simple, yet profound awareness of your precious inner being.

SILENCE THERAPY

We need silence like we need air. Silence is your inner space of great power. Silence is the void where thoughts are cast into the wind and the mind dissipates into stillness. If you are quiet enough, you can hear the flow of the universe. Notice, there's an aspect of you that is the witness to silence. Who is the mighty one that perceives all of this beauty? Show me this one, you can do it! This is the magnificent part of you that I am interested in knowing. A busy mind reacts to even the slightest stimulation. Know that if you don't react to any observation or event, you remain in silence. What prevents you from connecting to your inner being is mind noise and incessant thinking that I call "turbulence." Imagine the turbulent waters of a deep ocean. If you were to submerge yourself in the deep, you wouldn't see anything. But, if you can quiet the turbulence in your mind, you will find clarity instead of confusion. Silence therapy, stillness, and meditation all reduce stress, overthinking, and imbalance. If you are stressed out, turn off your television, put down your iPhone for a day, disconnect from social media for a week or two— unplug. Do whatever you need to do to create space between you and your overactive mind.

The forest is an example of a place where you can go to lose your mind and find your soul. Trees soak up all sounds in the forest. It is there that your thoughts, emotions, actions, and experience can be observed from a place of silence. Whenever you create the time and space to listen in silence, you can actually hear your spirit speaking.

The Four Most Powerful

Behaviors Are All Silent:

1) A smile
2) A look
3) A touch
4) A taste

EXERCISE #6
Press The Reset Button

Get aligned with your mind, heart, body, and soul.
Quiet your mind by adding 10 minutes of
purposeful silence to your day.
Close your eyes. Breathe deeply in silence.
Visualize your mind as a blackboard and begin to erase all the
thoughts and ideas that are taking up valuable space in your mind.
Place your right hand over your heart and feel your heartbeat.
Stay as the witnessing presence of this action.
When you reach ten minutes, you have finished this exercise.
Now open your eyes as if you are waking up for the very first time.

SOLITUDE AND STILLNESS

Solitude is a fountain for healing. The mind is like a dense forest. The essence of meditation is when one thought ceases and a future thought has not yet risen. In that gap, the space between thoughts, you find yourself in a deep state of silence and stillness. This gap usually doesn't last very long before a new thought or a movement arises. Don't reject the movement of your mind, merely shift your attention away from your thoughts. Likewise, don't focus on being still, but rather continue in the flow of your pure presence. We are all a part of and have access to the universal stream, the Mind of God. Think of the energy of your emotions as waves in the ocean. Of course there are rough waves, as well as gentle ones. In your life, strong emotions like anger, desire, and jealousy will come to you. A spiritual practitioner recognizes them not as a disturbance or obstacle, but as learning opportunities. A great hack is to see right through them as soon as they arise, see what they really are, the vivid and electric manifestations of mind-energy itself. Gradually, as you learn to do this, even your most turbulent emotions fail to seize hold of you and will dissolve. See your emotional waves as both rising and falling back into the calm of the ocean. For masters of meditation, their body becomes completely still, like a piece of wood.

> *I used to close my eyes at the time of meditation.*
> *Then I thought: "If God exists after closing the eyes, why should*
> *He not exist while the eyes are open?" I opened my eyes and saw*
> *the Divine Being everywhere. Man, animals, insects, trees, moon,*
> *sun, water, earth, and in and through all these,*
> *The Infinite Being is manifesting himself.*
> *~ Ramakrishna*

STILLNESS THERAPY

It has been said that "stillness is the language of God speaking and everything else is a bad translation."The state of stillness happens when you cease reacting to anything. Stillness requires no effort, concentration, nor skill— you simply need to remain present without reacting to whatever is happening around you. Be the witnessing presence of your environment. If you are looking to practice stillness, don't start a single thought, your thoughts are merely movements of your mind. Out of stillness, the altitude of the greater you appears. In stillness you can see things clearer and you are better able to act on time, instead of time acting on you.

SLEEP THERAPY

Sleep is very important. We sleep for two-thirds of our life. It is in sleep and in prayer that you communicate with your subconscious self and have conversations with God. Sleep is the time when the male consciousness seeks its lover, otherwise known as your subconscious self. Sleep is the normal state of the subconscious. When the sun goes down try to minimise the amount of light exposure you get. Use candles, lamps or dimmer lights instead. This is because bright lights trick our brain chemicals into thinking it's still daytime, we need darkness in order to produce melatonin, our natural sleep hormone. If you are wanting more relaxing and deeper sleep, increase your melatonin intake.

> *Sleep is healing balm for an empath's body. It calms the nervous system.*
> *As a self-care rule, honor the sleep time you need*
> *to replenish yourself every night.*
> *Take power naps during the day when possible.*
> *Sleep heals like nothing else can.*
> *~ Judith Orloff, M. D.*

EXERCISE #7
Sleep Therapy, 10 Easy Steps

1. **State your intention to fall asleep.**
2. **Make yourself a cup of organic Mugwort tea.**
3. **Create space for silence and relax your body in stillness.**

4. **Unplug from all electronic devices.**
5. **Minimize your exposure to light.**
6. **Close your eyes.**
7. **Focus on your breath. Breathe deep and slow, even and calm.**
8. **Make your last thoughts before sleeping only positive thoughts.**
9. **Be at peace.**
10. **Give yourself permission to rest your mind and drift off to sleep.**

SOUND THERAPY

Dr. Jeffrey Thompson, a Neuroacoustic practitioner and chiropractor in Carlsbad, California, has developed a therapy in which he produces a precise sound frequency that affects the brain center, which causes the body to drop into its parasympathetic nervous system, or "healing response." When you are stressed, your body activates your sympathetic nervous system "the fight or flight response." On the other hand, your parasympathetic response is the "rest and repair mode," in which your body is best able to heal.

EXERCISE #8

Go to a concert or listen to a song.
Listen intentionally to a single instrument
and follow their part through the whole song.
While listening, connect yourself to the emotion
of the musician and the notes of the different instruments.
For instance, listen to the bassline of a song
the whole way through. Notice how each instrument has
its own vibrational frequency and when they are
joined together, a symphony is produced.

**From this point forward, stop listening to the music
you hear with just your ears and try to feel
the music inside of your heart.
Music ushers in a vibration that actually lifts
people's spirits and touches their souls.**

SOUND BATH THERAPY

Tibetan singing bowls are a collection of metal and crystal vessels that emit different beautiful musical tones. They are used to enhance meditation, relaxation, and healing. Tibetans have been using these instruments, considered sonic frequency technologies, for more than 2,000 years. Recently, North America and the rest of the world has caught on to the many health benefits of sound baths. In a sound bath, your attention is initially drawn to the transcendental tones of the singing bowls. As the vibration of the music turns into a moving energy, you can actually feel the musical tones travel to you and through you. People use words like "cleansed" and "cleared" to describe their sound bath experience. Many people feel like they are completely submerged in sound. Some feel as if they are being washed by virtual waves of water. It's as if the sound waves of the singing bowls actually become a visceral thing.

There's no one common reaction to a sound bath, everyone seems to interpret it differently. During a session, you are sure to feel relaxed, sink into meditation, or have a transcendent experience. Some people experience a profound emotional release. It is not uncommon to hear people laughing or crying when they become overwhelmed. Whenever buried emotional pain is released from your body, love can replace the void. Sound baths are an immersion in sound frequency that result in healing of the mind and cleansing of the soul. It is often a soulful experience with impactful results that can last for days or even weeks.

EXERCISE #9
Sound Bath Therapy

If you've ever been to a sound bath, then
you will be really excited about this exercise.
Book a sound bath session. If you feel adventurous,
add CBD or Cannabis for a mind blowing experience.
Reset and recalibrate through the healing
qualities of sounds, music, and vibration.

MUSIC THERAPY

Music is the one thing that unifies our entire society. Everyone can recall a song or concert that changed their life. Music manipulates energy fields in our bodies through vibration. Whenever we absorb sound vibrations it raises our energy. Music has a therapeutic effect on the trillions of cells in our body and is capable of shifting our emotions. Sometimes, music is the only therapy the heart and soul needs to change our emotional state.

VOICE AND SONG THERAPY

Expressing yourself through your voice in chanting, conversation, reciting poetry, rapping, and singing are each soulful experiences. Singing is an emotional release. You have been given the gift of your voice, every song that you sing is a blessing. Harmonize with the presence of Source Energy in your heart. Chanting has been around for centuries. Chanting God's holy name helps us to attain spiritual happiness and escape a material existence.

What is "Om"?
OM is the song of God.
OM is the first born soul.

OM is the parent of all sounds.
OM is the perfected absence of thought.
OM is the silence within the heart of peace.
~Edg Duveyoung

DANCE THERAPY

When we move our hips from side to side, swirl, spin and shake, we are essentially moving into the flow of life. When we dance to our favorite music and really let it loose, we are letting go of our fears and cares. For those few minutes we are on a higher spiritual level. We express our unique spirit through movement. Dancing celebrates the release of your past hurt and struggles. Additionally, dancing holds a special importance in the archives of love. Close body synchrony allows two partners to show off their sensuality and vitality via the symmetry and balance of their movements. Chemistry is enhanced when dance partners make eye contact and feel one another's inner energy. Rhythmically moving together allows dancers to tune in to each other's vibration.

EXERCISE #10
Dance Therapy

Treat yourself to a group or single-partner
dance class. Put your ass into it!
Give it everything you've got. Dance like nobody's watching.
These classes are a safe space for the full
expression of your inner being!

PLAY THERAPY

Play therapy is a form of therapy used primarily for children. That's because children may not be able to process their own emotions or articulate problems to their parents or other adults. A trained therapist can use playtime to observe and gain insights into a child's problems. The therapist can then help the child explore their emotions and deal with any unresolved trauma. Through play, children can learn new coping mechanisms and how to redirect inappropriate behaviors. Children typically benefit from play therapy, but it's also used in adults. Empaths tend to be overly serious, but we also love to play. Be playful with your loving partner and let the world see your inner child.

Play therapy may be helpful in a variety of clinical circumstances, such as:

- **Facing medical procedures, chronic illness, or compassionate care.**
- **Developmental delay or learning disabilities.**
- **Problem behaviors in school.**
- **Anger management or aggressive behavior.**
- **Family issues like separation, divorce, or death of a close family member.**
- **Natural disasters or traumatic events.**
- **Domestic violence, abuse, or neglect.**
- **Anxiety, depression, grief, or PTSD.**
- **Eating and toileting disorders.**
- **Attention deficit hyperactivity disorder (ADHD).**
- **Autism spectrum disorder (ASD).**

EXERCISE THERAPY/KINETIC MOTION

One of my favorite ways to raise my energy is through exercise. Physical activity promotes a healthy life. Exercise raises the heart and respiratory rates, accelerates metabolism, burns fat, eliminates toxins, and elevates your mood. Frequently, when I leave an exercise class or gym session, I feel high on life. The feeling of being excited, unstoppable, and energized are the vibrations we receive from exercise. Movement is essential to life. Without movement there is stasis which leads to death. Walking, hiking, running, skating, biking, yoga, Tai Chi, martial arts, boating, sledding, skiing, and snowboarding all elevate your energy using motion and movement.

CHAPTER 5

MULTI-SENSORY HEALING THERAPY

Part 2

Sun Therapy	Hot and Cold Therapy
Nature Therapy	Prayer Therapy
Nutritional Therapy	Smile Therapy
Water Therapy	Laughter Therapy

SUN THERAPY

N uclear fusion is the source of the sun's energy. At the sun's core, where temperature and pressure are very high, hydrogen atoms fuse into helium atoms and release energy in the form of Gamma rays. This is the nature of the sun. We harness and benefit from the sun's brilliant energy in so many ways. The sun's energy is harnessed alike by plants, trees, rain, rivers, and also by the wind. The sun's intense energy warms the atmosphere, the earth's surface, and our great oceans. This natural process produces gigantic and powerful heat waves and pressure fronts which govern global weather patterns and stir our powerful ocean currents.

Since the moment you were born, every bit of natural food that you've ever eaten has been nurtured and blessed by solar energy, including: vegetables, fruits, and grains. Even the feed for the animals whose meat you have eaten are all grown through the process of photosynthesis, the transfer of light into energy. Exposure to sunlight is needed by human beings for many different reasons. The rawest reason is the role of sunlight in the creation of vitamin D, which is very important for our bone development. Another thing is mood stimulation, most humans will get depressed when not exposed to enough sunlight. The less sunlight we see in the winter months, the more likely we are to develop Seasonal Affective Disorder (SAD). Symptoms of SAD can be extreme: mood swings, anxiety, sleep problems, or even suicidal thoughts all arise in the absence of exposure to sunlight.

NATURE THERAPY

As McGill University neuroscientist, Daniel Levintin explains: "The digital age is profoundly narrowing our horizons and our creativity, not to mention our bodies and physiological capabilities." Modern life has made all of us, along with our kids, distractible and overwhelmed. On average, humans consume 74 gigabytes of data every day. After school, teens spend vastly more waking hours on screens than off them. And due to the COVID-19 pandemic, kids are mostly in homeschool and are now on screens all day long. In today's world, we don't experience natural environments enough to realize how amazing they can make us feel. Studies show that being outdoors makes us healthier, more creative, more empathetic, more apt to engage with the world and with each other.

Nature is the mirror of the soul. There's a direct correspondence between our interior and exterior worlds, between the soul and what our eyes see. Nature, as it turns out, is good for everyone. Getting daily sun exposure through sunlight induces the release of serotonin from the brain which regulates our mood. Serotonin also helps with our overall well being. Aristotle believed walks in the open air brought clarity to his mind. Darwin, Tesla, and Einstein each walked in gardens and groves to inspire their ideas. When you walk in nature, it's as if you're wearing rose-colored glasses. In nature everything is a little brighter, more positive, and there's a lot more connectedness to Source. In nature, our brains tend to rest and thoughts diminish. It is common to feel refreshed, energized, and inspired when outdoors. This sequence happens every time you watch a beautiful sunset, listen to birds chirping, hear the pouring rain, or appreciate a beautiful landscape. Nature scenes pull us into the dimension of presence and joy. We've known for a long time that athletes and artists can easily access flow states during a performance. The idea is that the rest of us can also reach that desired "zone" by connecting with nature.

NUTRITIONAL HEALING

The single most important element of your healing plan is your nutritional intake. You've got to find out what's feeding your disease and then starve it. I have come to the understanding that food is our main source of energy. When you are feeling depleted, de-energized, depressed, or deactivated, you have to start refueling, recharging, and replenishing your energy stores with high quality foods. Shifting your attention onto the quality of items you are consuming is important in your healing. Most people know which foods are healthy and which foods are not. But, in actuality, what's healthy for one person, may not be healthy for another. It's all based on your genetics. It's best to find a custom strategy for you and your individualized nutritional needs. The healthier and more organic the food is, the greater the energy that you will absorb and feel.

Eat well to live well. Don't skip meals. Try to eat natural plant-based foods with life already in it. These are foods fueled by the sun and grown from the earth. Alive foods have a glow. They are fragrant, delicious, energizing, organic, and free of chemicals in preservatives. There's no desire to over eat them. Alive foods give us pure energy which feels balancing. This diet promotes vitality and stimulates your immune system. The combination of juice therapy, eating live foods, drinking herbal teas, and taking herbs and vitamins are excellent ways to create the new, healthier version of yourself that you desire to become. Respect your body and give it the attention that it deserves.

> *For every human illness somewhere in the world*
> *there exists a plant which is the cure.*
> *~ Dr. Sebi*

BLESS YOUR FOOD

Before you eat, it's very important to bless your food. Blessing your food is a wonderful way of uplifting the energy of what you and your family are about to consume. You are fortunate to have food in a world where so many people walk in hunger. Pause for a moment to express gratitude for the hidden gift of life in your food. Pray that your food nourishes your body and gives you strength. Thank the farmers for picking your fruits and vegetables. Pray for the souls of the fish, chicken, or meat that you are about to consume. Blessing your food activates the vital life force in the nutrients of your meal. Eat mindfully with a grateful and humble heart.

EXERCISE #11
Food Blessing (say aloud)

Thank you to the universal life force for blessing us
with this meal sprinkled with unconditional love.
Thank you to the food sources and supply chain workers
that assisted in bringing this meal to the table.
Thank you to all the hands that prepared this food.

**May this meal nourish every aspect of our
minds, bodies, hearts, and spirit.**

BODY PH

The pH scale ranges from 1 (highly acidic) to 14 (highly alkaline), while your body's pH usually hovers between 7.35 and 7.4. Unfortunately, most of the foods that people consume today are full of sugar, preservatives, and genetically modified organisms, which all contribute to acidity in the body. The most alkaline foods are vegetables as well as some fruits, grains, nuts, and alkaline water. Helping your body neutralize some of its acidity is crucial for maintaining your overall health and also preventing and treating cancer.

THE HEALING POWER OF WATER

Water is life. Just like the earth, the human body is composed of around 75 percent water. The unique relationship of water and health has been emphasized in virtually every ancient culture. The healing power of water and its ability to carry divine information and memory has been known for centuries and many therapies have been based on using this knowledge. At its core, water is a basic human element and it performs many life-sustaining tasks. For example: it supports complex biochemical reactions, provides structural support for cells, and is the major component in blood and all other bodily fluids. Additionally, water helps to eliminate dangerous waste products from every part of the body.

There is an amazing connection between water and your brain. The human brain is nearly 90 percent water and brain function is directly influenced by the makeup, balance, and ph balance of its water. The nature of water is feminine. It curves and moves in spirals, amazing vortexes, and also in figure eights. The water within our bodies is in constant motion, it moves in response to the vibrational energy of the moon and planet. Water is essential to life on earth. If it ever becomes still, it stagnates and attracts the energy of disease and decay. In the absence of water, life simply ceases to exist.

WATER TIPS

- **Start everyday with a glass of water to flush your system and to bring new life to your being.**
- **Drink a minimum of six glasses of water per day, more if you're stressed out or when you are exercising.**
- **Hold water to be sacred, vow to protect it against disrespect and pollution.**
- **View water as alive, the giver of all life and a source of vitality.**
- **Use water in ceremony to heal, cleanse, and purify yourself.**
- **Anchor your emptying work by seeing yourself in the ocean being baptized by the water and feeling cleansed and refreshed.**

The Four Important Symbolic Lessons Water Teaches Us:

1. *What you see often is your projection.*
2. *What is soft can also be powerful.*
3. *Persistence can break barriers.*
4. *Change is always happening.*
~ *Yung Pueblo*

WATER AS A HEALING TOOL

Water has been revered over thousands of years for its powerful spiritual and healing nature. Water possesses powerful cleansing and purifying properties. In water therapy, see your healing in relationship to an ocean. Visualize Source Energy as the ocean. Next, open your mind to receive your healing as an incoming wave into your existence. See the wave washing over you, cleansing you of your emotional suffering, physical pain, and spiritual dis-ease. See your cleansing as a purification process with the intention to rid your body of any toxins. Let the wave of healing come to you, pass through you, transform you, and leave you cleansed; only God can do that so beautifully and so well.

> *Make a ceremony out of your bath. Light candles and incense,*
> *have soft and inspiring music playing. Bless your bathwater.*
> *Use the bath to release all negativity and anything that blocks*
> *the free movement of light, love, healing, or peace through your*
> *body temple. Add seven drops of the essential oil Frankincense*
> *to the bathwater to open your crown chakra.*
> *Frankincense attunes you to the Divine.*
> *~ Queen Afua*

WATER GIVES LIFE

Water's role in the world is both life giving and life sustaining. In my work as an energy healer and spiritual teacher, the energy of intention plays an important role. Water becomes my ally; after every healing session I join my client in drinking water that carries its pure vibration to enhance the goals of the healing. I hope that in time, modern culture will come to honor water and its spirit as much as ancient tribes have done in the past. That is my desire and that is my intention.

> *Emotion is energy in motion.*
> *Water in the body, whether it's the great ocean*
> *that bathes every cell; the rivers of blood,*
> *lymph, and cerebrospinal fluid; the little streams*
> *of the capillaries and minor nerves; or the great lakes*
> *of the stomach and the pools of the eyes,*
> *stop functioning optimally if there isn't enough of it*
> *or if it becomes too still.*
> *~ Masaru Emoto*

EXERCISE #12
Water Blessing
(say aloud)

I would like to share with you this declaration of gratitude for water.

**It was taught to me by a friend and as your friend,
I am passing it along to you. The intention of this
blessing is to purify the water before you receive
it.**

**"I take this the water of the earth and declare it the water of life.
I take this water of life and declare it the water of light. I take
this the water of light and declare it the water of love.
I am the master of all that I am."**

HOT AND COLD WATER THERAPY

Water therapy is as old as humanity itself. Water is a natural medicine that benefits the whole body. Almost every warm-climate civilization has at sometime used baths for therapeutic reasons as well as for pleasant social interaction. Water therapy is an energizer which helps the body to heal itself and prevents many other health problems from occurring. Types of water therapy include: hot tubs, cold tubs, jacuzzis, and hot steam saunas. Scientists say that we feel better in water because the seas are our true ancestral home. Others like the feeling of relaxation in water to the memory of the amniotic fluid we were suspended in before birth.

Sea salt baths are amazing tools of healing. For hundreds of years, sea salt has been recognized as a secret tool to detox anything that is not serving us. I like adding one cup of pink Himalayan sea salt to my warm bath. The more salt there is in the water, the greater will be the feeling of relaxation and refreshment.

During your healing bath, pour a bowl of spiritual wash over your head and let the wash run down your face, chest, and body. Call on the Divine Creator for a renewed body, a renewed mind, and a renewed spirit. I've always felt calm, relaxed, nourished and clear after doing this. I believe it clears the body's energy system, enhances flow, and allows the chakras to express themselves more clearly. All you have to do is sit back, relax, close your eyes, and enjoy your soak.

Cold bath rejuvenation is a great treatment to shock and reset the body. It is effective in reducing pain and inflammation. Cold showers are effective at stimulating your tired body. Cold water therapy can stop a cold before it starts. It reduces fever, enhances circulation, generates energy, relieves pain, vanquishes nervousness, helps you to sleep, and even helps you to feel sexier. In short, cold baths can revive, restore, and re-energize your body.

EXERCISE #13
Floatation or Isolation Therapy

Research companies that specialize in isolation therapy and choose a location that works best for you. Indulge in a sensory deprivation experience and allow yourself to enjoy the journey inward. This mimics your first experience ever, as an aquatic being in your mother's womb. The practice of floating in a salt solution eliminates the mind's need to navigate gravity. In this environment, the mind can redirect its thoughts and focus inward.

PRAYER THERAPY

Prayer is communion with God. Through prayer, a way forward is created before you. Ask and it is given. When your prayers go up, the blessings come down. Prayer is an unstoppable force. Prayer is not a psychological task, it's a spiritual practice. It is a step in the direction of gratitude and love. It is the art of moving your thoughts away from seeing your current situation as a problem and beginning to see solutions in your mind's eye. When friends call me and tell me of a problem, I respond to them with compassion and empathy. We pray on it and then turn the problem over to God. Prayer literally shifts your attention away from a problem state and into a spiritual energy-based state of being.

The 5 Most Essential

Steps of A Prayer:

1. **Thank God**
2. **Praise God**
3. **Ask God**
4. **Receive God**
5. **Be one with God**

BELIEVE IN THE POWER OF PRAYER

You can believe in the power of prayer because it is both powerful and true. When you are learning the art of prayer, your persistence is necessary. Pray daily and pray often. If your desires are not fulfilled today or into next week, don't give up on them. Anything and everything is always possible, including miracles. All of your prayers are being heard and answered at Godspeed. Learn how to pray with faith and conviction. Give thanks and praise for all of your blessings. If you can master the art of prayer, you can bend your world towards any ideal that you want to experience. Don't just use prayer to ask for things that you want, be unselfish in your requests. Pray for those less fortunate, pray for those in need of a healing, and pray for those that need a blessing. Be careful not to live in a constant state of desire, that is unhealthy. Slow down your mindstream and start believing in your prayers. Prayer strengthens your divine relationship with God. When you send up a prayer, maintain an unshakable faith in the Most High to carry out your task. All things are possible for those that believe.

EXERCISE #14
Affirm Your Prayer

- What is your prayer today?
- What are you asking God to do?
- Affirmation is the key activator of any prayer. See whatever you are asking as already present in your life.
- Release your prayer into God's hands and worry no more.
- Be patient and allow your request to manifest at Godspeed.
- Be gracious to God and be thankful for the opportunity to live another day on this beautiful earth.
- Pray often and bow to gratitude.
- Imagine how you would feel if your prayers were already answered, then be that.

The power of prayer penetrates the deepest point in the universal field. It can be felt thousands of miles away and is our greatest source of hope, inspiration, and strength. The objective of prayer is for you to be taken into and dissolve in God. Remember that prayer without action is in vain. May your prayers always bear the fruit of your desires.

The more you praise something,
the more you appreciate something,
everytime you feel good about something,
you are telling the universe: "More of this please,
more of this please."
~ Abraham Hicks

EXERCISE #15
Night Prayer

Before bed, turn your attention towards a feeling of accomplishment and gratitude for what you did today. Lift your vibration with self-love.

1. **Relax. When you are asleep you no longer are in control and no longer have the freedom of choice.**
2. **Your quality of sleep is determined from your last conscious view-point of yourself. Make your last thought before you go to bed a good thought.**
3. **Your subconscious sees you exactly how you view yourself.**
4. **Don't think or speak of your problems just before you sleep.**
5. **Affirm to yourself that you are an infinite soul in a body and that you are unlimited.**
6. **Your mood before bedtime determines how you will meet your subconscious mind during your sleep.**
7. **Be thankful and state what you are grateful for prior to retiring.**
8. **Praise God.**
9. **Focus on your breath and breathing.**
10. **Close your eyes and drift asleep.**

SMILE THERAPY

Smile is the most pleasing five letter word. Smiling allows you to communicate without using any words. You can smile silently with your face, your eyes, or both. Your smile releases your divine light. The purest smile is done through your eyes. Are you expressing your inner joy often enough? Use your smile more to radiate and release your joy. Your smile is your emanation of pure love and light. Make it a point to smile, even in the face of adversity. Let your joy be seen by the whole world. The world is in need of more smiling faces. A smile from someone is a gift to you from their soul. When you smile, try to trace it back to its source, in the center of your being. Smiling releases neurotransmitters called endorphins from the brain. These endorphins brighten your mood. The more you stimulate your brain to release these neurotransmitters, the more relaxed and happy you will feel. If you don't practice smiling, your face will freeze. I have seen many people with their face literally frozen in a permanent frown. When you practice smiling, you exercise and train your facial muscles to contract with joy instead of frowning with sadness and pain.

> *The secret to living well and longer is eat half, walk double,*
> *laugh triple, and love beyond measure.*
> *~ Tibetan proverb.*

LAUGH THERAPY

Laughter is a spiritual practice. Laughter always helps to wash away the pain of a broken heart. Laughter generates powerful waves of pure energy capable of reversing any surrounding negative energy field. The action of laughter triggers the release of neurotransmitters from a person's brain which manifests as a pleasurable feeling. Laughter is capable of changing people's moods and always brings one's attention back into the present moment. Laughter is contagious and like smiling, it sparks endorphin levels. Laughter is a powerful antidote to stress, pain, and conflict. Nothing works faster or is more dependable than bringing your mind and body back into balance than a good laugh.

EXERCISE #16
Laugh Therapy

Take the time to watch a comedy movie, stand
up act or sitcom, and laugh your ass off!

Give yourself the freedom and the space to laugh
out loud in uncontrollable bursts.
Remind yourself how great it feels to laugh
and truly enjoy the moment.

CHAPTER 6

MULTI-SENSORY HEALING THERAPY

Part 3

Crystal Healing

Touch Therapy

Reiki Therapy

Acupuncture

Aroma Therapy

Hug Therapy

Kissing Therapy

Sex Therapy

Love Therapy

CRYSTAL HEALING: GEMS, CRYSTALS, AND PRECIOUS STONES

Precious stones are ancient beings buried deep inside the earth's surface. They are part of the texture and beauty of our planet and they are here holding space for our growth and expansion. Shamans all over the world have always had crystals in their possession. Crystals are becoming increasingly popular among New Age practitioners. The interest in crystals is not limited to quartz. People are paying exorbitant prices for precious stones which on the surface only have ornamental value. Crystals connect us, even if it's in an unconscious way, to experiences of purity, clarity, radiance, brilliance, beauty, and timelessness. Keeping them around in your space is extremely influential to your vibration, just being around them inspires you to vibrate higher and shine brighter. If you don't have any experience with crystals, get a clear quartz crystal and get in touch with its consciousness. See it as a life form and communicate with it. Still your body tensions, emotions, and thoughts as much as possible and be one with the crystal. This can give you a lot of insight that normally would not have come to you, because of the organic nature of the crystal. Crystal consciousness brings you in contact with all matter with its crystal forms, crystalline structures, molecules, atoms, subatomic particles, and quantum energies.

CHARGING YOUR CRYSTALS AND STONES

When we use crystals for energetic healing, our ability to detect subtle energies increases. Remember that crystals themselves need healing and recharging too. Crystals collect our emotions, pain, and energies to create a positive place for our souls to soar free. Every time we touch them, every word that we speak in their presence, and every time we call on them during a sacred healing session, they're performing the blessed service of rejuvenating and restoring. Crystals and stones need to be charged because the energy that they carry is not unlimited. When you use crystals and stones for healing, energy work, and other purposes, the energies they possess can be drained or used up. To remedy this, crystals and stones should be cleansed and charged regularly before and after use. This will ensure that they are in top condition and working well. This will also clear any negative energy from the people who are around the crystals and stones.

To cleanse your crystals use any one of the following methods:

WATER - Hold it in running cold water for a few seconds or up to a minute.

SAGE – Hold the crystal over the sage smoke for a few seconds to be cleansed.

SOUND – Use a singing bowl to use sound vibrations in order to cleanse crystals by placing them next to the bowl, or even inside the bowl.

EARTH – Bury or partially bury the crystal in the earth, in a garden, or in a flower pot. Keep it buried overnight or ideally for 24 hours for complete cleansing.

SOLAR POWER CHARGE

All crystals and stones will benefit from the power of the sun. Yellow is the color of the sun's energy, and all you need to do to cleanse and charge your crystals and stones is to leave them out in sunlight for 24 hours. This will allow your stone to bathe in the light of both the sun and the moon. The more often you use a stone, the more energy it collects. A good rule of thumb is to clear all of your stones at least once a month. Many charge their crystals every full moon. When we care for our crystals, we're caring for ourselves. We're allowing energy that's inharmonious with our lives and intentions to leave in a peaceful and healing manner. Taking these small measures allows us to be more mindful in our interactions with the stones, with ourselves, and with others.

TOUCH THERAPY

Of all sensations, touch is my absolute favorite. Many people today are hesitant to shake hands because of fear of transmitting germs and viruses. Human touch, the exchanging of physical energy is essential to our physiology and livelihood. Hand shakes, hugs, and kisses are mediums by which humans create bonds and connections. In the end, social media likes, comments, and emojis will never take the place of human touch. The feeling of touch is an essential need to feel safe and loved. Skin is our largest organ system of the body. Human skin is a rich network of blood vessels and nerve endings. The hairs on your skin are energy detectors and visual evidence of your mood. In times of stress and anxiety, arm hairs stand up. In the cold, goose bumps appear upon our skin. The reason is that when the skin is touched, the brain pairs it with a chemical signal and a physical response. Additionally, human touch affects our mood. No one has to look any further than the animal model. When animals are petted and nurtured they purr and respond by relaxing.

EXERCISE #17
The Movement From Touch, to Light Energy
(A partner is required to complete this exercise)

1. **Give yourself permission to touch someone and also to be touched.**
2. **Give your verbal permission and consent to explore and expand boundaries.**
3. **State your intentions for this exercise to increase your awareness of the power of touch.**
4. **See yourselves as energy.**
5. **Open your minds and extend your hearts.**
6. **Sit on the floor facing one another.**
7. **Reach out to grasp both your partner's hands.**
8. **Look into their eyes.**
9. **Synchronize your breathing.**

10. Feel their energy field. Feel yours. Feel the merger of the two energies.

REIKI THERAPY - REDUCING AND REMOVING BLOCKS OF RESISTANCE WHICH OPEN CHANNELS OF HEALING

Reiki is a Japanese healing technique that works holistically on the whole body, mind, and spirit. Dr. Mikao Usui, a Japanese seeker of spiritual truths, brought the Reiki method of healing into human awareness in 1922. Reiki is simply a relaxing treatment where natural healing vibrations are transmitted through the hands of the practitioner. During a Reiki session, the practitioner lightly places their hands on or just above you seeking to transmit universal life energy. The purpose of a Reiki treatment is to relieve stress, pain, and emotional blockages. Reiki balances subtle, invisible body energies and accelerates natural healing.

In Yogic tradition, the human body has seven energy centers called chakras. Energy is constantly flowing through our bodies and moves through the seven chakras, even though we don't physically see it. Each chakra has a role in balancing some aspect of our life. When all seven of these energy centers are open and healthy, so are we. Throughout childhood and through our life experiences, we often create "energy blocks" in our chakras. A block is a place where energy is trapped. If you are dealing with a block, you need to get the energy moving, which is exactly what Reiki does. For instance, hypothetically, if you happened to receive repetitive criticism for your singing as a child, your fifth chakra (the throat center) may close down. This restriction could limit your creative expression or ability to speak up for yourself. Trauma, fears, and negative experiences can lead to long-term imbalances in your energy system and manifest into insecurity, stress, anger, or disease. This is where energy healing comes in. Reiki activates the energetic system and cleanses the constrictions in your system. Our bodies are in constant flux between balance and imbalance. Balance is not static, it's constantly moving. Reiki has been described as "the healing touch" and brings balance to the body. Your inner awareness of your body-mind constantly provides subtle signals and clues to your overall wellness. Everyone is capable of detecting energy levels in their bodies, but when we are feeling stressed, anxious, or depressed, we sometimes need the assistance of another to release the resistance. Energy work helps to release these energetic blockages. In Reiki energy healing, the practitioner's hands are used as an instrument of light.

EXERCISE #18
Foot Massage

Get a foot massage. Remember that your feet contain many powerful reflexology points and acupuncture meridians that help to center you. Reward your feet and honor them with rubs using lotions, CBD oil, and heat. You will feel soothed, relaxed and rejuvenated.

ACUPUNCTURE THERAPY

The general theory of acupuncture is based on the premise that there are patterns of energy flow (Qi) through the body that are essential for health. Disruptions of this flow is believed to be responsible for dis-ease. The stimulation of "acupuncture points" is activated by the penetration of the skin by very thin, solid, metallic needles, which are manipulated by hand and or accompanied by electrical stimulation. Inserting needles in several of the 365 accessible acupuncture points, can bring the energy flow back into balance. Each session may last 30 minutes to an hour, with the needles being retained for 15 minutes or so. Depending on the condition being treated, the frequency of sessions may be from two to six sessions. While there's no evidence that acupuncture is a miracle cure-all, it does seem to have many supporters and the evidence supports its use for the treatment for people who may have multiple conditions and illnesses. Energy travels along fascial planes in the body related to meridians. The fascia is a thin physical layer underneath the skin that holds your muscles and organs in place, it acts like the switchboard for the nerves in the body. These healing networks extend throughout every part of the body. Energy blocks impede the flow of your energy chakras. The placement of Acupuncture needles into the skin releases energy blocks, triggers the release of natural pain-numbing chemicals, and increases blood flow to target areas. Where blood goes, energy flows. On a personal level, I feel relaxed but also recharged after my sessions. There's a reason it's been around for more than 2,500 years and as research grows, so will our knowledge of exactly what it does.

AROMATHERAPY

Essential oils have been used throughout the ages for healing. Aromatherapy is like music therapy, it's full of different notes and frequencies. Each scent has a color and healing vibration. A good blend is to have all three of these elements in harmony. Visuals tend to get all the claims, but nothing hits the brain's emotional neurons more powerfully than scents. I offer you the notion that the practice of inhaling essential oils is a pleasant way to shift any resistant emotional patterns from a negative to a positive vibration.

EXERCISE #19
Emotional Clearing Ceremony With Essential Oils

Perform this ceremony with the intention to create movement with your feelings. Give permission for any old, undesired feelings to disappear and allow new ones to enter. The aroma of the oil creates spontaneous movement of your emotional current. If you've never experienced aromatherapy before, step out of your comfort zone and try something new, you'll be glad you did.

1. **To clear any undesirable emotional pattern through aromatherapy, begin by first identifying the feeling or emotion that you wish to replace.**

2. The most important element of aromatherapy is starting your healing with a sincere and powerful intention.

3. Next, identify the emotion that you wish to attract.

4. Create an affirmation that creates space to shift yourself out of your undesired emotion. Your affirmation then becomes the bridge to shift away from a negative emotion to a positive one.

5. The next step is to let go of the negative pattern from your cellular memory.

6. Place three drops of oil into the palm of your hand. Rub your hands together clockwise three times to activate it. Once activated, the oil knows what to do.

7. Take three slow deep breaths and inhale the essence of the oil. As you inhale, focus on the intention that you are seeking and exhale whatever you wish to release.

8. Imagine the fragrance of the oil penetrating all the cells in your body.

9. Lastly, close your eyes and say aloud: "I feel the oil working and moving to clear the unwanted energy inside and outside of my body."

10. For maximum effect, inhale the fragrance two or three times a day for 7 consecutive days.

White Angelica is an essential oil used to open the heart chakra. To cleanse your inner field, put a drop or two of it in the palm of your hand and rub your hands together three times. You may also want to run your hands down the front and back of your body. Since your energy field is larger than your physical body, holding your hand several inches away from your body allows you to quickly clear your energy field.

For a quick refresher, spray rosewater on your face and throughout your room. The delicate scent of rosewater is simply lovely. I find it effective and soothing for an emotional hangover. Inhaling lavender or spearmint essential oil is also uplifting as well. You can also select an essential oil and put it in a diffuser which spreads the scent in the air. The sublime scent of these oils purify your energy and the energy in the room.

Scents like lavender and rosemary cause a drop in subjects' cortisol level (known as the stress hormone) and increases blood velocity to the heart, which is a good thing. At the beginning of each day, clearing your chakras with oils is a great way to line up your energy field or to recap and unwind before retiring for the night. For difficulty sleeping, I highly recommend placing lavender oil on your pillow or placing it in an oil diffuser in your bedroom before sleep. My routine is that I place the oil on my temples and the release points on both sides of the rear base of my skull before I retire to bed, all the while focusing on my intention for a restful and deep sleep. Doing this clearing procedure immediately before bedtime allows your subconscious to process your intentions during your dream state.

HUGGING THERAPY

When the right person hugs you it's like medicine for the soul. "Hugging Meditation" was invented by Buddhist monk Thich Nhat Hanh. He describes putting your entire being into a hug. Hugs are meant to be given and received with all your mind, body, heart, and soul, while breathing consciously.

Hugging Mantra by Thich Nhat Hanh (say aloud)
"Breathing in, I know my dear one is in my arms alive.
Breathing out, she is so precious to me.
If you breathe deeply like that, holding the one you love,
the energy of your care and appreciation will penetrate into
that person and he or she will be nourished
and bloom like a flower."

EXERCISE #20
The Anatomy of a Good Hug
(Find a willing partner for this one!)

1. **First set the intention to transfer love during your hug.**
2. **Ask permission to hug your partner, you can use either verbal or nonverbal communication.**

3. Stretch your arms open wide and make yourself deeply available by opening your sacred heart space.
4. Make eye contact and stay connected.
5. Close your eyes on impact.
6. Steer your partner towards your left side.
7. On the initial embrace put your chest into theirs and press against them closely to generate a heart-to-heart encounter.
8. Exert no tension, allow yourself a brief moment to enjoy the hug.
9. Stay grounded to the earth with your feet flat on the floor.
10. Release the hug and disconnect slowly. Disengagement shouldn't be sudden or abrupt.
11. Be mindful not to back-slap or pet their back by habit- instead, relax into and out of the hug.
12. Close your hug experience with a compliment to your partner.
13. Express gratitude for your partner's presence and prowess.

KISSING THERAPY

The lips have more nerves per surface area than any other part of the body, followed by the tongue and fingers. The supersensitive top border of the upper lip is sometimes called "cupid's bow." Kissing on the lips for any extended period of time is widely considered the first step of sexual intimacy. Kissing is a mood elevator. You know that high you feel when you're head over heels for a new love and spending time canoodling with them? That's the effect of the dopamine in your brain's reward pathway. Dopamine is released when you do something that feels good, like kissing and spending time with someone you're attracted to. This and other "happy hormones" make you feel giddy and euphoric. The more you get of these hormones, the more your body wants them. For some, this may be more apparent at the start of a relationship, especially if most of your time is spent in a lip lock. Kissing also causes a burst of the hormone oxytocin. It's often referred to as the "love hormone," because it stirs up feelings of affection and attachment. Along with the dopamine and oxytocin, which makes you feel affectionate and euphoric, kissing releases serotonin, another feel-good chemical. It also lowers cortisol levels so you feel less stressed and more relaxed, making for a good time all around. We all have the urge to merge. Your lips are super-sensitive, which explains why a good liplock can feel so incredible, says Gloria Brame, PhD, author of Sex for Grown-Ups. Most importantly, kissing must be consensual. First try brushing your lips against your partner's without actually kissing them. While it sounds weird, breathing is also another component of kissing. Keep your slightly-open lips close to theirs and breathe in and out rhythmically in synchronicity. Amp up the sensation by alternating between soft, sensual kisses and deep passionate French kisses. Open mouth and tongue kissing are especially effective in upping the level of sexual arousal, because they increase the amount of saliva produced and energy exchanged. The more spit that you swap, the more turned on you'll get. While you are kissing, pay attention to what your partner is doing and how they are responding to your kisses. Body language is a good gauge to go by. If your partner is leaning into you and encouraging you, it's a great sign. Follow what feels good. As the kissing heats up, don't be afraid to switch up locations. A good kiss might involve a series of kisses down his or her neck, earlobes, nipples, and lower body to stimulate their erogenous zones. Chances are your partner will follow your lead.

SEX THERAPY

Sex is physical, emotional, and spiritual intimacy combined. The quest for intimacy is the main alluring factor for most physical connections. The underlying innate urge to procreate underpins all the biology and chemistry which lure us into having sex. Sex is medicine and orgasms are truly one of the healthiest ways to release stress and escape the pressures of the world. Orgasms are simply amazing and are the ultimate act of pleasure, the ideal release, and a spontaneous trigger for astral projection. A climax is a rollercoaster of excitement and ecstasy, the ultimate rush. Climaxes stimulate your brain's pleasure center, releases sex-hormones, and heightens your excitement, imagination, and fantasies. A truly amazing orgasm can make you feel like you are having an out of body experience. Sex is a ritual of surrender in which sex partners exchange their thoughts, feelings, and energies. Remain aware of the true mystical inherent powers that sex possesses, it's like skipping dimensions and floating along the cosmos.

You are sexual, but you are also spiritual. During sex you become a spiritual sponge for the consciousness of the other person, so it's important to be mindful of who you lay with. After intercourse, do you feel whole and connected with your partner? Sexual activity without love is called empty sex. If you satisfy your body, but don't satisfy your mind, heart, and soul— are you really being fulfilled? A deep sexual connection is when your body, mind, heart, and soul, are all fulfilled. With the addition of an emotional and spiritual connection, sexual intimacy connects you more deeply with one another. Move towards deeper spiritual partnerships by being more selective with whom you share your body with. Psychiatrist and philosopher Sigmund Freud once said: "Sexuality is the key to the problem of the psychoneuroses and of the neuroses in general. No one who disdains the key will ever be able to unlock the door." May you manifest someone who connects with you on all levels: emotionally, physically, sexually, and spiritually.

Ten Benefits of Sex

1. **Eases stress**
2. **Decreases anxiety and depression**
3. **Improves self-esteem**
4. **Provides a sense of euphoria and overall well-being**
5. **Enhances physical and emotional intimacy**
6. **Stimulates the immune system**
7. **Immediate and natural pain relief**
8. **Excellent sleep aid**
9. **Great exercise**
10. **Reduces erectile dysfunction in men and vaginal atrophy in postmenopausal females**

LOVE THERAPY

Love therapy is medicine for the soul. Spiritual medicine is the incorporation of love therapy into your healing program. Spiritual beings come to experience love with every cell of their bodies and beyond. This love is not one rooted in romance, but rather as a pulsating wave with immense invisible divine force. It is very hard to feel loved or realize how another person loves you, when on a core level you hold a fear deep inside, that you aren't lovable or don't really deserve to be loved. This fear blocks you from fully loving yourself and impedes your ability to give love to others. Love therapy is focused on finding and releasing your most deep-rooted fears so that your love can be freed. In love therapy, you are both the patient and the therapist. You are more than capable of treating yourself, you are a natural born healer. You have been healing yourself and others your whole life. The art of healing requires belief. You must first believe that you can be healed by love. Love is who you truly are. Each being is a divine manifestation of God. The fire of love burns in the heart of everyone. In love therapy, the first objective is to work on accepting and loving yourself. Once you are fully loving yourself, you are able to give love to others from the overflow. Love therapy aims to discover and process specific fears that may be causing you anxiety, panic attacks, over-reactions, and over-sensitivity. Love is medicine for your struggles. It is truly amazing how your circumstances will change by opening your heart and practicing self-love. If you find it challenging to love yourself or have emotional barriers that make it difficult for you to love, you may find the support of a therapist beneficial as you explore the reasons behind your difficulty.

CHAPTER 7

THE ENERGY OF PLANET EARTH AND THE HEALING POWER OF THE UNIVERSE

THE KEY TO ACTIVATING THE IMMENSE POWER OF THE UNIVERSE TO WORK FOR YOU

Invite infinite wisdom, divine will, and universal consciousness into your life. You accomplish this by realizing that you can't shoulder all the burdens in life by yourself. When you sustain faith in a higher power, it eases you into the state of surrender. Start seeing yourself as an important energetic part of this universe at large. Know that the web of the universal field is always supporting you. You hold the key to activating its secret great power, all you have to do is invite it to act on your behalf.

BEGIN TO SEE THE UNIVERSE AS ALIVE WITH ENERGY

There is one vibratory field that connects all things. Our universe is one infinite, conscious, intelligent, and compassionate entity. Quantum physics today gives us the picture of at least twenty different quantum fields interpenetrating each other. Each field has its own particular properties. The entire universe is built of them and there is nothing else but these fields. The energy force that holds all fields together is universal love. Love is energy and energy is power. The electro-magnetic universal field is constantly sending you signals, but it also follows your commands. The question is how do you begin to connect with this hidden energy field and use it for your benefit? Start by seeing yourself in terms of energy. Learn to come into alignment with your higher self, which always raises your energy and level and heightens your awareness. Your higher self is your God Essence. As you begin to identify as your divine energetic nature, you will begin to feel your way through life and encounter a lot less resistance. When you have mastery over your awareness and attention, you will gain mastery over your mind. Now aligned with your energetic self, you will be able to detect other people's vibrations and have the choice of how to respond to them in the absence of judgement. Don't stop shining your inner light and do so without apology. You improve the energy in any room by just being your authentic energetic self. Be powerful and vibrational with your intentions and presence. Be an ambassador of goodness and a light of love. Remember that whatever you put out into the universe always comes back to you in return.

EARTH'S MAGNETIC FIELD

The magnetic field of earth originates from its fiery molten core and extends deep into outer space. By this light, earth is always having a conversation with the cosmos. By aligning yourself with earth, you extend your consciousness to include the intelligence of the universe. As an awakened being, you already know that you have a conscious energetic relationship with the planet. You are literally immersed in and surrounded by earth's magnetic field. It is widely accepted that when you come into alignment with earth's core, you become energetically grounded by a superior natural magnetic force. Research suggests that we are all affected by varying degrees to the changing rhythms of earth's magnetic fields. Some people are ultra sensitive to these changes. Those individuals tend to experience more anxiety, increased fatigue, or mental confusion, especially during earth's magnetic storms. When you enter into resonance with the core of the earth, you become more conscious of the planet as a living entity. Forming a direct union with earth's core allows you to enter into a mental and spiritual relationship with it. Through your planetary alignment, you receive energetic balance and stability in your life. The way you align with the planet is by bringing earth's energy into your conscious awareness. Imagine a highway of energy starting from the crown chakra at the top of your head that extends straight down into earth's core. Also imagine that this invisible highway extends from the top of your head into deep space. The essential thing to understand is that you are always in resonance with the core of the earth. When you consciously illuminate this relationship, you become aligned with the immense power of Mother Earth.

INNER EARTH ENERGY

Now that you have the ability to get in alignment with the planet, it will bring stability to your presence, even in the midst of increasing chaos around you. This new consciousness will awaken your "inner earth energy" and bring you into greater alignment with the universe. Similar to being in resonance with the core of the earth, you can also stabilize yourself in relation to the "Mother Galaxy." This process requires your acceptance that consciousness itself extends far into deep space. Know that you can always call on the power of the universe and use it to balance your inner energetic field. In other words, use the energy of your outer energetic field to bring your inner energetic field into balance. With this new skill, you will ride life's unpredictable waves with a greater degree of mastery.

> *Beyond our sun are other suns, giving light and life to planetary systems, not a thousand, or two thousand merely, but multiplied without end. All arranged around us at immense distances from each other, attended by ten thousand times ten thousand worlds, all in rapid motion; yet calm, regular and harmonious, all space seems to be illuminated and every particle of light a world. All of this vast assemblage of suns and worlds may bear no greater proportion to what lies beyond the utmost boundaries of human vision, than a drop of water to the ocean.*
> *~ Elijah H. Burritt*

EARTH CRISIS: HEALING THE PLANET

The condition of the earth is in peril. The quality of our air, our oceans, and our lands are in jeopardy. At this time, forest fires are raging in Australia, the polar ice caps in Antarctica are melting, rivers of plastic flow in India, and war rages in the Middle East. Planetary healing is going to require collective intervention on behalf of us all. Together we create movements. Ask yourself: "What can I do to help Mother Earth?" Can you feed her birds? Can you clean her local park, beach, or forest? Can you use less plastic or contribute more to recycling? Can you convert to solar energy? All of these steps help you to become more supportive of the world around you. Cleaning up your outer world also helps you to clean up your inner world.

Teach your children about: "The Three R's"

1. **Reduce**
2. **Reuse**
3. **Recycle**

The American bald eagle is on the verge of extinction. Even the polar bear on its ice floats has become easy game for flying sportsmen. A peninsula named Udjung Kulon holds the last two or three dozen Javan rhinoceroses. The last known herd of Arabian oryx antelope has been machine-gunned down by a sheik. Blue whales have nearly been harpooned out of their oceans. Pollution ruins bays and rivers. Refuse litter beaches. Dam projects threaten Colorado canyons, valleys, and every place of natural beauty that can be a reservoir for power. Obviously the same scientific progress that is so alluring to me, is destroying qualities of greater worth.
~ *Charles A. Lindbergh*

EXERCISE #21

Global warming, overpopulation, water and air pollution, deforestation, global political conflict, and wars, are all impacting and diminishing the reserve energy sources of our precious planet. It's imperative to ask yourself, "What am I going to do to make earth a better place to live?" "Can I commit to zero emission transportation?" Specifically write down three things you can start doing to help heal the planet.

1. _____
2. _____
3. _____

Earth Pledge (say aloud)
"I, (say your name), pledge to commit to
doing my part as a naturalized citizen of the earth,
to maintain the beauty, power, and integrity of the planet,
for the preservation of life- for me, for you, and our future."

HARVEST FOR THE WORLD

We must grow our own food, that is how we will survive this earth crisis. Part of healing the planet means curating clean soil and growing organic foods. This growing of plants and foods gives life to earth and improves the quality of the soil. Hippocrates said, "Let food be your medicine." Research shows that dietary habits influence disease risk. While certain foods may trigger chronic health conditions, others offer strong medicinal and protective qualities. Eating whole, nutritious foods grown from the earth is important because the planet's unique substances work synergistically to create an effect in the body that can't be replicated by taking any supplement. Living off the earth has been and will continue to be, the most sustainable medium for survival of humanity.

CLIMATE CHANGE AND GLOBAL WARMING

The rapid increase in global warming is because of man's over reliance on animal products. Surpluses of animal food products results in industrial pollution. Greenhouse gases trap heat inside the earth's atmosphere in terms of global warming, which contributes to fires, deforestation, drought, flooding, and other extreme weather disasters.

As awful as this pandemic is, climate change could be worse.
If you want to understand the kind of damage that climate change will inflict,
look at COVID-19, and spread the pain out over a much longer period of time.
The loss of life and economic misery caused by this pandemic are on par with
what will happen regularly, if we do not eliminate the world's carbon emissions.
By 2060, climate change could be just as deadly as COVID-19,
and by 2100 it could be five times as deadly.
~ Bill Gates

CALLING ALL LIGHTWORKERS
AND ENERGY HEALERS

As lightworkers we must contribute to raising the vibrational frequency of humanity on the planet. Fill your body full of energy and light as you breathe in the whole sky. Each one of us are energy healers. The current earth crisis requires deep prayer and meditation from everyone worldwide. Additionally, we must hold space for the recovery of our planet and for the belief that God will save humanity. The world is in need of a cure. I believe that the solutions for the human condition today are going to come from our young minds. Our miracles will come from visionaries and from those who support the healing of the planet.

THE SIX ELEMENTS OF THE UNIVERSE

Fire	**Earth**	**Air**
Water	**Wood**	**Metal**

UNITY CONSCIOUSNESS AND PLANETARY HEALING

You are the world and you cannot separate yourself from the world. Individual transformation is also global transformation. When a single person transforms his or herself, there is a concurrent global shift that happens on our planet. When you finally realize that we are all one, this is your true awakening. Your conscious awareness is rising. When we become one with the world, we become one with one another— this is "unity consciousness." The earth is a living organism. I thank the universe for its gift. It's forests are the lungs of the planet. The rivers are like its arteries. The rain is like its tears. The oceans are the blood flowing through each of us. The mountains and forests are earth's body and the shifting sands of the deserts are earth's soul. Human beings are a part of one greater organism, consciousness itself.

Nature itself is the best physician
~ Hippocrates

EARTHING: CENTER YOURSELF BY WALKING BAREFOOT

Every step that you take makes an imprint on the surface of earth which is felt all the way to the depths of the earth's inner core. The addition of your personal energy also changes the earth's energy field at large. Whenever you're stressed out, the earth's energy is medicine. Walking barefoot in nature is called earthing or grounding. In short, grounding is putting your body in direct and uninterrupted contact with the earth. This means that skin needs to be in direct contact with soil, sand, rock, or water. From a scientific perspective, the idea is that the earth has a mild negative charge to it. Over time, especially in modern life, our bodies build up a positive charge. Direct contact with the earth can even out this positive charge and return your body to a neutral state. Walking barefoot allows electrons from the earth to flow into your body where in theory they neutralize overblown free radical and inflammatory damage. The end result of earthing is that your body is molecularly and vibrationally enhanced. Now that you have a better understanding of the science behind earthing, you can begin to walk with a sense of greater purpose. When you add the ancient spiritual practice of earthing to your spiritual practice, you add yet another tool to your tool belt to become a radiant example to the world of how a liberated person walks and lives.

EXERCISE #22
Grounding/Earthing

Grounding is an essential practice to keep you strong.
Use it to anchor yourself whenever you get thrown off balance.
Being in nature is the best place for you to heal and recharge.
Take off your shoes and walk barefoot in the sand, grass, or soil.
Feel the earth under your feet.
Experience the powerful energy of the earth's magnetic core.
Know that there is no separation of energies.
You are one with the planet and the entire universe is inside of you.

When we are in love with someone or something, there's no
separation between ourselves and the person or thing we love.
We do whatever we can for them, and this brings us great joy
and nourishment. When we see the earth in this way,
we will walk more gently on her.
~ Thich Nhat Hanh

CHAPTER 8

MEDITATION AND BREATHING TECHNIQUES FOR A CALMER, HAPPIER LIFE

DON'T HOLD ONTO ANYTHING, MAKE EVERY BREATH A SPIRITUAL PRACTICE

One of the most profound teachings I have learned in my spiritual journey is also the shortest, "I have arrived." When you return to your center through breathing, you return to the present moment, your true home. Once you arrive in the Now, there's no need for you to struggle to arrive anywhere else. You have the ability to connect with your soul through conscious breathing. Breathe in the present and exhale the past. In life, your first breath is in, your last breath is out. What leaves your body in death is not physical, it's spiritual. Breath is sacred, breath is life, without breath there is death.

Having a consistent breath work practice is the best thing you can do for vitality and wellness. The practice of conscious breathing can help you deal with your emotions and develop a real and lasting spiritual intimacy with yourself. Practice your breathing techniques every day. "Prana" is the energy force of the universe that you are blessed to inhale. Keep your breath deep, quiet, and even. On exhalation "apana" is created, a downward flowing energy responsible for rooting, grounding, and elimination. The opposing energies that we find in the breath of rise (prana) and fall (apana), create balance and can be found everywhere in nature: day and night, summer and winter, space and earth, and movement and stillness.

EXERCISE #23
Make Every Breath A Spiritual Practice

- **First close your eyes and settle down. Let your entire body release and soften.**
- **Throughout this meditation, remain focused on your breathing.**
- **On your in-breaths, inhale peace and calm.**
- **On your out-breaths, commit to letting everything go.**
- **Focus your attention on releasing any lower vibrations out of your body-mind.**

- **Make it your intention not to hold onto anything.**
- **Breathe in and out through your nose.**
- **Feel the positive energy of love coursing through your heart and body.**
- **Make every breath you take a spiritual practice.**

EVERY BREATH IS A MIRACLE

Breath is the connection between the body-mind and soul. Every beautiful breath that you take here on God's green earth is a miracle. Be grateful for each day and celebrate the gift of life. Whenever you find yourself in nature, practice your breathing techniques.

> *Breathing Mantra (say aloud)*
> *"And so it begins, the eyes are closed,*
> *the mind is quiet, the body is still,*
> *the breath is calm, the vision is inward,*
> *the soul is centered, the ego is lost,*
> *the broken heart heals,*
> *the wounded spirit is mended,*
> *inhale~calm, exhale~ease,*
> *love is real."*

You are love itself. When you begin to look for love, find love, feel love, be love, and show up in that light consistently, you will reach your maximum energy state. In this capacity, you will begin to shine the light of love onto everything and everyone. Start looking to add love to each one of your experiences. We increase our love vibration by finding love and tuning into love's frequency. Everyone and everything is a divine manifestation of God. It's all one love and one united energy.

EXERCISE #24
Conscious Mindful Breathing Mantra

Breath is the connection between your body-mind and your soul.

1. Place your hand over your heart and take a deep breath.
2. Breathe in and out fully and completely.
3. Make a sigh as you exhale and release whatever energy you are holding.
4. On your next breath, inhale the beautiful prana of the universe.
5. Say aloud: "I am loving awareness."
6. Each time your mind wanders, notice this and become a witness your thoughts and feelings. Breathe along with those thoughts and know that they are not you. Gently bring your awareness back to the natural flow of your breath.
7. Breath awareness is the heart of meditation. It is a way to settle and balance your mind and become present in the moment.
8. Use your breath to dissolve into the mighty universal field.
9. In between your breaths, in your mind's eye, say: "I am timeless, birthless, and love everlasting."

TIMELESSNESS

Your body, mind, and memories belong to time, but the aspect of you that witnesses your body-mind is beyond time. Put some space between you and your experience, this gap is known as timelessness, the formless space of awareness. Inside all of your breaths, you are timeless and formless. Begin to trace every thought back to its origin, which is always your busy mind. When you follow your thoughts back to their starting point, they begin to lessen their frequency and eventually go away— and your mind comes to a rest. Whenever you are able to quiet your mind, it creates space in your being and allows your soul to come forth and take the lead. An empty mind is a magnet for spiritual transformation. Don't be afraid of emptiness, it's your natural state. Be empty of all concepts of others. Be void of judgement of others. Be empty in every situation that you face. Everything collapses on the field of emptiness. Slowly focus your attention inward. Simply observe that everything arises from within you. Make it your practice not to react to everything and anything. Stillness is stellar.

LIVING IN THE PRESENT MOMENT

Not a single person can stop you from experiencing the beauty in the present moment. Every moment is divinely blessed. Our mission is to appreciate each moment we are granted. Staying present allows you to shine and thrive. When you live in the past, it keeps you unfulfilled. Scarcity blocks you from abundance. The more you resist what's happening in the moment, the more you suffer. Complete acceptance of whatever's happening for you right now, good or bad, happy or sad, is the key to the elimination of all fear and anxiety occupying your mind. Choosing certainty over uncertainty relieves stress and anxiety. Choose life, choose love. Love is the only certainty and only love is real.

THANK EACH EXPERIENCE THAT COMES TO YOU

One of the ways that has helped me not to associate pain with my past choices has been to thank each experience that has come my way. I realize that it's a great blessing to take a breath this morning and to be alive. I am grateful to be a free being and also to have the freedom of choice. Every day I awaken, I speak gratitude for experiencing another day on God's green earth. Gratitude cleanses and creates space. Being thankful clears any clutter from my mind and creates for me a clear path forward. The past and future are memory and imagination. Healing represents the end of conflict with yourself. True freedom can only be realized by living in the present moment. Today, I declare health, healing, and wholeness for all.

MEDITATION IS A TOOL FOR HEALING

Make sacred time everyday to release anything that is weighing you down spiritually. Meditation centers you and brings peace into your being. In spiritual traditions, meditation is seen as an essential tool of healing for a number of reasons. First, when you close your eyes it quiets the mind by redirecting your attention inward. This action reduces endless mind chatter which gives you a sense of inner peace. Once you learn to quiet your thoughts, you increase your capacity for concentration and increase your ability to control your desires and regulate your behavior. The normal chatter of your ego uses up a great deal of mental energy. Likewise, it takes a lot of energy to maintain the ego as a structure. So when thinking becomes quieter, the ego becomes weaker and a large amount of energy is suddenly freed. This energy naturally redirects itself into perception and higher awareness. Meditation also leads to an increased sense of the vividness and beauty of everyday objects. It has been linked with several healing benefits including: a reduction in negative thinking, decreased anxiety, decreased stress responses, a decrease in depression rates, and an overall feeling of well-being. The practice of meditation is self-healing in that you get to choose when and where you do it. With the high cost of prescription drugs, the lack of long-term pain management options, and an increase in the prevalence of chronic stress, meditation serves as a useful role in the holistic health industry. Think of meditation as an important tool in your medicine bag. The more you meditate—the more balance, truth, and inner harmony you bring to light.

THE BENEFITS OF MEDITATION

Meditation consists of generating three kinds of energy: mindfulness, concentration, and insight. These three energies give us the power to nourish our happiness and take care of any of our suffering. Finding freedom is never easy in this busy world. Despite our challenges, we all must find ways to unplug from the many pressures of our daily grind. Unplugging for some is reading a book, for others it's listening to music, and for others it's simply spending time alone in meditation. Although meditating works anytime, try meditating in the early morning. You will find that your brain will operate much more efficiently throughout the day with the addition of a morning meditation. Meditation acts to empty your mind and purify your consciousness. If you are indoors, visualize yourself surrounded by a beautiful scene in nature. Make sure that your indoor space is well-ventilated, fresh oxygen is fuel for healing. Outdoor meditation yields additional holistic benefits due to exposure to the elements of air, sun, wind, water, and earth. The heavenly sky enhances your ability to heal. Personally, I love meditating at the beach. When you sit near the ocean, try to synchronize your vibration with the frequency of the waves. Affirm your purpose of meditating and visualize your healing taking place. Invite positive energy to adjust your mood set point. Meditation brings balance, joy, and peace— so consider incorporating it into your daily self-care routine.

THE NEUROBIOLOGY OF MEDITATION

The way meditation works is it neurochemically stimulates the parasympathetic pathway, the body's relaxing state. Contrarily, meditation depresses the excitatory sympathetic "fight or flight" pathway of the nervous system. This energetic shift into homeostasis and balance is the optimal bioenvironmental state for body-mind healing to take place. Science has proven that meditation changes brain and body chemistry in a positive manner. When we change the condition of our inner world, we also change the condition of our outer world.

> *The thing about meditation is that*
> *you become more and more you.*
> *~ David Lynch*

MEDITATE ON INNER PEACE

The key to meditation is acceptance. The acceptance of the life force within you, all around you, and beyond you. The inner peace that you are searching for is already inside you. When your heart is heavy, come into meditation. Be done with anything that doesn't bring you peace. One of the natural benefits of meditation is that it places you in a state of zero resistance, which restores your balance. Acceptance of the divine flow of life is essential to discover your inner peace. Allow your body to drift into the silent inner dimension of Presence. Feel the calm waves of peace flow over you and through you. Let serenity become your vibration. Breathe fully and deeply like the rolling waves of the ocean. At the end of your meditation, appreciate that the energy of your body-mind has been cleansed, balanced, and fully restored. Realize that you are newly filled with peaceful energy and divine light.

CHAPTER 9

SURRENDER TO LOVE

SURRENDER TO LOVE

Chant love, because only love can save the day. Surrender is the spiritual process of letting go of all your attachments and the willingness to give up all things, including any mindset that no longer serves you. In surrender, you begin to dissolve and remove all obstacles, both imagined and real. Surrender is the shift from saying no to saying yes to life. Say yes to the moment and whatever form it takes. In order to become truly free you must clear all inner resistance. The antidote to your inner resistance is found in surrender. Surrender to what is. Surrender to truth. Surrender to the present moment and surrender to love. Surrender means surrendering your ego, nothing more or nothing less. What's left behind is the real you, the pure self. The only action that is not self-centered is a surrender to love. Surrender to love means, how often are you going to allow love to act on your behalf? An amazing part of your life begins when you surrender to love. Love is not lightning in a bottle, love is all around you waiting for you to believe in it, it's already there. Surrender is the fragrance that love sheds on the sleeve of devotion. The moment you know yourself to be love itself is the very moment that you realize that you've been love all along. Finding love is the way to find your freedom. As you deepen your practice of love, you can't help but follow the alluring scent of vitality. Love is a calling to become more alive. When you awaken from your slumber to the divine energy in your sacred heart, life is never the same again.

Healing Mantra (say aloud)
"I surrender to the Universe.
I surrender to Divine Light.
I surrender to the Supreme Creator.
I surrender to love.
I surrender every part of me
that has ever existed.
I surrender all of my thoughts, emotions,
resistance, memories, and attachments
to break free from my body-mind.
From this day forward, I pledge
to respond to my life's circumstances
the same way that God would."

VULNERABILITY AND LOVE

Vulnerability is not a weakness, it's a door that love walks through. Vulnerability is the gateway and birthplace for love. When you are vulnerable, you become a vessel for dynamic change. You shift into vulnerability by pushing your ego aside and following your heart. Being vulnerable is a critical step in your spiritual journey. Vulnerability exposes your sacred heart and soul when you surrender to love.

The I-Am Mantra (say aloud)
Beloved Father Who Dwells In My Soul At The Center Of My Being,
Who's Name Is "I am." I Surrender To You All That I Have,
And All That I Am.
~ Mooji

REFRAIN FROM JUDGEMENT

Don't be tempted to judge or act on everything that you see. Judgement always requires an action. It requires a look, stare, comment, approval, or disapproval. It's so easy to judge, but you can't judge another person and love yourself at the same time. When you judge another, you withhold love from yourself. Judging is a job of the mind, observation is a property of the soul. The way not to judge someone or something is to remain the witness of your experience. You may still see dysfunction, but there is no need to take action on it. The idea is to create more space between your thoughts and take a break from judging. Judgement is never helpful, no matter how justified you think it is. Look less with your eyes and simply feel with all of your heart. Let life happen in front of you freely. Drop your mind into your heart, in a moment you will be in such peace.

Love is Light, that enlightens those who give and receive it.
Love is gravity, because it makes some people feel attracted to others.
Love is power, because it multiplies the best we have, and
allows humanity not to be extinguished in their blind selfishness.
~ Albert Einstein

THE HEALING POWER OF LOVE

Eventually every situation brings the realization that interactions in the physical world are opportunities to grow in the spiritual dimension. Every interaction with everyone you meet are all providing life lessons for your spiritual advancement, each situation is for your higher learning and higher evolution. As you grow, you learn that spiritual evolution doesn't happen in the head, it happens in the heart. Find ways to tap into the divine love in your sacred heart, the greatest healing energy of all.

Love elevates your consciousness as well as the hearts and souls of those around you. The divine power of love is undefeated. Remember that love is always one choice away. You can choose to act out of love, or act out of hate. No matter what you are experiencing, no matter how painful, continue to choose love. You always have a choice between fear and love. Love is expressed through feelings and actions of compassion, empathy, and kindness. Fear is expressed through low level emotions like envy, jealousy, anger, and hatred. Life presents you with a continuum of experiences. Love is a choice you must make hundreds of times each and every day. Love is quite simply an addiction to your heart.

THE CHEAT CODE FOR LIFE

The cheat code for life is L.O.V.E.
L is for love yourself and also everyone else.
O is for the obliteration of negative thought patterns.
V is for the vision of who you wish to become.
E is for the evolution of your soul.

THE POWER OF LOVE

Love is the most powerful agent of change there is. Love changes people, circumstances, and everything in between. Love is the powerful invisible force that cannot and will not be denied. When love is applied to a situation, positive things begin to happen. If you choose to become a believer in love, it will help you to find your purpose. Love is purpose power. Love guides you to the deliverance of your magnificent gift.

CHAPTER 10

THE CONSCIOUS MIND, THE SUBCONSCIOUS MIND, AND DEPROGRAMMING

THE CONSCIOUS MIND

The mind is both non-physical and immeasurable in its power. You have only one mind, but it has at least two different aspects. Let's refer to these two dimensions as your conscious mind and your subconscious mind. The development of human consciousness includes the accumulation of wisdom, knowledge, and experiences, along with an increased awareness of our unconscious mind, which already possesses that knowledge. It is a process of the conscious mind coming in to synchrony with the unconscious. Your conscious mind and subconscious mind always flow in simultaneous operation. The conscious mind is also called the objective mind which includes your current field of awareness. Your conscious mind is deeply personal and selective, it's the part of you that decided to read this book right now. It's the part of you that makes all the decisions, like what you eat for breakfast or whom to call on the telephone.

PATTERNS PURPOSE AND CREATION

The human mind is a maker of 3-D patterns in a multi-dimensional world. Our intellects cannot grasp facts unless they are first organized into a pattern or image. Science is the art of discovering the pattern already laid down by nature and also finding out how it was done. Creation is the act of establishing meaningful patterns through which a purpose might be achieved. Patterns bring meaning and adding meaning to your life brings purpose. Discovering and understanding why certain thought patterns are laid down the way they are is one my missions in this manuscript of *Love and Healing.*

GETTING OUT OF THE MAINSTREAM, DEPROGRAMMING, AND DEEP DIVING

The human brain that has evolved through millions of years is the common brain of humanity. Your mind comes preloaded with thoughts and beliefs that are then shaped by your conditioning. Similarly, note that a baby bird already knows how to build a nest. Its DNA is preprogrammed with the instincts, knowledge, and ability to build a nest for its survival. Your programming hinders your search for the truth of who you really are. Your situation is not who you are, who you are is pure love personified. You are programmed to look at the particles and physical aspects of yourself instead of your invisible energetic self. It's your task to learn how to close your eyes and see beyond your world of form and object reality. What you need the most in your life is unseen. Fortunately, there is always enough space for you to pull back as the witness to see the programs that are currently controlling your thoughts, emotions, feelings, and actions.

The real you is pure and untouched. When you depattern away from your normal responses, you invite new possibilities into your life. You are consciousness. Cease judging every event that happens to you and accept the divine flow of the universe. Try seeing yourself as always evolving in the most divine way.

DISMANTLE YOUR DEFAULT PROGRAMMING, UPGRADE YOUR IDENTITY

You are not responsible for the abuse you suffered as a child, but it is your responsibility as an adult to investigate and unearth why you are still reacting to it. You continue to be triggered by this unhealthy past and continue to choose and execute your defensive programming. As long as you remain defensive about your past, the universe will continue to create other challenging experiences until you face your trauma and free yourself. I recommend doing your inner child work to diagnose and repair the damage that you have suffered. Defensive programming hinders your growth and expression of your truth. We are programmed to run our old hard-wired programming. When you dismantle your network default settings, dissolve faulty mindsets, and depart from your old responses, you create space for the arrival of new possibilities and higher level outcomes. Disintegration of your default networks frees you to become selfless, energized, and supercharged. Take a leap of faith today and begin to upgrade your identity. You create your new identity by improving your mindset and by starting to choose differently than you have done in the past.

EXERCISE #25
Thirteen Questions To See If You Are Enslaved To Your Programming

**The intention of this exercise is to gauge your current
position on your spiritual journey. The goal is to
eventually answer "yes" to each of these questions.
When that day comes, you will have
become the Master of Your Mind.**

1. **Are you able to detach from thinking?**
2. **Have you learned to become a witness to your emotions?**
3. **Have you learned to wear your smile?**
4. **Do you believe in yourself?**
5. **Do you believe in a higher power?**
6. **Can you perceive surrounding energy fields?**
7. **Are you a great manifester?**
8. **Do you practice unconditional love?**
9. **Are you able to use your inner power to heal others?**
10. **Do you believe in oneness and equality?**
11. **Have you reconciled with your past?**
12. **Are you unafraid to die?**
13. **Do you believe in rebirth?**

THE SUBCONSCIOUS MIND

*The interface between God and man is at least in part the interface between
our unconscious and our conscious. To put it plainly, our unconscious is God.
God is within us. We are a part of God all the time.
God has been with us all along, he is now and always will be.*
~ Scott Peck, M.D.

Your subconscious mind is the part of your mind that functions below the surface of your awareness and is a thousand times more powerful than your conscious mind. When you sleep, your subconscious remains awake, it literally never rests. Even when you're unconscious under anesthesia during surgery your subconscious mind remains alert and aware. As I've said before on many occasions, your subconscious and it's intellect is like a biological "juke box" which will automatically playback any memory or recording whenever the right button is pushed. Your subconscious mind does not originate ideas, but it does accept and keep those which your conscious mind feels to be true and gives form and expression to them. Every feeling you have or entertain makes a tiny subconscious impression.

Your subconscious meticulously carries out ideas you have about yourself every single moment. The great majority of your thoughts spring forth from your subconscious by the association of ideas. One thought literally spawns another. The subconscious is the womb of creation, it is the greater you.

95% of who we are by the time we are 35 years old, is a memorized
set of behaviors, emotional reactions, unconscious habits, hardwired attitudes,
beliefs, and perceptions that function like a computer program.
~ Dr. Joe Dispenza

Your subconscious mind also stores your memories as well as the teachings and lessons of your parents, friends, relatives, teachers, religious figures, books, radio, television, advertising, and many others. Your memories are recorded, strung together, and labeled either "painful" or "pleasurable." This is how your memories are accompanied by exact biochemical emotional sensations whenever you are triggered.

Your subconscious holds all your values and beliefs safely intact. It efficiently has instant recall of your typical responses and behavioral patterns. Your conscious and subconscious regularly communicate with each other whether you realize it or not. Your subconscious is resistant to sudden change. This is especially true when you attempt to change a long-standing belief or attitude. This is because of your programming. Your subconscious also controls your body functions like your heart rate, blood flow, digestion, and respiratory rate. Many of the tasks it knows how to do are built in at the time of your birth. Other tasks are taught to it by your conscious mind, tasks like handwriting, painting, and playing piano. The memory of how to write your handwriting lies in your subconscious. Your stories are written from your subconscious.

Early life trauma negatively affects your inner child and damages your self-confidence and self-esteem. This level of hurt leads to a loss of self-respect, insecurity, and the onset of addictive behaviors to cover up your pain. Time doesn't heal all wounds. It just gives them the opportunity to sink into your subconscious mind where they can affect your thoughts, emotions, and behaviors. Deep emotional wounds become trapped in time and buried into the bottom of your subconscious. Emotional disturbances, especially suppressed emotions, are the cause of much dis-ease. At the root of things, your subconscious mind is what most influences your behavior. You behave just like who you believe yourself to be.

All creation occurs in the domain of your subconscious mind. Subconscious impressions literally determine the condition of your world. Carl Jung wrote, "highly consciously sensitive people are more influenced by their subconscious minds than others, which gives them access to important information that contains prophetic insight." That being said, it's difficult to access your subconscious mind to make beneficial changes because of your mind's security system. What heals you is to go inward, accept yourself, forgive yourself, love yourself, and address your attachments.

Imagine yourself living your best life. Visualize what that dream life looks like for you. You can achieve whatever you set your mind to do. Remember that all dreams require an activation code. Dreams must be transferred from your subconscious into your conscious mind to manifest, otherwise they will remain dormant in your subconscious. The way you activate a dream is first by getting into alignment with your higher self. Your higher self has the codes to unlock your subconscious desires. By this light, now is the time to get into universal alignment and activate your dreams.

WILLPOWER

Will is a quality of consciousness. Conscious-will is the ability to act, or refrain from acting, in reference to your painful or pleasant memories, hopes and fears, and likes and dislikes. Your willpower is a natural and creative power. In exercising your will, it starts with a strong desire to accomplish a goal or fulfill a dream. In a sense, conscious-will is powered by a vivid visual imagination. It's by sheer willpower that men and women alike have accomplished the unthinkable and the impossible. Impossible is merely a word that you don't have to accept. Will is a strong desire from deep within you that's capable of creating a powerful sending force that sparks the manifestation of an idea. Willpower transforms a single wave of energy into a particle of living matter. Once alive, the penetration of your dream project will only travel as far as you drive it. Always remember that you are a masterful manifester. You are the miraculous one that moves thought energy from the invisible wave to the visible particle universe.

EXERCISE #26
An Exercise In Courage

My challenge for you is to be courageous, bold, and fearless.
Make the choice today to do something that you've never done before.
Choose something that will push you to the edge of your fears.
Aim to go beyond your comfort zone.
Try activities that make your heart race and
push you to the limit, such as:
rock climbing, white water rafting, parasailing,
scuba diving, skydiving, etc.

YOUR MIND IS PROGRAMMED

Your mind is like a very complex computer and your thought patterns and behavioral sequences are like pre-installed programs in a computer. Some of these programs you inherited and some were installed by you. For example, maybe the first time you ever ate chocolate, you enjoyed the taste so much that you began to eat it often and to this day, you've formed a pattern of eating chocolate on a regular basis to feel a certain way. Some programs were installed by your parents, teachers, and friends. For instance, a teacher might have exposed you to classical music as a child and now as an adult, you deeply appreciate listening to and collecting classic music because of the way it makes you feel. Just like the programs of a computer, that can be activated with the right commands, the programs of your subconscious are also ready and waiting to be activated. Changing, installing, or deleting a computer program is a relatively easy task, but it isn't so easy to alter the programs of your mind. Your subconscious mind comes complete with a filter, a protector that acts as a built-in security system. This filter screens new thoughts and behaviors and makes sure that you really want what you say you want. This security system works to keep your beliefs, personality, and your sense of reality consistent. It also keeps you from constantly changing your mind and from accepting any and every suggestion that comes your way. If not for it, you would end up in a state of confusion. But what if you simply want to add a program, a new attitude or behavior that appeals to you? Hypnosis offers an expedient method for that change. Hypnosis disarms or bypasses the security system of your subconscious mind just long enough to slip in new beliefs. Hypnotherapy is a process that allows you to instruct your subconscious mind to make beneficial changes to your mind, body, and behavior.

GETTING PAST THE DOORMAN (AKA THE BOUNCER) OF YOUR MIND

You might say that your subconscious mind has a doorkeeper, a bouncer of sorts. Take a journey with me and imagine yourself outside a nightclub. Inside the club where everything is happening is your subconscious. It's your desire to get into the club, but first you must find a way to get past the bouncer. How you approach a strong doorman of a popular club is similar to how you must approach your subconscious mind to change a particular behavior. When you first approach a nightclub, the doorman or bouncer looks you over to see if you are a good fit for the environment inside. Similarly, when a new idea or suggestion comes up to the doorman of your mind, that idea is examined and weighed to see if it fits in with current programming. If the new idea doesn't meet that standard, your idea is rejected and the doorman turns you away. Now imagine if you could get a beautiful woman to talk to the bouncer on your behalf. She could use her low sultry voice to distract his or her attention away from the door just long enough to let you slip by them without them noticing you. This is very similar to how self-hypnosis works. It calms, quiets, and distracts the doorman of your mind so that you can get inside, make some changes, and then leave. A doorman can always be sweet-talked and lulled to distraction. In fact, the doorman may enjoy the experience so much that he or she looks forward to it again. Likewise, hypnosis is so pleasant that it becomes easier and easier every time. It becomes something your mind enjoys and actually looks forward to.

CHAPTER 11

THE TECHNIQUE AND BENEFITS OF SELF-HYPNOSIS

This chapter is for anyone that wants to eliminate a bad habit or needs a potent valuable tool for positive personal change. Are you looking for positive personal change? Hypnotherapy gives you a fast and easy method for improving the quality of your life in so many areas.

The Definition: Hypnosis is a state of narrowed attention in which suggestibility is greatly heightened.

THE HISTORY OF HYPNOSIS

Hypnosis has been around for several hundred years. The art of hypnosis has proven itself to be both safe and efficient tools for growth and self-change. It's a phenomenon that's being used today as a powerful life-changing therapy. Millions owe a profound debt of gratitude to hypnosis for their turn around and success. In life, it's not always always the smartest person that wins, it's the one that uses all their tools most efficiently. I owe a great debit of credit to self-hypnosis, which has helped me to significantly improve my focus and drop several negative habits. If you are willing to open your mind to include the possibility of reaching and positivity influencing your subconscious, then you are really going to enjoy this chapter.

The term "hypnosis" was coined by Dr. James Braid back in the 19th century and the field of clinical hypnotherapy has been developing and spreading ever since. In the late 1950s, the American Medical Association approved hypnosis instruction for inclusion in certain medical schools' curriculum. The therapeutic use of the practice of hypnosis turns mere hypnosis into hypnotherapy. Indeed hypnotherapy has the ability to make profound changes in one's habits by influencing the mind at its deepest level.

MISCONCEPTIONS ABOUT HYPNOSIS

Hypnosis has its army of skeptics, both casual and adamant, mostly because of media misinformation. Who can forget some of the versions of hypnosis made famous by stage entertainers and movies. One misconception is that hypnosis is mind control. The idea that you surrender your will to a hypnotist is nonsense. Actually, the participation of your willpower is crucial for effective hypnosis. Another myth is that when you are brought out of hypnosis, you won't remember what went on during the session. While this is a possible phenomenon, it is rarely seen. Most people fully remember everything that was said to them during hypnosis. Another fable is that hypnosis is a supernatural practice. Hypnosis is not a product of the occult. All things considered, in my personal practice, I chose to focus on self-hypnosis rather than hypnosis done by a conductor.

Self-suggestion is a movement and doorway to your inner mind. It's important to recognize that hypnosis doesn't create actual changes in subjects, what it does, is that it creates a favorable state of mind that's highly conducive for making positive changes. Hypnosis is not a magic wand, it's simply a state of mind in which you are able to learn new things much quicker with greater execution. Self-suggestion helps you to unlearn any unwanted habits that no longer serve you. It helps to see your unwanted behaviors being blown away by the wind, crushed by a boulder, or burned by fire.

SELF-HYPNOSIS (SELF-SUGGESTION)

In self-hypnosis there is nobody feeding you suggestions, you do it yourself. Plainly speaking, self-suggestion is the process of putting yourself under, followed by giving yourself auto-suggestions which aim to strengthen your performance. Self-hypnosis is a form of auto-suggestion in which you feed your subconscious commands while you're in a fully relaxed, but awake state. I believe that there is no simpler way to make significant changes in your life than by self-hypnosis. Almost every leading book on personal development, from Napoleon Hill's book *Think and Grow Rich,* to Tony Robbins book *Awaken the Giant Within,* acclaim the tremendous value and impact of self-hypnosis. Be adventurous, be open, be flexible, and be willing to add self-hypnosis to your healing essentials kit.

YOU'VE BEEN SELF-HYPNOTIZED MANY TIMES BEFORE

The truth is you have already hypnotized yourself many times before! You've entered hypnosis spontaneously literally thousands of times depending upon your age. We all slip into transitional states everyday but the mind does not label these situations as hypnosis. Daydreaming is nothing but a state of hypnosis, perhaps light but sometimes deep. When you concentrate intently on anything such as reading a book, watching television, or a movie, we tend to slip into a trance countless times a single day. In any religious ceremonies, particularly if there's music and ritual, many in the audience will enter hypnosis spontaneously. Almost anyone who drives a car can recall this familiar situation happening, which is extremely conducive to hypnosis. Imagine yourself out on the open road, relaxed behind the wheel, your eyes fixed on the white lines of the highway, you hear the background noise of the monotonous hum of the car's motor, and suddenly you realize that you passed through a small town but you don't remember the drive! You have been in hypnosis, experienced symptoms of amnesia, and then awakened yourself. There is no fear here, only the realization that you can fully operate safely and successfully while deeply relaxed.

Music is also a powerful tool for a deeper trance. The tempo, volume, and lyrics all work to synchronize your mind. We can all recall a memory of someone vibing out to music as if no one was watching, this is a great example of a trance state achieved through music. Another example of music as a powerful hypnotizing agent is found in the example of a "singing commercial" where advertisers incorporate the song's rhythm and lyrics along with subconscious subliminal suggestions, which leave you wanting to buy the item.

Potential Health Benefits of Self-Hypnosis

- **Reduces stress in your mind, body and spirit**
- **Cures bad habits like smoking, drinking, and drug addiction**
- **Helps you to lose weight**
- **Promotes emotional mastery**
- **Reduces your fears and anxiety**
- **Elevates your mood and improves symptoms of depression**
- **Improves your memory and mental abilities to learn and create**
- **Enhances your dreams. Your dreams become more consistently nurturing, self-enhancing, and positive.**
- **Fly without fear**
- **Cures fear of heights**
- **Improves your overall performance**
- **Charges your body with a new exhilarating energy and vitality**
- **Brings on a brighter personality**

- **Manifest more money**
- **Have greater sex**
- **Helps to make a success of your relationship/marriage**

Healing then, is accomplished by uncovering, neutralizing,
and erasing any false images of thought, and letting the perfect idea
reflect itself through the subjective mind into the body.
~ Dr. Ernest Holmes

CONDITIONING

When you teach a dog to do a trick by making him do it over and over until she is an expert at it and obeys your order immediately, you have "conditioned" her or taught her a new set of chain reactions in which thoughts and muscular movements follow, one after the other. Similarly, you can train your subconscious mind to perform tricks in a similar way.

EXERCISE #27
AutoSuggestion

What is it that you want to autosuggest to yourself?
State aloud: "The change I want to make in my life is:

_____

Now that you have written your own autosuggestion,
take a few moments and read it aloud three times.
Now name three actions that you can take today
to help you accomplish your goal.

1. _____
2. _____
3. _____

CONTROL YOUR MIND AND YOU CONTROL YOUR LIFE

Hypnosis is not just about trance, relaxation, or skills development, it's also about making positive changes in your life that align with your highest desires. The first step of self-suggestion is to reach a relaxed state. Once you are able to come into full relaxation, you can insert suggestions and reprogram your subconscious mind. More specifically, in a heightened state of suggestibility— positive ideas, values, and intentions can be presented to your inner mind to bring about beneficial behavioral changes.

Your conscious mind acts as a filter for your subconscious mind. Any hardwire change in your life has to be done through the reprogramming of your subconscious mind. However, as your subconscious mind cannot be approached directly, remember that you have to use creative methods to bypass the security system of your subconscious mind. This is where the artistry of hypnosis and self-hypnosis can serve and assist you. In hypnosis you will begin tapping into the hidden powers of your higher mind. The powers that you've only had glimpses of are now brought to the surface for you to use for your benefit.

Hypnotherapy is essentially a way of reprogramming how you think in order to influence your actions in a positive manner. Self-hypnosis allows you to bypass your conscious mind and introduce positive suggestions into your subconscious. This is powerful because your subconscious mind is more than ten times as powerful as your conscious mind. If you can gain better understanding and control of your subconscious mind, you multiply your inner power. If you can learn to master your mind, then you can master your life. I find hypnotherapy to be a useful tool for healing unconscious behaviors. Most people live an ordinary life because they have the habit of using their limited belief as their space of creation, negativity blunts creativity. Self-inquiry assists in the identification and understanding of our shortcomings. One of the easiest ways to uncover your misbeliefs is to use self-hypnosis. Start by asking your subconscious mind to reveal your blocks to you. Asking for permission to access your subconscious mind assists in its arrival. You'll be surprised how inner reflection is capable of revealing what should've been obvious to you for years.

I believe that if you can learn the simple and safe techniques of self-suggestion, you can acquire the power that leads to a positive mindset, increased vigor, greater wellness, success, improved self-control, and a more loving and peaceful existence.

From this point forward, you don't even know how to quit in life.
~ Aaron Lauritsen

The Four Pillars of Self-Hypnosis

1. **Autorelaxation: The process of reaching the state of full mental and physical relaxation.**
2. **Autosuggestion: How to give suggestions/commands to your subconscious mind. New autosuggestions must be morally acceptable to your subconscious belief system, or they will not be carried out**
3. **Autoanalysis: Self-analysis skills are critical. It's important to uncover which of your limiting beliefs are affecting your performance.**
4. **Autotherapy: Sparked by relaxation, self-hypnosis aims to create a positive mental and energetic shift in your subconscious that improves your psyche and performance.**

Self-hypnosis pays huge dividends of a richer and happier life. In self-hypnosis we align with our thoughts and actions at our deepest level. You can use self-hypnosis to acquire more of your personality and unleash your greatest potential. Start seeing yourself as timeless and limitless and begin to believe it at your core.

Suggestions for Self-Hypnosis

- **Set aside 15-30 minutes for your hypnotherapy session.**
- **Identify your intention for your hypnosis.**
- **Find a quiet place where you will be undisturbed.**
- **Slowly become less aware of your surroundings.**
- **The first goal is full physical and mental relaxation. Once your body relaxes, your conscious mind automatically relaxes and you become more receptive to suggestion.**

- Anyone can slip into a "trance", it's a natural state of being. Visualize your conscious mind shutting off. Stop analyzing things and simply float off to a calm and relaxing imaginary place.
- Make your suggestion. It's better to work on only one thing at a time. Autosuggestions may be made verbally but it's not required, thinking them is enough. Always tell yourself that the thing suggested is pleasant and good.
- If you can add a visual image to your verbal suggestion, it will make the suggestion 10x more potent. Word your suggestions with only the end result in mind. The more you practice and repeat your self-suggestion, the more successful it will become and the more easily you will be able to reach a hypnotic state.
- Fear of loss of control can prevent your induction and hold you back from deeper hypnosis.
- Remember that hypnotherapy works amazingly well for a lot of people and it can work well for you too. Results depend on your belief factor and also on how much you practice.
- Trust and expect that self-hypnosis will open your mind to greater capabilities and more favorable outcomes.

AUTOSUGGESTION

The most famous proponent of autosuggestion was Emil Coue', a French hypnotist who lived from 1857-1926. He taught a simple mantra, "Every day, in every way, I'm getting better and better." He advised his subjects to repeat this mantra every morning when they rise and also at bedtime every night. He believed this autosuggestion set in motion both mental and physical effects that helped his patients heal. He believed that giving general non-specific mental suggestions is superior to commanding your subconscious to achieve a specific end. He believed in the power of the mind to overcome almost anything and he famously said, "I've never cured anyone in my life. All I do is show people how they can cure themselves." Coue noted that whenever he dispensed medication, more patients got better when he praised the effects of the medication than when he didn't. The simple idea was that patients could have "thoughts of illness" or "thoughts of cure." The method he taught relied on the principle that any idea exclusively occupying the subconscious mind, turns into reality. The subconscious never fails to express that which has been impressed upon it. The moment it receives an impression, it begins to work out the ways of its expression.

The top 3 reasons for failing to discover results in self-hypnosis are due to:

1. **An underlying fear of hypnosis**
2. **Misbeliefs about what hypnosis feels like**
3. **Impatience and lack of practice**

EFFECTIVE SELF-HYPNOSIS

Learning how to hypnotize yourself might seem uncomfortable or even impossible to you right now, but in time you'll find it easier and eventually you'll begin to wonder how you ever got through your week without spending some time going inwards. The effectiveness of self-hypnosis depends on several factors including: strong motivation, an open mind to hypnotherapy, and a commitment to diligence. I am not suggesting that self-hypnosis replace psychiatry, I am merely advocating its use as an adjunct therapy to improve people's overall well-being.

DR. CLAYTON'S STEP-BY-STEP TECHNIQUE OF SELF-HYPNOSIS

Self-hypnosis programs your subconscious mind to achieve supreme self-confidence and self-mastery.

1. **Plan for your session to last 15 to 30 minutes, that's a good start. The reason that a time frame is given is so that your expectation(s) can be set and reached in a short amount of time.**
2. **Expectation is a foundation for self-hypnosis success. Expect to experience self-hypnosis and also expect to reap benefits in a short period of time.**

3. To start the process, loosen your clothes and sit or lie down on a chair or sofa. What's most important is that you are comfortable, relaxed, and momentarily free from the stress.

4. Both hands should lie straight along your body. Don't cross your hands or legs and don't lay them on each other.

5. Relax your body one muscle group at a time until your entire body is calmed. Let all your muscles go as loose and as limp as possible. The more you can relax, the deeper you'll be able to go into hypnosis. Repeat in your inner mind, "I am going deeper into hypnosis."

6. Find an object that you can focus your attention on. Clear your mind of all thoughts and just focus on your object.

7. As an alternative, you can focus on the flame of a candle for 2-3 minutes. The candle flame is a wonderful deepener and induces a lovely calm feeling.

8. Sense your eyelids becoming heavy and slowly closing. Close your eyes.

9. Shift your focus to your breathing. Breathe deeply and evenly. Mentally tell yourself that every time you breathe out, you will relax a little bit more. (say aloud): "The deeper inside I go, the quieter I become. With each breath I am feeling better and better."

10. Use visualization to put yourself further under. Start by visualizing a blackboard full of your thoughts in writing. Visualize your chalk writings on the board being erased, one by one until your board is empty. When your blackboard is finally empty, you have created the space for Presence to arise.

11. Say inwardly, "I am now in the state of complete relaxation." Sense your body getting lighter as if you are floating on a cloud.

12. Once you've reached a comfortable hypnotic state, repeat your dominant suggestion. Focus on your statement looking out from your mind's eye and then repeat it in your thoughts three times. Keep it simple. Your statements need to be very straightforward and no more than a few words long.

13. Keep your suggestions positive. Your statements need to be of a positive nature to influence your higher mind.

14. Simultaneously, visualize the end result that you desire. Imagine what it would mean to have sustained and successful action on your suggestion. What would change for you? Picture yourself acting on your suggestion later today, next week, and even next year.

15. In your mind's eye, state: "When I awaken, I will feel fantastic."

16. Relax and clear your mind one last time before bringing yourself out of your session by taking a few deep energizing breaths. Open your eyes and let your session end naturally.

CHAPTER 12

RAISING CONSCIOUSNESS TOOLS OF THE EGO, MINDFULNESS, AWARENESS AND PRESENCE. WHAT'S THE DIFFERENCE?

CONSCIOUSNESS IS ANOTHER NAME FOR THE INTELLIGENCE OF THE MIND

Consciousness is your Divine Intelligence. Indeed it is consciousness, thought-energy, which creates everything you take to be your reality. The terms "consciousness" and "awareness" are often used interchangeably, which often results in ensuing confusion and misunderstandings. Essentially, consciousness can be regarded as your mind-based energy field which includes the presence of objects, whereas the term awareness refers to the non-physical universe without objects. Consciousness can be considered as the "relative nature" of your mind, since its transitory, changing, and dependent on your internal and external conditions. Whereas, awareness is generally regarded as the divine reflection of the "absolute nature" of your mind, since it is your unchanging background. Don't become so fixated on your identification with your transient consciousness as the "doer" in your story. If you do, you'll come to believe that your job and personality define who and what you are, hence you will suffer. Suffering happens whenever you cling to the impermanent aspect of who you are. When you embrace your magnificent true nature, your suffering ends.

Consciousness has no shape of its own.
It's like water, it's nature is to flow. It will take
the shape of whatever concepts you point it to.
~ Mooji

Most people can accept the idea that consciousness is inside their body, but can they also accept the notion that the body also lies in consciousness? If a person sees their body as their only identity, suffering will come. Consciousness also includes all things which you can see or perceive. As you relax more and grow to see yourself beyond the physical nature of your body, you won't feel trapped inside your body anymore. Your conscious mind is like a projector. The world you see is a projection of your ego-mind, which is also known as your "condition." Everyone's conditioning is in need of some healing. Whatever energy doesn't pass or filter through your conscious mind is the "unconditional" part of you, this is known as your inner essence. This unborn or eternal aspect of you is what watches your condition, this is your pure self.

> *If the expansion of consciousness does not loom large*
> *in the human future, what kind of future is it going to be?*
> ~ *Terence McKenna*

Your mind projects a world that you subsequently take to be real. Why? Because you habitually get attached to your thoughts and feelings and then you look outward at the effects. Because of this, you fail to recognize the hidden source of your projected world. Let's discuss the one who is behind all the projections that you see, show me this one. This is the one I want to surrender to, the Creator of all before me. This is why the wise suggest that you frequently delve into your inner essence. It is through God-realization that you can fully understand how you create your own suffering, and learn how you can free yourself of it. What I am speaking of is the concept of becoming a student and a devoted practitioner of consciousness. Learn the difference between consciousness and awareness and align with your true nature. The other is a false narrative and a collection of images that have you believing you are something that you are not.

> *Self Awareness Mantra (repeat aloud)*
> *"I am completely aware of my personality*
> *and the singular physical aspect of myself.*
> *At the same time, I recognize the non-physical aspect*
> *of myself beyond this room, beyond this chair that I am*
> *sitting on, and beyond what I currently perceive.*
> *I trust that everything is unfolding for me*
> *for my greater good. I am a part of the great history*
> *of the universe and I rest in knowing that*
> *I am one with all there is."*

THE EGO

The ego is your lower level of consciousness, nevertheless it's very important in your development of self-esteem, self-respect, self-preservation, and self-love. Sages believe that the ego was created by the soul in order to experience this sweet earthly existence. Your ego loves you, aims to protect you, and believes it's always striving for your betterment. For the ego it's a race to become a winner in the game of life. Winning is defined by garnering more attention, fame, or fortune. The problem with the ego's stance is that it places you in the position of always being right. This finger pointing mindset keeps you from coming into the recognition, acceptance, and forgiveness of your own contribution to your dilemmas. Your ego seeks to balance you. If you are sad, it tries to make you happy. If you are happy, it will try to keep you happy. If you are neutral or bored, your ego aims to entertain you. People with extra large egos are imbalanced and largely unconscious. Self-absorption is so limiting and only serves the needs of your lower self.

Ego is truly dangerous because it tries to keep you in personhood and away from the light and wisdom of your higher self. It is often described as the dance of a snake. The real you was placed in a trance long ago. You awaken from the trance by pushing your ego-identification aside and awakening to your true self. The source of the idea that "I am the body," is ego. Fortunately, ego is balanced by the self. The ego is like a finger that you hold up to block the searing rays of the sun. A mere finger trying to hide the sun is the same as the ego's attempt to hide your higher self. Your ego is threatened by your spiritual awakening and tries to prevent your soul's expression, so that it can remain in control of your life. Ego encourages you to control your situations, but your soul asks for your surrender. The only thing that can save someone with an ego-based identity is a conscious awakening.

Opinion is really the lowest form of human knowledge.
It requires no accountability, no understanding. The highest form of knowledge
is empathy, for it requires us to suspend our egos and live in another's world.
It requires profound purpose larger than the self kind of understanding.
~ Bill Bullard

Comparison is the main tool of the ego. Your ego is always inviting you to compare yourself to someone or something else. In one ear the ego whispers "you are great." In the other ear it whispers "you deserve better." Thus you are never satisfied with where you are. Whenever this happens, it succeeds in parring your identity to whatever self-image that you are currently defending and protecting.

All you need to know and observe in yourself is this:
Whenever you feel superior or inferior to anyone, that's the ego in you.
~ Eckhart Tolle

Resistance is also a tool of the ego, which keeps you unsatisfied with what is available to you in the present moment. When you live in the ego's shadow of scarcity, it blocks you from forgiveness, acceptance, and joy. Conflict is yet another tool of the ego. Take away the problems and complaints in some people's lives and there is little left to be joyful about. Your defense against your ego is peace. If you do not want the interpretation of the ego to run your life, then ask for peace and your mind will become still. The ultimate lesson is the same, to know thyself. Unselfishness, service to others, and assisting humanity are actions which unlock the higher self.

The ego relies on the familiar.
It is reluctant to experience the unknown,
which is the very essence of life.
~ Deepak Chopra

CONSCIOUSNESS EXPANDS

Since conscious energy is always moving, it cannot comprehend the motionless and so it falls into silence and stillness. The mind has many abilities, but there's only one consciousness, the unborn aspect of you. Consciousness is everywhere and everlasting. Even if one million bodies perish, consciousness does not perish. Expanding your consciousness requires becoming more aware of the entire universal field. This training and learning is done through immersion into silence and stillness. The goal of healing therapy is to become more aware that you are a part of the single ocean of consciousness. Realize that you are one with consciousness and that consciousness is always expanding inside of you.

The source of wisdom and power, of love and beauty is within ourselves,
but not within our egos. It is within our consciousness. Indeed, its
presence provides us with a conscious contrast which enables us

> *to speak of the ego as if it were something different and apart: it is*
> *the true self whereas the ego is only an illusion of the mind.*
> *~ Paul Brunton*

The 4 P's:

1. **Path: You are always on your path, the key is to not to try to control your destiny and trust that the universe has your back.**
2. **Purpose: Everyone has a divine reason for being here. When you find your special gift, your purpose unfolds.**
3. **Persistence: Everything in life is proportional to the amount of work you put into it. You will eventually reach your goal if you never quit.**
4. **The Dimension of Presence: Presence is the proof of God in you. When you come into the state of Presence, you are in alignment with your divine soul.**

OBSERVATION: THE ROLE OF THE WITNESS

If you take a step back and let your thoughts come and go without attaching any personal significance to them, it will become apparent that you are not your thoughts, but the living witness of your thoughts. You are not the passing traffic, but the space in which traffic flows. What remains when all grasping and wanting falls away is pure awareness, the motionless timeless background. It is your true nature prior to, during, and after your thoughts, memories, sensations, perceptions, and experiences. It is in this state of Presence that you can come to rest in this breathtaking stillness. The only inner voice is silence itself.

> *So long as the ego thinks of himself as the "doer" and the master*
> *of the house of the heart, the Real Master does not enter there.*
> *The mercy of the Lord is the surest way to God-vision.*
> *~ Ramakrishna*

The witnessing element of you stems from your soul. The view of the witness is like sitting in an audience watching a movie instead of being in one. The witness inside of you is your centering device, your rudder in the game of life, your soul, your Divine Intelligence. The healing journey asks you to remain as the witness of your experience. When you find yourself out of spiritual alignment, remind yourself to stay as the watcher, this is the fundamental principle of self-awareness. In your new role, continue to watch your projections manifest from the inside-out. Soon, any sense of separation in your identity will fade away. There has never been any real separation in you, only oneness everlasting. You and your inner being are truly one.

The ability to observe without evaluating is the highest form of intelligence.
~Krishnamurti

EXERCISE #28
The "Question Yourself" Exercise.

Ask yourself these three questions.
Write your response to each:

1. **Are you living up to the expectations that you've set for yourself?**
2. **State what issue or issues are most difficult for you right now.**
3. **What are your biggest shortcomings and how do you overcome them?**

The ego-mind can not keep up its attack on you
under the power and scrutiny of observation.
~ Mooji

AWARENESS IS ANOTHER NAME FOR YOU

Sri Ramana Maharshi states: "You are awareness, awareness is another name for you. Since you are awareness, there is no need to attain or cultivate it. All that you have to do is to give up being aware of other things that are not the self. If one gives up being aware of them then pure awareness alone remains, and that is the self. The self, our Being, is awareness." Awareness is silent, peaceful, and unafraid— meditate on it as your truth. Loving awareness is another name for the soul. Choose to be aware of your awareness. Whenever you disengage from identification with your stream of thoughts and object consciousness, a space is created for your higher awareness to shine forth unobstructed. This is one of the purposes of meditation, to release attention from your passing neural parade and to focus inward. Awareness is always within. You can't be made to be more aware, but your mind stream can be quieted so that your awareness can shine through. When you meditate, things quiet down because the noise level of your mind quiets down. You are already unchanging awareness. Nothing needs to be changed or improved in awareness, which is already perfect and is always present.

Awareness Mantra (repeat aloud)
"All I am is loving awareness.
Anywhere I look, anything that
touches my awareness, I will love.
In the absence of judgement, my true self arises.
I immerse myself in the sea of love."

MINDFULNESS

Mindfulness is paying attention to what is arising in you in the present moment without clinging to it. Mindfulness is the full engagement of your five senses. Once you become aware that your senses are fully engaged, you arrive in the Now. The practice of mindfulness teaches people to observe their thoughts and feelings without judgement or getting hooked on them. Mindfulness assists in eliminating old thought patterns that keep you rooted in the past. The idea is to be present in the Now in order to watch the falling away of any illusions. Mindfulness is also the cure for forgetfulness. Whenever you lack attention to detail, you become susceptible to forgetfulness. Forgetfulness is a disease. Inattention activates the default setting of your mind which is forgetfulness. Our default network is responsible for mind-wandering and day-dreaming. Mindfulness is on the other side of this wall.

Mindfulness will help you with non-judgemental observation.
This will help you to lower your stress level.
You only need to take a breath to enter the kingdom of God.
~ Thich Nhat Hanh

PRESENCE

There is the temporal version of you and the transcendent version of you. The transcendent and forever version of you is always connected to the timeless dimension of Presence. Presence has been described as the realm beyond your five senses and mindfulness, it is both emptiness and fullness at the same time. Presence is the proof of God in you. When you come into the state of Presence, you are in alignment with your divine soul.

Beyond all tastes is the juice or nectar of the fruit of presence.
This taste quenches all thirst and conquers all situations.
~ Mooji

Presence is thoughtless surrender. Presence is to be free of any self-image. Presence is the promised land of freedom. Beyond ego, beyond fear, beyond pain, and beyond your past, is the state of Presence. Presence also lies beyond your thoughts, emotions, and feelings. Everything emerges from Presence. Greater than any theory, place, or discovery is the dimension of Presence. Without Presence there is no life, no existence, no world, no you, and no me. You can choose to live in a state free of any suffering. You can choose to reside in the kingdom of God. The best place to meditate on God is in your sacred heart. Unhappiness can only cling to the little version of you. You can fully be your greater self whenever you recognize yourself as Presence.

Only Presence can free you of the ego,
and you can only be present Now,
not yesterday or tomorrow.
Only Presence can undo the past in you and
this transforms your state of consciousness.
~ Elkhart Tolle

Imagine the dimension of Presence as a material medium such as water or clear fluid. This medium is homogeneous, unified, whole, and undivided, exactly like an ocean. This homogeneous medium is consciousness fully aware of itself. It's like a breathable intelligent matrix that we move around in. It is not aware of itself by reflecting on itself, but by being itself. To continue the physical metaphor, it is as if all the atoms of this precious medium are alive and self-aware.

Your ability to remain present as the witness of your experience is proportional to the amount of presence power in you. In order to become present, simply remain as awareness itself. Mindfulness is another tool that you can use to reach your higher self. Start by using your five senses to gently come into mindful awareness. Just beyond the state of mindfulness, you can slip into the dimension of Presence.

> *A man's spirit is his self.*
> *That entity which is his consciousness.*
> *To think, to feel, to judge, to act,*
> *are functions of the ego.*
> *~ Ayn Rand*

SELF-REALIZATION

The desire for self-realization burns in the hearts of many. This is the search for one's hidden inner truth. Your gift of self-reflection is one of your greatest powers and your personal journey is among the noblest causes. See yourself as a work in progress. Along this magnificent journey are many gifts, treasures, and rewards. The journey is never easy, but the lessons you receive are always worthwhile. The landscape is full of obstacles, both imagined and real. The sweetest gifts happen when you realize your true nature and begin to feel absolute divine bliss.

Each human soul is a child of God, but most don't realize it and therefore they live ordinary lives. When a person realizes their true nature and embraces a conscious path, they become fearless and learn to become a realized soul. Awakening is the shift in your identity from ego to soul. It's not about killing your ego, you are merely killing your identification with your ego. The worldly illusion that we see with your eyes is orchestrated by your ego-mind which attempts to block you from ever finding your truth. Your identity will always be tied to whatever you turn your heart to. The shift from an ego-based identity to a soul-based identity happens through the power of love. The task is to move in alignment with love. Ram Dass says, "Love comes from your soul and all other emotions come from your ego." If anyone has become absolutely free from egotism, you must know that that person has seen and realized divinity.

According to thought leader Maryann Williamson, "Enlightenment has become a mainstream impulse. Enlightenment is not a learning process, it's an unlearning process." It is the remembering of your true nature, a true transcendence of the human mind. In the end, an enlightened mind is a mind free of conflict, with no wanting, no direction, no motive, or need to achieve anything. Without motive, the mind is quiet and still; you reach the level of the watcher, the witness of your experience. You come to this state in time gradually, life after life. Alignment with your timeless self is the biggest threat to your ego's existence. Remember that your ego can only exist in the reflection of space and time. The self is infinite and everlasting. An unbound soul knows the sweet fragrance of awakening coming into being. Divine miracles await the discovery and understanding of your limitless inner essence.

CHAPTER 13

SELF-IMAGE, SELF-RESPECT, SELF-DISCIPLINE, AND SELF-LOVE

SELF-IMAGE

There are many people who suffer from a poor self-esteem. One of the end products of this feeling of inferiority is insecurity, which is essentially fear. Lower energy characteristics are: shyness, passiveness, dependency, and a tendency to withdraw. These behaviors are rooted in childhood. If poor self-image is an issue for you personally, don't worry. Simply believe that it's entirely possible for you to overcome any inferiority or poverty complex. You can lift your attitude through self-analysis and study how many of your issues trace back to your childhood, but you've got to do the work. Expect to dig deep and experience painful memories in order to discover the roots of your pain.

If you can change your self-image, you can change your life. Other people don't determine your self-worth, you do. Supreme new thought leader, Dr. Wayne Dyer says: "Love empowers you to higher levels." Don't despair that you may not be happy today, God is not finished with you yet. You are valuable to your family, job, children, and the world— and don't you ever forget it, you are loved by so many. Often society doesn't celebrate their heros until long after their deaths. There are countless artists, writers, and creators that die without ever receiving their glory, but their work is no less brilliant. There is more to come from you, your journey is never over. Your mind may tell you otherwise, but believe it in your heart that you are worthy of being respected, loved, and celebrated. To start with, have the intention to speak with more clarity and confidence. When you speak your truth, you cease being afraid of the people listening to you. Remember that once you start believing in yourself, so will others.

EXERCISE #29
Positive Mindset Exercise

**Setup and framing of how to develop a new
positive mindset and change how you
feel about yourself. How to become the person
that you've always wanted to be:**

1. Keep an open mind. Push yourself beyond your comfort zone.
2. Humble yourself often and lift others in spirit. Have faith in a power that's greater than you.
3. Speak in front of a mirror. Get used to being observed by others.
4. Read aloud to yourself and pretend that an audience is listening. Speak and project from your soul.
5. Center yourself in love. Trust that the universe is delivering to you exactly what's needed to evolve.
6. Lift your voice in song and praise.
7. Be of service to those less fortunate. Be assertive in everything you do. Smile a lot.
8. Eat foods from the earth and drink alkaline water that fuels and energizes your body-mind.
9. Get in your best physical shape. Start training, moving, exercising, walking, and running.
10. Keep yourself neat and well groomed. When you look good, you feel good. Feeling healthy and thinking positive boosts your confidence and self-image.
11. Start conversations with people. Maintain good eye contact during your conversations, looking away is a sign of hidden insecurity.
12. Don't be afraid to make mistakes, just make sure that you learn from them.
13. Don't listen to your inner critic, instead follow your soul's path.
14. Repeat this affirmation: "I am confident in my abilities to express myself."
15. Say "I MANIFEST" aloud three times.

HEALING A NEGATIVE BODY IMAGE, THE DILEMMA OF OBESITY

As a physician, fighting obesity is one of my main objectives. As a society, if we can reduce obesity rates, we can heal millions of people. Obesity increases the rate of cardiovascular disease and it affects millions of people worldwide. Obesity shortens lifespans and kills people. Many obese patients are overweight because of the habit of overeating. Obesity often results when someone loses their ability to self-regulate their food intake. The body should be treated like a temple. Healthy food choices promote overall wellness. What you put into your body is very important, constant poor food choices result in disease. Many obese patients suffer from body dysmorphic behavior and experience hidden sadness characterized by the obsessive idea that some aspect of their own body or appearance is severely flawed. Overconsumption is like eating to fill a big hole in one's spirit. There will always be someone who can't see your worth, just don't let it be you. Being overweight is not unchangeable. Change requires a strong desire, hard work, and discipline. Whatever size or shape your body is today, it's important to accept and love yourself. Self-love is the most important love of all. God doesn't make mistakes and you are here to do great things. See yourself as constantly evolving and work towards becoming a greater version of yourself. Being overweight today does not have to be your reality tomorrow. Cease allowing food to be your master. You must find a way to resist temptations and correct poor lifestyle habits. Everyone has the power to change, including you.

Many obese patients have co-existing psychosocial issues that they are trying to bury by eating. In many cases, eating is a way of armoring oneself against stress or depression. Eating makes people feel better, it's pleasurable and at the very least, it's a temporary substitute for true happiness. If you have a painful relationship with food, exercise, or the way your body looks, there are ways that you can stop your suffering. Eating disorder treatment can help you take steps to change this self-destructive pattern and learn to create a healthy, positive relationship with food and your body. It's also important to obtain a medical evaluation, which should include tests for hypertension, diabetes, and hormonal disorders. Locate and join a local health and wellness community that's aligned with your fitness goals. It's easier to train and get into shape when you are inspired to mirror the proper habits of others. Whether you feel that you can change your ways by yourself, or if you need a wellness community, or professional help, decide to change your life right now. Today is the day to take back your glory. When you are in alignment with your powerful higher self, you can receive the necessary motivation, inspiration, self-love, and discipline to receive transmissions from Source. These pure vibrational signals of love call for optimal health, a healthy diet, and blessings beyond comprehension. The actual weight loss only occurs after your identity is transferred over from your body-mind to your higher self. When you stay as the self, your consciousness gets elevated and unconscious behaviors like overeating and inactivity can quickly be eliminated.

Dignity is how you export yourself to others.
Dignity is our inherent value and worth,
as human beings, we are born with it.
Respect on the other hand it's earned through
one's actions. When you honor the dignity
of others, you increase your own.

SELF-RESPECT

Self-respect is the way you think about yourself. Self-respect it's not the same as egotism. Egoists are in need of outside verification of their self-worth. Those with true self-respect don't need verification and justification from others. Repair and deepen your relationship with you and your body by learning that you deserve to treat yourself with compassion, love, and respect. It's never too late to change. Making decisions in your life is similar to making a sculpture and the sculpture is you. The tools you use to carve out your sculpture are your choices. The choices you make in life shape you along with your beliefs on self-worth, self-esteem, and self-love.

We can only attract things into our life
that we truly believe that we deserve.
If your subconscious mind has limiting beliefs
and thinks that you don't deserve something,
then that something will elude you for as long
as you don't discard this limiting belief.
Repeating this simple yet powerful affirmation will
certainly help you dispel all your limiting self beliefs:
"I am worthy. I deserve all the good things in life.
There is nothing too good for me."
~ Reverend Ike

Self-Respect Practices

- Let go of being codependent and let go of focusing and meeting other people's needs as a means of feeling better.
- If you consent to sacrifice your self-respect for someone else, you will always have to compromise your integrity to keep that person. To do that is choosing to live in a self-imposed prison and that's the most unkind thing you can ever do to yourself.
- Set boundaries. Don't sell yourself cheap and don't tolerate; nonsense just to save a relationship. Love yourself first before your partner, because if you don't love yourself, how can you give real love to someone else?
- Make sure your cup is full before giving to other people. The more you take care of yourself, the better you become at taking care of others.
- Let your needs and self confidence be important enough to you, not to feel bad about being the number one priority in your life.
- Know this truth in life: everyone is not going to love you. You don't need other people's approval to feel good, instead aim to be respected.
- Give yourself the approval you need to do the things that make you proud of who you are and the person you've become.
- You deserve to be happy. Happiness begins by staying true to yourself and your principles.

YOU ARE ENOUGH

You possess the one commodity that cannot be bought, sold, or traded. Your soul is a gift from the Creator sent straight from heaven, dipped like a candle in blessed love and light. Nothing but your fears can stop you. Even your circumstances don't matter, only your vibrational alignment matters. Staying connected to Source Energy enables you to operate at your highest level. Trust that your inner strength and fortitude simply will not let you fail. You are blessed and destined to pass all the tests of time. You are divine love itself. You are indeed enough!

Eleven Conscious Steps to The Greater You

1. The law of attraction is always in effect. Your thoughts become things and what you believe is what you receive.
2. Pay attention to your emotions and follow your intuition. Stay as the witnessing presence of your experience.
3. Energy is real, everything is energy. Source is power. Vibrations are real. Tune into your own personal frequency and vibration.
4. Follow the path of least resistance.
5. Let go of any fear that you're holding onto and be fearless.
6. When a crisis arises, see it as an opportunity to learn, pivot, grow, and transform.
7. Higher levels of consciousness is always within your reach. You are never not evolving.
8. Return to your sacred heart. The way to the center of your heart is to surrender to love. Love is the expression of the divinity of God in you.
9. Focus your attention on the present moment. Mindfulness matters. Journey inwards always.
10. Seek the universal alignment of mind, body, heart, and soul. Your soul is the source of your power, wisdom, and healing abilities. At the soul level you are whole.
11. You are always on your path. There is a divine plan already in place for you. Know that awakening to your higher self is positively inevitable.

SELF-LOVE

The importance of self-love cannot be overstated. If you don't love yourself, you can't love others and you can't stand to see others being loved. Admitting that you don't know how to love yourself is how you begin to love yourself more. Your journey into self-love leads you to your sacred heart space where love resides and fear dissolves. When you truly love yourself you become a lighter version of yourself and one with the Divine. Love is your original language and it is divinely encoded into your DNA. You are always loving, even when you think you are not. Love is literally the fertilizer to grow your happiness. Learn to appreciate the profound love that you truly are and love yourself to death.

If you find yourself angry and hateful, it is because you are lacking in self-love. The more you choose love over fear, the closer you come to your awakening. Your concept of love originates from your soul, but after decades of human conditioning love gets covered by layers of self-defense mechanisms. Once you go inside to heal the source of your inner pain, your true nature is revealed. This single action replaces your anger and hate with love. Learn to love whatever arises in you. Show compassion to yourself and others. Love deeply, don't be late to the realization that life is short and real opportunities for transformation are few.

Love is your superpower. Never hold back on love. When you give love by loving others your cup doesn't diminish, it actually increases. The universal supply of love is infinite, you cannot run out of it. Love always attracts equal energy. The quality of love you experience is directly proportional to the amount of self-love that you have. You will always attract the same type of love that you hold in your heart.

We have always had
a promise in place. A promise to uphold a love
for ourselves. This is the level of self-love that we are committed to.
No one deserves your love and affection more than you. Don't believe
that part of you which says you don't deserve this or you don't deserve that.
You are deserving of all of your dreams. Failure to love yourself
enough results in sadness, dysfunction, and personal suffering.
True love is unconditional. When you search for love merely
to fill a void in yourself, love cannot find you.
Love can only find you when
you become the love
that you
seek.

LOVE YOURSELF UNCONDITIONALLY

Learning to love yourself unconditionally is one of the greatest lessons of your spiritual journey. Treat yourself with compassion and forgive your shortcomings and past failures. Keep watering yourself, you are still growing.

Love each and every part of yourself, even your dark emotions that you don't currently understand. You are one magnificent miracle in the process of a spiritual awakening. Wisdom and understanding are gifts of your transformation. You are an expression of love born from consciousness itself. You are worthy of receiving immeasurable love and living a peaceful existence.

Mantra of the Day (say aloud)
I am good enough. I am not my past.
I am willing to open my sacred heart.
Today is the day to start healing my past.
I totally commit to healing my emotional self.
In my healing, I welcome abundant love
into my heart and soul.
I will share my love with the world.

COMPASSION FOR YOURSELF IS WHAT YOU RECEIVE WHEN YOU LOVE OTHERS AS MUCH AS YOU DO YOURSELF

In my own journey, the most impactful action I've ever taken was my decision to love myself more. As a result of that one decision, I was able to free myself of everything that no longer served me. I stopped worrying and began to see my difficult situations as temporary and changeable. I stopped talking so much and began to listen more. I stopped being angry and began to show more compassion towards myself and others. I stopped judging people and started to love everyone as they are. I stopped staying busy which was making me tired and I found the value of stillness in meditation. I vowed to stop reacting to everything in my experience and I started to become a receiver to all that is good. Soon I began to see less with my eyes and I started to feel my way through life. I stopped living from my mind and began to follow my heart.

COMPASSION AND EMPATHY

Compassion is not empathy. Empathy occurs between two separate beings when one person thinks sympathetically of another. Compassion is experiencing another's emotion as one's own with the wisdom of oneness. Another person's suffering is experienced as one's own suffering. If you are compassionate to everyone you come across, then you will receive abundant love in return. It takes complete faith in God to love everyone you meet. When you perceive yourself and others as souls, you bring love, truth, and compassion to your interactions with others— then you become the mirror of their soul. Learn to feel with your heart instead of only seeing with your eyes. Let go of the difference between individuals and see oneness; see God in everything and everyone. Realize that waves are just smaller parts of the ocean and are all one in the same.

> *The foundation of the Buddha's teachings lies in compassion*
> *and the reason for practicing the teachings is to wipe out*
> *the persistence of ego, the number-one enemy of compassion.*
> *~ The Dalai Lama*

EXERCISE #30
Commit To Loving Deeper And Making Yourself Feel Loved

- **Write down three main goals to accomplish every day.**
- **Acknowledge yourself. Allow yourself to feel good about the goals you plan to accomplish.**
- **Start with simple goals that are reasonable and attainable.**
- **Identify and distinguish between the goals that you need vs. the things you want. Choose goals that you need and have procrastinating starting.**
- **Visualize how you plan to spend your days, it acts as a screenplay for your subconscious mind.**
- **Activate your plan.**

CHAPTER 14

DESIRE, EXPECTATIONS, ATTACHMENT AND DETACHMENT

THE PITFALLS OF DESIRE

Desire is simply the actions of your five senses bringing a stimulus to the mind. If you love the object that enters the mind, you will desire it again. If it becomes a love of yours, you will seek it out over and over again to satisfy those desires. Suffering is not caused by desire, suffering is caused by unfulfilled expectations around a desire. The removal of desire is not the goal, the removal of your attachment to the outcome is the goal. Free is the one who is free of expectation. Yet, desire is also an integral force in life. This can be somewhat a contradiction for most people. In the state of not wanting anything, your mind-made identity slowly disappears into the vast intelligence of the universe. Don't want anything, seek nothing. For this moment, be void of desire. Don't entertain any thoughts, memories, or emotions. See all of them from afar. The one who perceives everything is the watcher, be that.

- **If you remain centered in your heart, desire is not found.**
- **Note that I am not speaking about daily essential practical desires. I am speaking of the kind of desire that leads to weakness, need, and the obsession that "I" cannot live without.**
- **Identify who or what part of you is the one experiencing this great need.**
- **Be quiet and hold this task in your focus. In the pure light of seeing, a great sense will be made of your situation. This state is known as wisdom and understanding.**

*Key point: You do not manifest your desires.
You manifest what you think and believe.

EXPECTATIONS

Expectations are what causes suffering. The expectation is that if we get what we desire, it will somehow end our suffering. This is untrue. Don't cling to any attachments or beliefs. Emotional addiction and attachment are the reasons why we need to detach. People generally say that one should be detached to avoid grief and sufferings in life. Attachment causes self-inflicted suffering, the worst kind. When you die, it is actually your attachments that die. In death, your attachment to your body-mind is severed. Your soul is liberated from its contract with your body and is free to return to Source.

ATTACHMENT

In Buddhism, one of the four noble truths is that attachment is the root of all suffering—it is the opposite of love. This flies in the face of Western philosophy, which tells us that attachment is synonymous with love. You see this manifested in the attitudes of so many people who will tell you that the quality of a relationship is not important, as long as the relationship continues to exist. The Western philosophy is designed to keep us attached, unhappy, and unfulfilled.

You must create separation from your emotions in order to heal your addiction of replaying past suffering. All suffering stems from replaying the emotional patterns of your past. Detachment from your emotions detaches you from the chains of your body-mind. You find freedom from the past by turning your attention to the timeless, thoughtless, and emotionless dimension of Presence. Full detachment is selfless love, also known as spiritual love. Attach to nothing but love.

EXERCISE #31

Look at where you are and see where you are stuck.
Most people are stuck in fear because of one thing or another.
Author Dr. Brene Brown invites you
to ask yourself three questions before
you verbally respond to anyone:

1. "Is it true?"
2. "Is it kind?"
3. "Is it necessary?"

EMOTIONAL ATTACHMENT

Your emotions are holding you back. Not the feelings themselves, but you have lost the distinction between your feelings and your true self. Your ability to manage your emotions, not suppress them but enable them to transform into higher quality feelings is beneficial for the advancement of your consciousness. I have learned that the most effective way to balance my own emotional nature and clear any unresolved issues is to access my sacred heart space and practice gratitude and compassion. Your sacred heart space grants access to feelings of compassion for yourself, compassion for others, gratitude, kindness, inner peace, understanding, and unconditional love.

EMOTIONAL DETACHMENT

The nature of emotions is temporary. Your emotions are simply energy in motion moving through space and time. When you see yourself in terms of energy, your emotions represent the energy of your past experiences coming alive again inside of you. The most effective way to manage your emotions is to release them. When emotions are acknowledged and expressed, they dissipate naturally. Let your emotional current flow through you. Be a vessel for your feelings, but don't hold onto anything. Your emotions are merely visitors which come into your space of awareness. One common failure results when people try to suppress their emotions. This suppression makes people cold and intolerant. If you suppress your truth, you can get stuck in time and become frozen-like. When you suppress your emotions they become illnesses in incubation within your body. Whenever you hold onto your emotions too long, you begin to suffer. In suffering your emotions, you remain trapped in your body-mind and become increasingly more unaware of your higher self.

Author Rolf Alexander puts it this way "An ape lives in his feelings, is his feelings, and possesses nothing which can detach himself from his feelings." In short, apes completely identify themselves with their subconscious images. Attached to these images are acquired pleasure and painful memories. As these images take form in the apes mind's eye, pleasurable or painful memories trigger their emotions. Alas, most men also live in this state, at least most of the time, but unlike apes, man can detach himself from his subconscious images along with their memories. In addition, this "something" can and will deliberately create images of things not present to the five senses, this something is called consciousness.

BALANCE

The path of life is not a straight line, there are many twists and turns that can occur within a day that can affect your vibration. You can be experiencing the most incredible day, yet a single phone call or event can destroy your mood set-point. Balance is the key to emotional intelligence. You must try to maintain an even keel when things don't go your way. Remember that you are an infinite being that is derived from Source Energy. Use your relationship with Source to stabilize your emotional self.

SEE YOURSELF AS ENERGY

The answer is simple, don't be a victim of your experience, become the witness of your experience. Learn to go beyond your thoughts and emotions into the realm of Presence. See all of your emotional states as temporary and ever-changing. Your reality is a reflection of your current level of consciousness. Reside as the aspect of yourself that is timeless and everlasting, reside as the self.

> *The miracle of the human mind is not only that it can observe,*
> *remember, and understand, but it can also learn to*
> *observe itself in performing these acts.*
> *~ Rolf Alexander*

As the witness of your experience, you maintain a higher perspective of the happenings around you which allows you to better navigate through life. Becoming the witnessing presence of your emotions is the entrance to higher consciousness. The way to get your power back is to understand that you create your own reality, it's you that holds the key. You have always had the power to dictate your outcomes. There is a deep functional relationship between your emotions and your ego. As long as you stay in your emotions, you remain stuck in the limited dimension of personhood.

Your freedom is on the other side of personhood. When you align with your higher self, you free your mind and consciousness to expand. Emotional attachment, codependency, addiction, and the certain suffering that follows, is why we need to practice detachment. I need you to get excited again. The most important lesson I can point out is that it's possible to observe your thoughts and emotions from a distance. These activities are going on without you randomly and automatically engaging. Observation without participation, this is detachment. The goal is to create a gap between you and your experience by remaining the witness of all this activity. The watcher that is you, is independent of all activity and passes no judgement. In this heightened state of being, you are no longer "a mind in action" with no separation from a thought to an action. Detachment can be learned and repeated.

Watch your thoughts from a place of silence. One mechanism by which inner peace is lost is negative thinking. Inner peace is your most precious possession, but it can easily be lost with the onset of a single angry thought or a sense that something shouldn't be happening. Become the witnessing presence of your thoughts. True inner peace is a deep state of aliveness. My theory is, a person becomes prone to depression when they become disillusioned with the perceived gap between the life that they once imagined for themselves and their current reality. In essence, the declaration of depression is an indictment on a person's past choices and decisions. Depression leads to inaction and restlessness. The key to recovery from depression is finding the motivation or drive to get your train back on the rails. Failure to get back on track results in a slow but steep decline. As soon as you recognize that you are depressed, take aggressive actions to change your circumstances until you begin to see growth.

CHAPTER 15

HEALING YOUR EMOTIONAL SUFFERING

WHAT IS EMOTIONAL TRAUMA?

Most people think trauma is only physical abuse, sexual abuse, abandonment, or other major events that occur in your life, but we as humans also suffer our emotions. *Emotional trauma is defined as: The mental stains embedded in one's mind due to a sudden, forceful and overwhelming experience.* Your emotional scars are not physical by nature, but rather invisible wounds that have caused you deep and lasting spiritual damage. Trauma specialist Mastin Kipp defines trauma as: "Any belief or event that disrupts your overall mental, physical, spiritual wellness, or ability to function in society." Many people are in denial about their hidden trauma. If you are uncertain whether or not you have old hidden trauma, ask yourself if you are experiencing trauma symptoms. Common symptoms of trauma are: excessive worry, anxiety, ADHD, PTSD, lack of motivation, apathy, dysfunction in relationships, depression, addictions, eating disorders, or any type of dysregulation of your emotions or nervous system.

Trauma is specifically an event that overwhelms the central nervous system which alters the way we recall and process memories. It is the current imprint of that fear, pain, and horror living inside people.
~ Mastin Kipp

EMOTIONAL SUFFERING

Science is now proving that negative emotions such as: anger, hurt, fear, depression, jealousy, and rage all affect your biochemistry in a negative way. Your body assists and amplifies your emotions through your memory by recreating your body's exact chemical state and reactions to past similar events. This is because memory is your body's version of identity. Healing starts with becoming more aware of your body's effort to increase your chemical reaction to current circumstances or events.

The greatest win is walking away and choosing not to engage in drama and toxic energy at all.
~ Lalah Delia

WHY YOU SUFFER AND HOW TO STOP IT

When you are in the habit of resisting change, you suffer. Suffering is a wake up call for spiritual growth and evolution. In times of struggle, you can resist change or embrace change, it's your choice. The question is: Are you willing to change? Are you looking for the key to escape your mind-made prison? Are you willing to shift out your old defective mindsets? You are programmed to suffer through your emotions. However, many of your emotional patterns are outdated, they are inherited from past generations. If you allow emotional suffering to endure for long periods of time, these same negative emotions can take over your life almost to the point of possessing you. In these cases, the real you can become unrecognizable. In time, a person can lose their self-esteem and become hopeless. Hopelessness often leads to addictions in an attempt to numb the pain, which leads to even deeper suffering. People who lose hope in their life are at risk of losing their aspirations and dreams. In extreme cases, intensive therapy with trained psychological or psychiatric caregivers can assist in healing these self-destructive emotions and teach self-care exercises that can help a person fully understand and cope with their circumstances. If you are suffering your past, don't give up, there is hope. If you can learn how to master your mind, overcome your emotions, and break the addiction to your suffering, a full recovery is possible.

> *All thoughts carry energy and a certain frequency.*
> *Change your thoughts and you change your life.*
> ~ Dr. Joe Dispenza

POST-TRAUMATIC TRANSFORMATION

Why is there such a strong relationship between turmoil and transformation? What actually happens when a person awakens in the midst of intense stress or trauma? Spiritual awakening happens when a person's psychological attachments slowly dissolve. This movement is not a sudden movement, but a gradual descent into deeper realms of consciousness. This might happen as a result of a sudden illness such as cancer, divorce, job loss, bankruptcy, addiction, or any other strong negative event. When your attachments (hopes, beliefs, and possessions) are fractured, your identity also breaks down. This can lead to intense inner turmoil, a sense of despair, a feeling of emptiness, and in severe cases— contemplation of your own death. Turmoil can be devastating, but many people can testify that it can also spark transformation. Many people emerge to their higher selves through struggle. The fire of transformation strips away the aspects of personhood that you no longer need. Now, light as a feather, you begin your ascension. Your liberation from personhood leads you the highest version of yourself, your infinite potential. You are the fullest expression of love. The surest thing about life is that there are crescendos and decrescendos coming to you and everything else in between. It's best not to get too high, but also don't get too low. Stay even and stay in the flow. What is meant for you, you shall receive.

> *God had brought me to my knees and made me*
> *acknowledge my own nothingness, and out of that knowledge*
> *I had been reborn. I was no longer the centre of my life*
> *and therefore I could see God in everything.*
> *~ Bede Griffiths*

THE STARTING POINT OF HEALING

The most common question I receive about emotional healing is: "Where do I start?" My answer is to start with wherever you are right now. Start by looking at the roots of your fears and emotional pain. Leave no stone unturned in this inquiry. Come into acceptance of your current conditions and situation. Whatever is happening in your life right now is attached to a lesson drenched in purpose. Be patient with yourself, all healing occurs in divine time. Begin to see, sense, and feel what you are looking to heal. Healing begins with the intention to transcend your current state. Start speaking your desires into existence. Go deep within. Self-inquiry asks you to have a look at your emotional past. Closely examine the negative fluctuations along your journey. Look into your long term memory to uncover any deeply hidden past trauma. Unpack your emotional baggage and lay it all out for self-examination. The aim of your self-analysis is to identify, understand, and come to peace with those past events in such an enlightened manner that they no longer impact you in a negative way. Ultimately, there is only one way to heal your suffering, you have to eliminate the cause of the suffering. If you attempt to resolve an instance of suffering without dealing with its root causes, more similar situations will arise that bring about more suffering.

From the altitude of healing, begin processing your traumatic past. Processing emotional trauma means to take an objective but compassionate look inside yourself to examine the moments of pain, stress, loss, and unconsciousness over the course of your life. Begin to see how such damaging content may still trigger negative fluctuations in your current vibrational state. If you have difficulty remembering your thoughts and feelings, I recommend starting a "Healing Journal." Keep it in a safe place and make daily insightful entries reflecting the overall plan and inspiration for your healing. Take things one day at a time and crystallize the vision of your desired future self in your mind's eye. Measure your daily progress in actions. Allow your intuition to guide you and let love handle the rest.

> *The people in your age group who didn't experience life altering*
> *trauma had an advantage over you, your brain was focused on*
> *survival, while theirs was free to grow and develop. You may feel*
> *behind, but it's because you were doing the best that you could.*
> ~ *Zoe Anne Aranda-Tafoya*

HEALING YOUR PAINFUL PAST

One of the first things to learn in regard to your healing is that your suffering has accumulated throughout your time here on earth. The roots of people's fears, insecurities, and anger begin in our infancy and are then lived out in adulthood. We must come to realize that a deeper cause of our suffering is the way that we hold onto the past. If you can stop identifying with your past history, all that happened in your childhood can be reconciled and forgiven. Doing your inner work is the key to reconciling your past. Higher levels of awareness, insight, and understanding helps to reduce your fears. This is why self-inquiry is so important. You are the key to unlocking the mysteries of your past. Whenever you reconcile with your painful past, you are instantly transported into the Now. All healing takes place in the present moment.

Every lesson has a price to pay. Take time to identify what you have learned from each of your disappointments. When you work through your old painful issues, you come to the realization that your past experiences can no longer hurt you. At that very moment, you are free of your past and you are presented with the opportunity to create space for a brighter future. Everytime you identify a lesson learned, your consciousness shifts higher. Learning is aligned with growing and evolving. You need not repeat your past mistakes to learn your life lessons. When you tap into love and gratitude, you can create new joyful memories which will begin to replace your traumatic memories. The more healing that you do, the easier it becomes. You have always had the innate ability to heal yourself. Believe that you can process your painful past, remember how to love again and redesign yourself into a greater version of you.

EXERCISE #32

ASK YOURSELF: "What are some of the labels I am carrying that are informing my cells how to behave?" List three health affirmations that you can start telling yourself each morning. For example: "I feel amazing." "My immune system is working for me 24 hours a day." or "I am so grateful to be healthy."

1. _____

2. _____

3. _____

AIM TOWARDS HAPPINESS BUT MAKE JOY YOUR TARGET

The difference between happiness and joy is that happiness is temporary, it comes and goes in waves, but joy is a state of being that you can reside in. In order to achieve any goal you need to have a final destination. Some people shoot for the moon with their aspirations and fall short, but they land on a star. By the same light, you can shoot for joy and fall short, but land on happiness. The secret to being joyful is shifting your energy from a lower vibration into the emotional state of gratitude and freedom. Make joy your target, move towards that goal by taking small steps each day and by making it your everyday mission to improve your happiness quotient. A mission without a target is susceptible to the winds of change, but a laser-focused eagle-eyed lock on your mission, cannot be stopped. So set your intention and target in the direction of happiness and let your final destination be in the realm of joy.

EMOTIONAL MASTERY: HEALING YOUR EMOTIONAL SELF

By healing your emotional self, you are not only stepping towards your own inner light, you are also making a contribution to the global healing of the planet. Everyone wants to feel free, no one wants to be a slave to anything or anyone. No matter what your age is, it's never too late to heal. Know that you can not be free if you remain caught up in your emotions. Being caught up in your emotions is to be trapped in the chemical residue of the past. Fortunately, in the midst of your suffering there are always rays of light. In the present moment, Pure Divine Light can never be stopped from coming to you. The life hack happens once you get tired of carrying your emotional baggage and you decide to become the master of your emotions. As a master of your emotions, you learn to differentiate between the sound of your intuition guiding you and your unhealed emotional traumas misleading you. Start becoming a witness to your feelings. Feel your emotions, but don't become them. Observe when your emotions arise and then take time to validate them. Acknowledge their arrival and honor your feelings. From this altitude, show empathy for your difficult emotions and also for yourself for feeling that way. After your witness, validate, and show empathy to your emotions, you can then consciously release them back into the universe.

As your body starts to trust the present moment and come into universal alignment more often, the tide of your emotional waves will lessen. This is what I refer to as "the wave of emotional healing." The end goal of your emotional mastery is to learn how to to transmute your past pain into life lessons. This is how you become a lighter version of yourself to reach the higher vibrational states of effortlessness and grace.

Feel the feeling but don't become the emotion.
Witness it. Allow it. Release it.
~ Crystal Andrus

LET THE VOICE OF YOUR HIGHER SELF BE HEARD

Most people don't recognize or experience the light of their higher self because they have never called upon it to take action on their behalf. If this is you, don't stress out— you can always become more aware of your soul. You can accomplish this by learning how to remain as pure awareness. The more you practice being the witness of your thought patterns and energy fields, the more adept you will become at closing the distance between you and your higher self. At your highest energy state, there is no separation between you and your God Essence. Your inner voice is your secret weapon. Let the sound of your higher self be heard. The voice of your higher self is never loud, it's always a whisper. The question is: "Why are you running away from who you are while pretending to be something that you are not?" Your higher voice is present to remind you of what you already know to be true. Your truth is that you are a mighty spiritual being experiencing itself in physical form.

The final resolution to suffering is enlightenment. The suffering caused by your past is small in comparison to the benefits of discovering your true essence. This is why it's important to work on the liberation of your essential nature. An emancipated person distances themselves from the lies and misdirection of others. A liberated mind maintains hope when others have none. An awakened being is as loving as a gentle breeze. An unbound soul knows the sweet fragrance of awakening coming into being. Awakening to your true self releases the happiness, joy, and peace necessary to balance all of your suffering. Spiritual awakening brings light to previously hidden truths. Unfortunately, enlightenment will not happen for everyone in this lifetime. So in the meantime, continue to do your inner work, be compassionate with yourself, and realize that most suffering is universal. This is the common human experience.

The Ten Phases of Healing Emotional Trauma

1. Set the Intention to Heal Yourself.
2. Visualize A Successful Healing.
3. Self-Analysis and Recognition of Cyclical Life Patterns.
4. Process Your Emotional Pain By Locating The Root Causes of Your Suffering.
5. Practice Gratitude, Mindfulness, and Present Moment Awareness.
6. Initiate Multi-Sensory Healing Therapies.
7. Practice Self-Love and Emotional Healing.
8. Find Your Flow State.
9. Claim Your Healing.
10. Share Your Light And Become A Healer For Others.

CHAPTER 16

HOW TO IDENTIFY YOUR TRIGGERS AND HEAL TOXICITY

WHAT IS TOXICITY?

Until a toxic man or woman addresses, processes, and heals their emotional trauma, they will continue to exhibit toxic behavior in every relationship they have. Toxic environments and toxic families produce traumatized children. Unhealed childhood trauma can lead to becoming a broken adult. Oftentimes, when parents are absent from the home or irresponsible in their choices, their children often get rushed into carrying adult responsibilities. Too many children have been damaged by having to "step up too soon." This premature leap into adulthood robs them of their childhood, builds mistrust, and leads to a loss of joy. Part of the magic of life is possibility, but if your upbringing was violent and traumatic you can be led to believe that the world is against you. This is a false limiting belief, the world is never against you— the world is yours. The universe scripts daily scenarios that reflect your current level of consciousness. The world that you see is the same world that you've created.

> *Triggers are like little psychic explosions that crash through*
> *avoidance and brings the dissociated, avoided trauma,*
> *suddenly, unexpectedly, back into your consciousness.*
> *~ Carolyn Spring*

THE PROPER MINDSET FOR HEALING

Your mind is what holds onto negative thought patterns and negative emotions. If a defective mental/emotional pattern is allowed to persist in your mind, it will soon show up in your physical body in the form of dis-ease. You remain in a "trauma pattern" when your attitude remains fixed, instead of being open to beneficial change. A resistant mindset is: "I want to stay the way I am." Alternatively, the ideal mindset for healing is: "I am open to beneficial change."

IDENTIFY YOUR TRIGGERS

Learn your triggers and how to deal with them. Your triggers are a bridge between a buried past memory and your present analytical mind. Triggers frequently cause you to overreact and impulsively respond to even the slightest stimulus. A trigger that manifests is a cry for help. It points to an area of your being in need of healing. Your triggers are always synchronized with a past traumatic event. The mind's association with past trauma keeps the event open to fester, to remain unresolved and trapped in a time loop. If a painful event once happened to you as a child, know that your emotions, feelings, and memories are still valid today. No one is immune to emotional trauma and everyone has something to heal and replace with forgiveness and love.

> *The process within our brains is a three-step loop. First, there is a cue,*
> *a trigger that tells your brain to go into automatic*
> *mode and which habit to use.*
> *Then there is the routine, which can be physical, mental, or emotional.*
> *Finally, there is a reward, which helps your brain figure out if this*
> *particular loop is worth remembering for the future: The habit loop.*
> *~ Charles Duhigg*

TRAUMA RESPONSES: TRIGGERS ARE YOUR GUIDES, WHAT YOU DON'T HEAL REPEATS

Every time you get triggered, a trauma is uncovered. If you project your reactions outward with your ego instead of going inward for self-examination, your triggers will continue to show up in the form of other people or similar situations. Our triggers are intelligent messages designed to wake us up to address our past feelings of failure. The more you step back as the witness, the more control you gain over your responses. Healing happens when you are triggered, realize it, and no longer react unconsciously. Healing a trigger doesn't mean that you won't ever be triggered again, the magic lies in your lack of response. When you are able to move past the story, through your emotional pain, past the memory, and then reach for a different response, you arrive at healing.

EXERCISE #33
Feeling Your Feelings

**After years of burying your feelings about your darkest past, it's
time to release them. This breathing exercise invites you to focus
on unlocking your energy blocks and opening your sacred heart.
Find a quiet peaceful place. Relax your body. Take three calm,
even, deep breaths. Align with your inner essence and release your
buried, uneasy feelings to the universe. Ask the Divine to dissolve
them and clear your path. Focus on the intention to release the
hold the past has on you. Aim to be free from time itself. Seek
liberation from your memory. Fill your heart with love. You can't
erase the past, but you can make the choice to remain focused
on the present moment and remain faithful of the future.
The goal is a feeling of pure love and inner peace.**

DEEP HEALING HAPPENS IN LAYERS

The deeper you go inside, the more you uncover the roots of your emotional trauma. It's okay to peel back your layers of hurt and pain to reframe your struggle. If you don't investigate your past, you will continue to spiral through the same emotional experiences and continue to be triggered by even the slightest reminders. If you remain open and curious while witnessing your rising emotions, you can trace them back to where they came from. Are you up for it? You're really just going back to the openness you knew as a baby for the purpose of reinstating your soul as your rightful self. Have the intention to bring more love, compassion, and understanding to yourself. This simple action assists your reactions to subside and stimulates your wounds to heal. Remember that healing comes in waves. The first signs of healing are that your triggers begin to surface less often, with less intensity, and last for a shorter period of time. Healing is a gradual process and not just a one time fix. True healing comes with a heightened awareness, practice, patience, and the grace of time.

CHAPTER 17

CALMING FEAR, ANXIETY, AND PANIC ATTACKS

STRESS

If you regularly experience low vibrational emotions like fear and anger, it will increase your stress level. Conflict and tension trigger the release of stress hormones into your bloodstream which create imbalance within the organ systems of the body. It's important to remember that we are all wired differently, so we all experience and process stress differently. Some of us handle stress well while others are severely affected.

The mind can go either direction under stress—
toward positive or toward negative:
on or off. Think of it as a spectrum whose extremes are unconsciousness
at the negative end and hyperconsciousness at the positive end.
The way the mind will lean under stress is strongly influenced by training.
~ Frank Herbert

Being positive and having a healthy mindset could be the difference between longevity and dis-ease. Every thought you entertain produces a chemical which signals the body to feel exactly the way you are thinking. In other words, your thoughts generate feelings and your feelings will generate more similar thoughts which creates a vicious cycle. It's wise to be mindful of the quality of your thoughts as soon as you awaken every morning. This can be the difference in what type of day you are going to have. Stress is associated with unhealthy behavioural coping strategies like: irritability, arguing, emotional eating, compulsive shopping, chain smoking, alcohol, and drug usage.

Fear has caused millions of souls their dreams and provided many
more with the only excuse that they have ever needed to fail.
Imagine your life if you could be unafraid.
Exchange your fear for faith and change your world.

Many scientific studies have proven that conscious minds have the power to influence cellular behaviour. Cellular behavior literally responds to your thoughts. The more powerful the emotional charge behind a thought, the more your cells react. An example of how the quality of your thoughts affect your body is that stress and fear lower your immune response which makes you more susceptible to viruses and illness. Your immune system is a collection of billions of white blood cells which travel through your bloodstream through your lymphatic circulation. These white cells move in and out of tissues and organs defending your body against foreign agents (antigens) such as viruses, bacteria, and cancerous cells. Chronic stress reduces the ability of your immune system to respond appropriately to outside invaders which can affect your overall health and quality of life.

If you are experiencing fear, anger, or other emotions that may increase your
stress level, then these unsettling thoughts are picked up by the brain.
The brain then stimulates the endocrine system to release hormones
that have an adverse effect on the immune cell's ability to divide.
This causes a decline in immune function which may result
in your becoming more susceptible to illness.
~ Patty Carrosicia, R. N.

The endocrine (hormonal) system in the body is also a major player when it comes to maintaining a healthy mind and body. Stress disrupts the natural order of your endocrine system which results in a chemical imbalance. If you are constantly stressed out, then all your energy will be used to stimulate the release of stress hormones from your adrenal glands. As a response, the functions of the other glands in your body will be reduced and less able to maintain overall chemical/hormonal balance in your body.

Your cells are either in a state of growth or
protection. If your mind is 'stressed out,'
then your cells are in a suppressed state, a.k.a breakdown mode—which
will leave your body wide open and more susceptible to illness or disease.
~ Bruce Lipton

Stress Management Tips

- **Keep a positive attitude.**
- **Accept that there are events in life that you cannot control.**
- **Be assertive instead of aggressive. Assert your feelings, opinions, or beliefs instead of becoming angry, defensive, or passive.**

- **Practice relaxation techniques like meditation, mindfulness, and deep breathing.**
- **Exercise regularly. Your body is able to fight stress better when it is fit.**
- **Eat healthy, well-balanced meals.**
- **Set limits appropriately and learn to say no to requests for your time that would create excessive stress in your life.**
- **Make time for hobbies, interests, and self-care.**
- **Get enough rest, relax, and sleep. Your body needs time to rest and recover from daily stressors.**
- **Don't just rely on alcohol, drugs, or compulsive behaviors to reduce your stress.**
- **Learn some relaxation techniques to use when you are stressed out. My favorite mantra is to recite and repeat the phrase "serenity now" three times whenever I am feeling stressed and overwhelmed.**

ANXIETY

Don't use your energy to worry, use your energy to believe in yourself. When you put your worries aside you create space for love and creativity. Being unconcerned doesn't mean being uninspired, calmness and security builds confidence and better serves you to manifest your brightest possible outcomes. When you are anxious, you are only worried and concerned because there is a part of you that's insecure and seeking your loving attention. Once you recognize that it's only your fragile ego that's overwhelmed, you can calm yourself by getting into alignment with your more powerful higher self to breathe in confidence and stability.

Factors that influence cell behaviour:

- **Thoughts**
- **Emotions**
- **Mindset**
- **Stress**
- **Nutrition**

- **Energy**
- **Exercise**
- **Rest**
- **Sleep**
- **Perception**

Anxiety is the experience of growth itself.
Anxiety that is denied makes us ill.
Anxiety that is fully confronted and fully lived through- converts
itself into joy, security, strength, centeredness, and character.
The practical formula: Go where the pain is.
~ Peter Koestenbaum

WHY WORRY

People worry because they are believing their negative thought patterns and so they start to feel anxious because their life isn't working out for them. Things get worse when you start believing that your dreams may never come true. This negative belief is the end result of incessant worry. The most important ingredient of manifesting success is having a powerful inner desire and drive to live out your dreams. Why worry? The only thing that worrying changes are the colors of the hair on top of your head. Being worried or concerned never solves your problems, it becomes the problem. Worry prevents clarity and does not allow for solutions to come forward in your mind. There isn't enough room in your mind for both faith and worry. You must decide which one of these opposite energies dominates your daily existence. If you choose anxiety, you are living in the future, and if you are regretful, you have been living in the past. Your best outcomes happen when you are living in the Now.

We are afraid of success.
We are afraid of failure.
We are afraid of love.
We are afraid of loss.
We are afraid of ourselves.
We are afraid of one another.

*We are afraid to see
what lies behind the
curtains of life.
Faith, hope, trust, gratitude, and love
is what frees us from ever doubting
ourselves again.*

EXERCISE #34

The goal of this exercise is to examine your thoughts and behavioral patterns with the intention of changing to a more positive mindset, tune into your higher mind, and find clarity in your purpose

- **What emotions do you dominantly feel about your current problem?**

  _____

- **How have your past choices contributed to your current circumstances and how have they held you back?**

  _____

- **How have your circumstances shaped your perception of yourself and your level of self-worth?**

  _____

- **What lessons have you learned so far regarding your current problem?**

  _____

- **What is your motivation? Do you have strong desires about your dominant intention or is it a weak desire?**

  _____

- **Is your higher self in full support of your thinking on this issue or is it divergent?**

  _____

- **Are you receiving pulses, messages, and inspiration from your divine inner being?**

  _____

Use your answers to these questions to drive your action plan forward. No plan can succeed until you implement it!

THE ROOTS OF FEAR

Fear can be crippling and its presence places stress and limitations on your potential experiences. Staying in the present moment is the key to lifting and eliminating all fear in your mind. Once you learn to become fearless, you become limitless.

There Are Two Core Fears:

1. Not getting what you want.
2. Losing what you already have.

Fear is what makes life difficult. It spawns the poisons of insecurity, doubt, greed, hatred, and ignorance. When you become trapped in fear, it's largely because you are living from the limited perspective of your lower mind. The human mind is part memory and part imagination. Memory and imagination are both illusory because they are equally time dependent and neither exists in the Now. You can only reach your higher mind in the present moment. At the root of fear is imagination, a fixation, something that doesn't yet exist in physical reality. Fear has often been described as false evidence appearing real. Don't look through the lens of fear and give in. Remember that only God's love is real in any situation. That mantra alone brings you into acceptance and inner peace. May your mind remain weightless and light as a feather for all eternity.

Common Fears:

- Fear of being alone
- Fear of being without
- Fear of being wrong

- **Fear of being disliked**
- **Fear of being disrespected**
- **Fear of failing**
- **Fear of being attacked**
- **Fear of being hurt**
- **Fear of being rejected**
- **Fear of being abandoned**
- **Fear of growing old**
- **Fear of dying**

You reap what you sow,
If you plant a banana tree you will grow bananas.
If you plant an apple tree you will grow apples.
If you plant fear and sorrow you will grow fear and sorrow.
~ *Unknown*

THE FEAR OF FALLING AND FAILING

The best thing about the presence of fear is that it's appearance and your reaction to it, lets you know that you're alive and that's a good thing. If you can't feel anything at all, then you might as well be dead. It's important to note that fear and excitement are similar emotions, the body literally creates the same neurochemical response to both. The reason you believe them to be different is because of your preexisting beliefs. Excitement and fear both activate the sympathetic nervous system (fight or flight), resulting in the release of norepinephrine and epinephrine from the adrenal glands. The next time you are in a fearful situation, play a mind trick on yourself by convincing yourself that your rising fear is actually the feeling of excitement. Try it, this mind trick works. Sometimes a new world problem can be solved by an old world answer. In ancient Taoism, healing is based on a "Secret Four-Word Treasure of Success." The four words are: *relaxed, tranquil, fearless,* and *carefree.* Use the information and techniques expressed in this chapter to attain this relaxed state of being. There is something reassuring about knowing about the scrutiny of science and the traditions of faith, that affirm the value of consistently reaching for a state of relaxation.

Inner Treasure Mantra (say aloud)
"I am relaxed.
I am tranquil.
I am fearless.
I am carefree."

PANIC ATTACKS

According to Psychology Today, a panic attack is "a sudden rush of fear and anxiety that causes both physical and psychological symptoms. The level of fear experienced is unrealistic and out of proportion to the events or circumstances that trigger the panic attack. Basically your fight or flight system is on overload and you are having a physical reaction to it. Your body is on red alert and your systems are overly stimulated. A person experiences an anxiety attack when they are exposed to a certain situation or "trigger" that makes them feel anxious. Your brain is the main reason for anxiety attacks. This emotional build up is your body's way of telling you it can't cope or carry on with what's happening to you.

Several years ago one of my patients who was an actress described her panic attacks to me. She was on the red carpet and had a panic attack when photographers paid more attention to a rival actress. They paid compliments and chose to photograph the other woman instead of her. As a result, she panicked and had to run off the red carpet. She was overcome with fears of inadequacy, embarrassment, judgment, shame, rejection, and failure which sent her into a spiral of toxic emotions. Panic attacks often create physical symptoms in the body like: a rapid heartbeat, nervousness, sweating, nausea, hyperventilation, flushing, and shaking, all which result in overstimulation and an impulse to escape.

Panic attacks typically last between 10-30 minutes. The first thing to counteract a panic attack is to self-regulate your breathing. When you breath too quickly, hyperventilation is capable of causing panic, imbalance, and occasionally a loss of consciousness. In order to overcome panic attacks you have to reframe them in the correct context. Panic attacks result from overreaction, so the goal becomes how do you restore calm to your body-mind once you're triggered? Consider redefining your definition of anxiety. Anxiety is merely the body's reaction to feeling unsafe.

No More Fear Mantra (say aloud)
"I will no longer fear my fears.
I will not allow fear to steal my joy.
I will grab fear with my hand and walk with it.
I will keep telling my fear, "It's going to be okay."

Relaxation Techniques To Use When Panic Strikes

1. First slow down your breathing. Try to deepen your breath to interrupt any new negative thoughts.

2. A sigh of relief releases built up tension before it can cause any negative effects in your body. On your exhale, release an audible sigh.

3. Initiate positive thinking. Assure yourself that you are safe and loved. Tell yourself that you're okay and that everything is going to be alright.

4. Shift your focus onto a nearby object, preferably something natural like a flower or a tree. Look at the object in detail and think thoughts of how beautiful it is. Focus on the object's beauty, color, and texture. This mindfulness technique will distract your mind away from it's negative state and shifts your frequency towards wellness.

5. Find something to be grateful about and speak your appreciation aloud. Begin to feel safer in your circumstances and surroundings.

6. Slowly bring your focus back to your body. Focus on your hands and feet. Shake your hands and wiggle your toes. Loosen your body to release any tension that you may be holding. Get your circulation moving to your extremities. Notice the tension in your neck and shoulders lessening. Sense your level of fear slowly dissipating and like a receding wave.

7. Get centered by grounding yourself. Shift your body weight over your feet evenly and straighten your spine. Relax your shoulders and if possible, close your eyes. Feel and appreciate the great magnetic power of Mother Earth moving underneath you and through you.

8. Mentally picture yourself after the panic attack is over being cool, calm, and collected.

9. Later that day, write out what happened, what triggered the attack, and how you handled it. Talk about your experience with someone you trust. This vulnerability initiates the process of healing.

THERAPY FOR ANXIETY.

In the case of generalized anxiety disorder, it's not just a matter of coping, there should be therapy going on to help the person understand their disorder and to develop effective management skills. Clinical psychology can be effective in treating panic attacks with: anti-anxiety medications, exposure therapy, systematic desensitisation, and mindfulness therapy. Exposure Therapy has remained the mainstay for the treatment of anxiety. The best way to get rid of anxiety is to start living in the Now. Stay in the present moment. In order to get over your anxiety attacks, you must get to the source of your emotional blockage. Once you figure out what's triggering you, you can begin working through the negative thoughts and beliefs that precipitate the attacks.

EXERCISE #35
Conquering Your Fears

What is your biggest fear? You must step fully into what you fear in order to transcend it. Whatever your fear may be, experience it from the window of observation. The more you witness the one suffering from fear (ego), the more you realize that fear is only an energy field that comes and goes, which is separate from you. If you can see a wave of fear coming to you and separate from it, then it will no longer be a part of you. Imagine yourself remaining calm in the midst of what truly terrifies you. Self-control

is strength. Calmness is mastery. See yourself remaining cool, calm, and collected in the midst of any and all chaos. Concentrate on keeping your normal breath rate and stay present in the Now.

Taking responsibility for fixing your inner resistance is paramount to deleting old thought patterns which are holding you back. From this day forward let each new thought of yours be accompanied by a sense of purpose capable of moving mountains. Stop procrastinating and second-guessing yourself. Now is the time for revision and change. Don't get caught standing still while everything around you is in perpetual motion. Step into your divine light, execute your plan, push through, and don't look back. There is no room for fear when you are seeking love and peace. Replace your inner void of fear with faith.

It has been said that there are only two true emotions, love and fear.
All other feelings are an extension of these two.
However, love takes precedence,
for it's only when love is absent, that fear is present.
~ Masaru Emoto

EXERCISE #36
Clearing Fear And Becoming Fearless

1. **Make sure you are in alignment of body, mind, heart, and soul. This is when you activate your great inner power, experience synchronicities, your intuition is activated, and you harness the power of the universe. From your center you can naturally follow the path of least resistance in the most pleasant state possible.**
2. **Belief Tree: "I am anxious" and "I am feeling unsafe." To exit this anxiety-based belief tree, ask yourself, "What falsehoods**

must I be believing in to feel this anxiety?" And finish this statement, "I feel unsafe because…"

3. Picture your future in the coming weeks, months, and years ahead. Choose the reality that you prefer. Focus with laser vision on those mental images and use them as your compass.

Life is a mirror and will reflect back to
the thinker what he thinks into it.
~ Dr. Ernest Holmes

UNCERTAINTY; EXCHANGE YOUR FEAR FOR FAITH AND CHANGE YOUR WORLD

It is commonly said that faith is the key that opens all doors. One who is lost can only find their way by faith. Faith is the seed of knowing with certainty that despite your condition, everything will work out in your favor. Without faith there is no hope of salvation and no place for the belief in a power greater than yourself. Faith means living life unmoved in the midst of uncertainty. The human mind craves certainty, it's uncertainty that creates doubt and compounds fear. Uncertainty is reality, but not knowing what's coming next can be absolutely terrifying. What we crave as human beings is clarity. Find hope in these uncertain times. In today's ever changing and unpredictable world, we must learn to live side by side with the unknown. Fear not, uncertainty is the condition that calls mankind towards brilliance and innovation, it is the birthplace of infinite possibilities. Step out on faith and know that your reality is formed from a combination of your thoughts, beliefs, and dreams. I know it's hard to trust the universe when all you've experienced in the past is evidence that you shouldn't have, but your circumstances scream for the universe to answer. Having faith doesn't mean that you will be spared of all pain. Faith merely means that you'll have company to sit with you during it.

Your beliefs can either limit you or set you free. I believe that anything is possible. Be mindful that whatever thoughts you believe, your reality will reflect them back to you. False beliefs are self-limiting and miscreated from fear. In order to change a faulty fundamental belief of yours, you must expand your consciousness. Let me assure you that you weren't born to fear life, you were born to live it! When you replace your fear with faith, you become centered in the transformational Light of the Divine. Once you import a fearless mindset, your fears are turned into courage and motivation— and you become unstoppable! Exchange your fear for faith and change your world.

CHAPTER 18

ADJUSTING YOUR MINDSET. ATTITUDE, ALTITUDE, OBJECTIVES, AND LIFE TRAJECTORY

KEEP A POSITIVE KEEP A POSITIVE MINDSET

Everything in your life starts with your mindset, your actions follow your thoughts. The worst poverty imaginable is poverty of the mind. Many times, the only thing standing in your way of accomplishing your goals are your limiting beliefs. Limiting beliefs play a key role in why some people tell themselves things like, "This is as good as it gets." or "Life is so hard." or "Nobody likes me." When you speak negativity, the universe conspires to deliver to you a matching reality. Remember that every cell in your body listens to and is influenced by your thoughts. Your thoughts trigger your emotions which are translated into energy. That vibration becomes the spark that creates your physical reality.

Kindness, gratitude, love, and compassion are examples of positive mindsets which lift your spirit. On the other hand, a negative mindset has the potential to negatively affect your life in almost every imaginable way. In order to shift out of a negative mindset and into a more desirable "abundance mindset," you will need to become more flexible, refocus, and be open and willing to see and do things differently than in the past. The presence of negative mindsets including: scarcity, fear, rejection, shame, worthlessness, and hopelessness hinder us all and prevent us from living in peace. Most people live their lives in the bubble of their comfort zone, but old ways don't open new doors. Your consciousness expands once you begin to see yourself in a more positive light. Envision yourself making progress everyday, in every way.

You are today where your thoughts have brought you;
you will be tomorrow where your thoughts take you.
~ James Allen

CHAOS ALWAYS ARRIVES UNEXPECTEDLY WHEN BAD THINGS HAPPEN

The thing about life is that nothing ever goes as planned. None of your catastrophes were expected, chaos always arrives unexpectedly. Think about your life for a moment, did you predict to be in your current situation? At some point you are likely to lose a job, close friend, car, home, mom, dad, relative, or child. These monumental losses are capable of shaking your foundation to its core. Know that you are an intelligent, strong, and resilient human being. You've got what it takes to be more than just a survivor. Aim to be successful in life and live from your dreams. Trust yourself, nothing can stop you from fulfilling your soul's purpose.

THE WORLD IS NOT AGAINST YOU

The world that you see is your creation. This is your world! Your reality is merely a response to what you are creating and what you are currently believing. Discard any disruptive thoughts and allow them to fade away. Make a habit of only building on thoughts that serve you and your purpose. You have everything it takes to conquer your biggest challenges. Have faith that your current situation will ultimately work out in your favor. If you have fallen, get back up again. Failure is not an option and God's divine grace is your inherent blessing.

HOW TO DEAL WITH PERSONAL FAILURE
LEARN TO FAIL YOUR WAY INTO SUCCESS

There is always emotional and physical pain ahead when you continue to stand in resistance to your hidden truth. This is why it's important to live from your center. Unfortunately, despite our best effort, failure will happen. Don't fear failing, it's not you, it happens to everybody. The silver lining of failure is that it creates an opportunity for new growth and expansion. Don't despair and never stop trying. Use your latest failure as motivation to move forward and steer clear of sadness and self-pity. Believe that it's literally possible to fail your way into success. Losers quit when they fail, winners fail until they succeed.

EXERCISE #37
Locating The Gift Inside of Failure

- **What would you say is your worst fail ever?**

_____

175

- **What did you learn from that failure?**

  _____

- **How can you implement this lesson into your new and improved life plan?**

  _____

**The most important lesson about failure is to always learn from it.
Analyze it, separate from it, delete it, heal it,
and then replace it with forgiveness and love.**

MINDSET HACK

Your past childhood trauma and conditioning has you thinking and believing that you have bad luck. Perhaps you were once neglected, abused, or told that you were not good enough, pretty enough, or tall enough. We are afraid of the past and we are also afraid of the future. We are afraid of hate and we are afraid of love. We are afraid of success and we are afraid of failure. We are afraid of ourselves and we are afraid of one another. We are afraid to see what lies behind the curtains of life and we are also afraid of remaining unchanged. Whenever you develop the habit of making excuses to justify your path of pain, you recommit to holding onto it tighter and reliving it. Simply choose to make changes to yourself that will shift your fortune. Let go of your hurtful past and choose to be free from it instead. This forward action of letting go is what allows you to grow. You are a divine emanation of the Creator. Your true nature is amazing and powerful beyond imagination. Open your mind to new mindsets, paradigms, and experiences. The idea is to develop and maintain a growth mindset, one that is free of past failures. Recognize that greatness is deep inside of you. You are powerful, resilient, and resourceful. A successful career and abundant future can be yours if you claim it.

When life knocks you down, try to land on your back.
Because if you can look up, you can get up. Let your reason get you back up.
~ Les Brown

ALTITUDE: YOUR FEELINGS ARE
FOOD FOR YOUR THOUGHTS

Modern science is beginning to prove what ancient wisdom has known for thousands of years, emotions are energetic waves. If you don't process them correctly they can negatively impact the energetic systems in your body. Your thoughts and emotions are intimately linked. The relationship between thoughts and feelings can be seen through this story that features a common house fly. Imagine that the fly represents your thoughts. It goes flying and buzzing around, it lands and starts feeding on something. That something is your emotions. Your thoughts feed and grow from your emotional current. Whatever you choose to give your power and attention to, has power over you. Don't let your emotions rule your life. Emotions are just energy fields. Observe your emotions both coming and going. Ground yourself in your center and see there is a hidden aspect of you that is steady, unshakable, and unchanging. This is the powerful altitude of your soul, the witness of your experience.

The law of self-fulfilling prophecy says that you get what you expect.
So why not create great expectations and the highest vision
possible of yourself and your world?
~ Mark Victor Hansen

POSITIVE THINKING

Don't let your current circumstances control your trajectory. Be encouraged that it's possible to overcome your current challenges and never give up. There is nothing like the power of positive thinking. A select group of positive thoughts form a mindset. Alignment with a positive mindset always encourages you to expand and grow, while a negative mindset tends to attract painful experiences. The more you focus on what you want instead of what you don't want, the smoother the journey. Anytime you are having a bad day, remember that you have the ability to change your thoughts and simply decide to have a better day. See your positive attitude as an invitation to spark and awaken your inner giant. The mere awareness of your innate power to shift into higher frequency thoughts and vibrations is all you need to change your mood. The key to mood elevation is to keep reaching for a better feeling inside each moment. Start to witness and monitor your inner speech. Honestly assess whether or not you're listening to the voice of your lower self or higher self? Remember that you are a spark of the Divine and your purpose here is important. You have a special gift inside to shine light to the world. Don't let your mind get in the way of your mission. Be inspired by your dreams to accomplish all that you are predestined to do.

Don't ever dim the brilliance of your inner light just to be accepted. Shine as you are meant to shine. Use your positive attitude to lift the spirits around you. Lead by example and show them what the greater you looks like, walks like, and talks like. Hold the belief that your nature is positive, not negative. Live life as the greatest version of you that you can imagine. Give love and service from your overflow. Maintain a source of positivity and keep the faith that you alone can change the world.

A CALL TO ACTION

Make today a day of change and transformation. Today represents an opportunity to choose to go deeper into spirituality. Up until now you've talked and focused on your wants, desires, and expectations. Awakening is in the nature of all souls. It's irrational to think that you can bring changes into your life without first changing your spiritual perspective and beliefs. You are not ordinary, you are extraordinary, so don't choose an ordinary existence. Inner change is the key that unlocks the chains of stagnation. Let this moment be an inspiration to change your life. From this day forward, have the intention to live a spiritual existence. Know that each lesson you experience in your life is divinely written to help and assist your evolution into universal alignment with your higher self. When you step into the vibration of your inner essence, not only do you become the greater you, but you also fulfill a piece of the collective spiritual needs of all humanity.

EXERCISE #38
You Are The Script Writer Of Your Life

1. Write down your negative self-talk. Describe all the times that you have abandoned your dreams and goals in life because of your fears. Read the letter aloud, thank it, and then burn it.
2. Write down a new script for your life going forward. Use positive affirmations and encouraging speech. Keep it within eyesight on your nightstand. Read it over and over again every night until you truly believe it in your mind and feel it in your heart.

LAW OF ATTRACTION

The energy that you are currently emitting is your point of attraction. Whatever state of being you are in, the law of attraction will add divine momentum to it. If you are happy, then happiness will follow you. If you are anxious, then anxiety will find you. Sadness will create more sad situations to feel sad about. Remember that your emotions are in fact a guidance system which is designed to guide you through life. Take note of your emotions throughout the day and remind yourself that you are not your circumstances. Surround yourself with the people and the environments which bring you happiness. When you experience negative vibrations, redirect yourself. Keep your positive energy flowing. Tune into your higher mind and trust your higher self to make the difficult choices in your life. Bless the lives of others and be blessed yourself.

YOUR IDENTITY, THE STORY OF YOU

Your story is important, it's literally amazing, but don't become identified or attached to any narrow narrative of your life. You are more than your story. Making a habit of retelling your story in casual conversations is a significant part of what supports and sustains you having a limited identity. There is freedom in being able to share your story with others, but becoming too attached to your story can stifle your emotional growth. Don't let opportunity pass you by. Too many people miss opportunities because they are too busy complaining about what happened to them. Don't become a storyteller of your problems. Visualize and tell inspirational stories detailing your strength, determination, heart, and spirit. Tell great tales of your victories and realizations.

God gives you opportunity.
What you do with it, is your gift to him.
~ T. D. Jakes

Complete identification with your thoughts and story constructs an identity known as the mind-made self. This story-based identity is, "The story of me." In this reality you become fascinated, fixated, and identified with a mindset which distances you from your higher self. While a story changes according to the storyteller, your truth is both unwavering and unchanging. In the world of form, arguing your limitations contracts your inner space and limits your rate of growth and transformation.

True Self Mantra (say aloud)
"I am not my story.
I am a dream come true,
a beautiful ray of sunshine,
a refreshing drop of rain,
a dynamic seed planted,
a dissolving grain of sand in
only a spec of time in
the calendar of forever."

THE MENTAL PICTURE OF YOURSELF

The mental picture of yourself that you hold of yourself today is the very seed that creates your harvest of tomorrow. Past experiences play a big part in our lives, but it's not so much about what happened to you, as much as it is, what's possible for you? Many people have a powerful, entrenched belief that we cannot escape our history. This is a false narrative. Who we really are is supercharged energetic beings with unlimited potential. Thus, don't ever sell yourself short, your greatest moves and adventures are yet to come.

Losing your identity with personhood can be a really scary thing. Replace your fear with faith, supreme love, and inner peace. Somewhere inside of you, a part of you is seeking freedom and shifting towards a limitless expansion, but the limited physical aspect of you is stunting your growth. Releasing the identification with your body-mind is liberating. At the level of your higher self, there's no identification with anything. Your essence is the light of consciousness behind your thoughts. You are the master of your mind and the co-creator of your universe.

Purpose Mantra (say aloud)
"I am here to watch the falling away of any
illusions and delusions I am holding onto
and reprogram my mind to serve in
the manifestation of my higher purpose."

YOUR INNER GIANT AND THE FIRE WITHIN

Don't use your imagination to try to create any vision of who you are, just stay as the self. This is your true "I-Am power." When you step back a short distance and begin to observe the happenings in your life, you gain perspective and clarity. I have learned on my journey that most people's identity is largely phenomenal, it is always changing. Realize that you are not the identity you are holding onto right now. Each day that you go out in the world saying "I'm a person," the universe will proceed to treat you merely as a person. Losing your identity with personhood can be a scary and dark thing. Replace your fear with faith in supreme love and peace everlasting. The real you is neither coming or going. The real you is always present, watching, and evolving. You are the mighty, infinite giant that resides inside your body temple.

Deep inside, there is a fire that burns within us all. This is the fire of thought vs. no thought, acceptance vs. desire, domination vs. unity, trust vs mistrust, stagnation vs. growth, and love vs. hate. This fire of transformation is capable of burning away any old beliefs that no longer serve you. The ultimate victor of this fiery blaze is already known, the real winner is you—The Greater You, the part of you that is infinite and everlasting.

Letting Go Of Your Ego-Based Identity

- **Recognize that there is a lower energy force within you (ego) that does not want you to awaken. This force must be met by the superior belief that there is nothing that can stop you from evolving into your higher self.**
- **Thankfully, your identity is always attracted and gravitating towards freedom, it must be this way. If you continue to resist your calling to higher consciousness, the whisper in your ear will eventually become a loud roar in your mind-based reality.**
- **There is supreme power in the recognition of your higher self. To find yourself is the greatest gift you could ever receive in life.**

AIM TO BE A WINNER AT LIFE

How do you explain something coming from nothing? You can't. You have to redefine "nothingness." You are the infinite being born to survive and thrive in this sometimes unkind world. You are simply unstoppable. Having the confidence and courage to endure the tough moments of life puts you in the winner's circle. To become a winner in life, you must reside in the present moment, where all things are possible.

How To Land In The Winner's Circle Of Life

- **You become a winner at life by consciously deciding to step into your divine inner light.**
- **You win by trusting and surrendering to a power greater than yourself.**
- **You win by showing gratitude for your very existence.**
- **You win with every breath you take.**
- **You win by lifting others.**
- **You succeed by overcoming what sometimes feels like overwhelming resistance on your path.**
- **You win by living a life of love.**

Along your journey, stay focused and stay in Presence. Always remember that there's always a calm and safe way through your violent storms. You were born with the will to overcome your circumstances. It doesn't matter if you don't know what tomorrow will bring, just believe that you can handle it. We are all part-scientists of sorts here to discover our divine hidden inner purpose. All the while displaying great courage, determination, gratitude, kindness, beauty, love, heart, trust, grace, dedication, and undying perseverance along the way. There are lots of challenges ahead, but you are destined for greatness. You are a natural born winner.

Your presence is a major key for so many people that you know and also for several others that you don't know. Your beautiful impact has a ripple effect in the universe. You are appreciated and loved more than you think. You are a natural born winner. Anything is possible if you just believe.

How can you become
more of what you want to become?
You can do it only when you feel that
you alone can never make yourself
what you want to become.
No human power can do it.
Only by the Grace that comes from above
can you do what you want to do and
become what you want to become.
~ Sri Chinmoy

GO BEYOND YOUR COMFORT ZONE

Today's uncertain circumstances require that you energetically rise up, not shrink. Courage is not the absence of fear, it's taking action in spite of fear. Now is the perfect opportunity to find out what your capacities are. Push against the bubble of your comfort zone. Your comfort zone is a product of your default programming which you must look to bypass to evolve. If you're looking for comfort, you will find greatness hard to find. Until you get uncomfortable, nothing happens. Discomfort is the main impetus for transformation. You are capable of doing extraordinary things when you tune in to your higher self. Don't continue to choose security over freedom.

Creation and manifestation cannot take place in the presence of stagnation. Trust and know with certainty that there's more for you than what you can see before you.

YOUR TRANSFORMATION ZONE

To enhance your creativity, commit to reprogramming and rewriting your script. Just beyond your comfort zone lies your "T-zone" (transformation zone), the realm of infinite possibilities. This is the edge of your fears. The T-zone is where you must take a leap of faith to shift into a higher level reality. Stretch to extend yourself beyond your T-zone and push beyond your limits. Make the choice to do something different today. Take more chances. For big rewards, you've got to take big risks. You are capable of doing extraordinary things whenever you decide to focus, drive, and push yourself.

Not so long ago I was afraid of finding greatness. I was more comfortable just being above average. I suffered from the affliction of self-sabotage. I suppose you could say that I traded in chance and opportunity for security, safety, and comfort. Never stop making moves to reach your inner greatness, even if you have to overcome your own self-destructive mindset. You are the only thing standing in the way of finding your truth.

Transformation Mantra (say aloud)
"Today is a perfect day for transformation.
I am a miracle magnet. I desire to attract
only positively charged circumstances,
particles, beings, and realities.
The past doesn't define me and I believe
that my future is unlimited. And so it is."

STRETCH-POWER-ACTIVATE

1. **Stretch: What is not growing is dead. In order to grow, you must stretch out of your comfort zone. Move to the edge of your fears, this is a movement towards the imaginary border where uncertainty meets possibility.**

2. **Power: Align with the power of love, use it to discover your signature gift.**

3. **Activate: Activation is the key agent of change in transformation. Make something happen today.**

EXERCISE #39
Plan of Action

1. **What do you fear the most?**

   _____

2. **What is your action plan to move beyond your fixed point?**

   _____

3. **What obstacles might you face and how do you plan to navigate through them?**

   _____

4. **What is your vision for the next five years of your life?**

   _____

5. **What standards are you unwilling to compromise on?**

   _____

MAKE A HABIT OF ACTIVATING YOUR HIGHER SELF

In this world, your highest opportunity is to recognize the truth of your higher self. Getting to this next level in your life is really a deconstructive process. Spiritual transformation asks that you get rid of any negative habits or routines that are creating a drag in your current state of being. Don't continue to allow unhealed emotions or repetitive life cycles to slow down your growth. The moment that you realize you have the power to co-create your reality, you are traveling downstream. All rivers lead back to the ocean. The next phase in your life includes the opportunity to orchestrate an epic shift in your awareness known as self-realization. Your time is now, your moment is at hand. The journey of awakening is a virtual bypass operation which shifts your mind-based identity into a soul-based identity. Don't stand in the way of your own transformation, make room for your greatness to come forth.

22 Ways To Shift Your Perspective To See Your Life As A Gift

1. Think and remain positive.
2. Remain open to the endless possibilities of life.
3. Trust in the goodness of life.
4. Be an agent of truth. Be honest, don't lie. Lying is a terrible habit that can become addictive.
5. Don't seek revenge, seek resolution.
6. Be genuine and authentic in your endeavors.
7. Resist temptation. Don't let temptation take over your heart.
8. Be kind-hearted. Don't say mean things, kindness matters.
9. Try to make people smile. Be a smile collector.
10. Be empathetic and be sympathetic to all, including those who have made mistakes in their past. The downtrodden need your blessings the most.
11. Don't ever doubt the power of love. If you choose to be loving, then realize that you must first learn to trust. Loving someone is giving them the power to hurt you, but trusting that they won't.
12. Don't be jealous or hate others, instead bless them.
13. Nurture your body with clean water and food from the earth.
14. Say these three phrases a lot: "It's okay" "Things are always working out for me," and "I'll be alright."
15. Don't give into fear. In every moment of indecision, choose love.
16. Trust your intuition, never stop believing in yourself.
17. Get out of your comfort zone, find your transformation zone.
18. Set new goals and then go about manifesting them.
19. Remember that hard work drives success.

20. Don't give your power away to anyone. Don't dim your light, or shrink in anyone's presence.
21. Remember that you and the universe are one.
22. What you cannot withstand or hold onto any more, surrender it to God.

CHAPTER 19

DENIAL, INSECURITY, ACCEPTANCE, AND GRATITUDE

THE PAINFUL CONSEQUENCES OF DENIAL

No one is perfect. Seeking perfection eventually causes people to bury their mistakes and flaws. You don't have to be perfect. Denial becomes a powerful and familiar coping mechanism for some of us who grew up in households that pretended everything was "fine." Perhaps the number one condition of suffering of human beings is their common use of denial. Denial results in self-inflicted suffering in the form of buildup of internal resistance. By justifying your pain, you commit to reliving it. What you don't let go of repeats. Spiritual teacher David Hawkins says, "What's unresolved gets called back by the universe and presents itself again." People often use denial to avoid dealing or feeling their way through painful situations. When you deny what is really going on in the moment, you stand in resistance to both the moment and to your higher self. Why not choose to let go of what's bothering you and be free instead?

True belonging only happens when we present our authentic,
imperfect selves to the world, our sense of belonging
can never be greater than our level of self-acceptance.
~ Brene Brown

HEALING INSECURITY AND SEEKING YOUR TRUTH

There is no perfect self. Your beauty lies in your imperfections and individuality. Never mind what other people think of you. You know who you are and what you believe in and that's all that matters. Being in truth simply means being yourself. We are taught as children to repress our feelings which creates separation from our true selves. This is how many people get lost in life. Some people repress their feelings about their struggle and their truth while trying to adhere to the illusion that they are perfect.

ACCEPTANCE

Complete acceptance of whatever is happening for you in the present moment is the doorway for the removal of all negative resistance in your mind. Once you fully accept everything the moment is offering you, you arrive to a powerful state of gratitude, presence, and healing. Sometimes our memories of past emotional trauma shakes our foundation. No matter what you have endured, acceptance of your circumstances is always the first step of your recovery. One of the best ways which has helped me to no longer associate pain with my past choices and experiences has been to thank each experience for the lessons it brought me. This simple action brings closure to the past.

Desire is beautiful along with its intentions and goals,
but it is the attachment to those desires that causes suffering.

All dreams require the imagination of a dreamer. Dream your dreams, but remember the most important step, the action of releasing them into the universe. This creates more inner space and allows you to move forward on your path of creating and manifesting new dreams.

GET COMFORTABLE WITH BEING UNCOMFORTABLE, BE WILLING TO EXPECT RESISTANCE

You will encounter resistance along your journey, so expect it. Expect the unexpected and when it arrives, see it for what it is, a challenge. Step to your crisis with faith, courage, and love. Give your challenges their proper attention, but remain focused on your goals and intentions. See your challenges as storms that will eventually pass. Whenever storms rage in your life, align with gratitude. Take notice of your busy mind and then get very quiet and still. Peace is found in silence and stillness. Know that you are resilient and buoyant enough to survive any crisis that you may be facing.

GRATITUDE TRIGGERS A CHAIN OF CHEMICAL REACTIONS WHICH REWIRES YOUR BRAIN

The simple action of gratefulness increases serotonin production in the frontal cortex of the brain. Serotonin is a pleasure chemical, in this way, gratitude rewires your brain to feel a more positive vibration about yourself and your current situation. The goal is to be literally filled with the spirit of gratitude. Whenever you are thinking of things that you are grateful for, it immediately brings your focus to the positive aspects of your life including all the things that are going well for you. Allow gratitude to occupy the same space as your shame, blame, and guilt. Trust that gratitude cleanses the spirit and heals the body-mind.

Everything that you've ever wanted in your life
already exists on the other side of gratitude.

The Nine Benefits of Gratitude

1. **Gratitude brings you into alignment with the universe.**
2. **Gratitude gives you the gift of perspective.**
3. **Gratitude activates your blessings.**
4. **Gratitude brings about humility.**
5. **Gratitude ushers in benevolence.**
6. **Gratitude cleanses the spirit.**
7. **Gratitude heals the body-mind.**
8. **Gratitude shines the light of love onto you.**
9. **Gratitude delivers the fragrance of grace.**

The other day I was sitting in my car bored, so I just put the car in park. I had nowhere to go and nothing to do. My mind wasn't in a state of creation, it was restless. Looking for something to focus on. I intentionally shifted my attention to the state of gratitude and instantly I came into a state of pure silence. I suddenly felt a flood of positive energy and creativity wash over me. I found myself swimming in my mind stream where anything was suddenly possible. Find the things that help you find joy in moments and do more of those. The more you choose to focus on gratitude and happiness, and the more time you spend really savoring the good stuff happening in your life, the better you'll feel.

Gratitude Mantra (say aloud)
"A grateful heart is a magnet for miracles to happen for me in my life.
My attitude of gratitude attracts positive energy to me.
I am always filled with gratitude and I am blessed to be alive.
For all that I am, for all that I can be, for all that I can do,

for those whom I love- thank you God for giving me all that I need.
I am truly blessed and highly favored."

THE POWER OF GRATITUDE IN ADVANCE

Most of the time when we say we are grateful, we do so by expressing gratitude for what has already happened for us. Next level consciousness invites us to express gratitude for delivering what hasn't happened to us yet. This slight adjustment creates a powerful shift in energy that invites a higher power to have influence over your manifestations. Gratitude in advance brings everything you want to you. First see a picture in your mind of what you intend to manifest. Keep visualizing your plan in it's completed state so that your brain cells begin to wire and fire together to turn your dreams into reality.

CHAPTER 20

HEALING SHAME, GUILT, AND BLAME. THE POWER OF FORGIVENESS

SHAME

The definition of shame is a painful feeling of humiliation or distress caused by the consciousness of wrong or foolish behavior. Shame is the feeling that you are not enough. Everyone carries the shame of something that either we did or what someone did to us. Once shamed, we carry the burdensome weight of guilt on our backs. The more shame a person carries, the heavier the load that they experience. Remember that you are not the shame that you carry and nothing that you bury can be healed. Shame says that, "Because I am flawed, I am unacceptable, and thus I am unworthy."

Shame is also intergenerational in many families, it is passed from one generation to the next. In some families, vulnerability and displaying emotion is considered to be a sign of weakness. Shame also triggers denial. In my own medical practice, I've had many patients assure me that they were fine, while their inner world would literally be collapsing on them. To heal from your past, be honest, mindful, and raw with yourself. You must find a way to shed the heaviness you are carrying in order to become a lighter version of yourself. Search for any hidden shame that you may have buried and lay claim to finding the life lessons behind your struggles.

Toxic shame is complex and it cuts like a knife deep inside of your core. Shame turns toxic when instead of trying for the best. you seek out friends, jobs, and partners that are as inferior as you perceive yourself to be. In extreme cases, your life could feel like a failure and the shame you bear will not allow you to improve. You may even begin to set yourself up to fail and feel that you deserve it. You bury the source of your pain so you don't have to remember that it happened and then you dishonor yourself with "don't talk about it anymore" type rules. As a consequence, you practice avoidance which further buries your true needs and feelings.

I am sending love to everyone who is trying to heal from a painful secret from their past. No amount of shame can change your pain, but you still have room to heal and have a bright future. You experienced what you experienced, but instead of feeling ashamed of what happened, be grateful for who you have become and all that you've overcome. Say yes to your healing! Free yourself from the prison of your past. The key to liberating yourself is opening up to others about your struggle. Shame lessens when you share your stories in safe places. Whenever you rise up to face and conquer great obstacles, you overcome them, which also inspires those around you. Your success enables friends and family members alike to believe that they can do the same in their lives. When you share your story, make yourself the hero. Let your narrative describe the value of being a survivor and not succumbing to the pitfalls of life. Tell tales of your magnificent adventures, revelations, and awakenings. Speak of your courageous fight to persevere in the eyes of overwhelming adversity. Tell why you believe you were placed here on the planet and share the keys to your bravest victories. Be a storyteller who speaks from your divine soul slowly remembering its divinity. Speak from your pure heart and share your truth. Along the way, don't confuse your identity with your story, the real you is unlimited.

Even if you've been victimized, you were not born a victim. You are a divine light, worthy of great love and inner peace. Switch your mentality from "I'm broken and helpless" to "I'm growing and healing." Adversity and struggle tends to bring out the best in people. You win the game of life by overcoming your steepest challenges. Push through your suffering with courage and precious grace. May you reach your glory yet remain humble. Now, sit back and visualize all the new energy you are attracting into your experience. Aim to empower yourself further. As you upshift your energetic frequency you'll notice that you are no longer the same person you used to be. You've shifted into a higher gear and evolved to a higher level of consciousness. Grace says that although I am flawed, I am precious and worthy. Grace is the energy that supports your spiritual journey. There is a force of Supreme Intelligence which is beyond words that always supports you and floats you in your beingness.

Authenticity is a collection of choices that we have to make everyday.
It's about the choice to show up and be real. The choice to be honest.
The choice to let our true selves be seen.
~ Brene Brown

EXERCISE #40
Complete the following statements:

1. What I am most ashamed of is... _____
2. My darkest secret is..._____
3. What I feel is holding me back is..._____

Picture yourself light as a feather. Feel the release of your dark emotions. See this exercise as a release of the past and forgive yourself. Give yourself permission to move forward and celebrate the new and improved version of you. I encourage you to continue this inner dialogue and expand on your answers in your healing journal.

GUILT

Guilt can take quite a toll on your spirit. Guilty feelings must be rooted out of your long term memory and replaced with self-love. When you commit a mistake and feel guilty, try to objectively see why it happened. Guilt is nothing but the review and judgement of your past actions and decisions by your ego. Guilt is not only felt, it is inherited and taught. It's like a crown that's passed down from generation to generation. It's a way of keeping every person in compliance with the social standards of that society. Until about the age of twenty-one, society and family members plant seeds of guilt in us all. Those same seeds grow and over time begin to root inside of you. Eventually, you start creating and manifesting guilt all by yourself, sometimes without any provoking reason. This is how guilt becomes a permanent guest in your beingness. Societal guilt is a way to keep individuals from straying away from the agreed common values which form the core of all societies. Every society has their norms and whoever deviates away from that is shamed. As with every other emotion, you must learn to accept the feeling of guilt, it's there for a reason. Feeling guilty doesn't mean you're a bad person, it means that you're emotionally healthy, human being and it's presence also means that your self-regulatory system is working.

One of the harmful consequences of immense guilt is that it creates energy blockages inside your being. It's harmful because guilt is invisible and eats one from within. Guilt can lead to depression and at worst, self-harm. Guilt isn't the most common reason for self-harm, but it's certainly a contributing factor. After all, guilt is a powerful trigger connected to past trauma. Self-harm is a form of self-release. I've had many patients who release their trauma by cutting themselves. The action of cutting brings them temporary relief and euphoria because the physical pain takes their mind off their spiritual pain. It's only reasonable to want a release from pent up guilt, but self-harm is not the answer. Self-harm is a cry for help. Cutting is a deeply troubling and disturbing habit that requires immediate referral to professional psychiatric therapy and behavioral modification education. The truth is that self-harm doesn't solve the underlying issue, the presence of profound guilt.

As with every other emotion, guilt serves a purpose. It tells you that you did something that is against your values. The real problem is not that you feel guilty, but that you choose to stay in that feeling without doing anything about it. Sometimes, doing someone or something wrong, can later become a beautiful lesson and a game changer for you. In this way, your guilty feelings have the potential to eventually spark your evolution. Take a look into the origin of your guilt. Just this new level of awareness and attention will open new doors for you and create the opportunity to never commit the same mistakes again. This is because, once you look deep into it and identify the source of your guilt, it tends to disappear. Whenever you face a great fear, you defeat it. Where your attention goes, energy flows. As long as you flow unobstructed like a powerful river, you will manifest greatness in your life.

EXERCISE # 41
The Elimination of Guilt

The elimination of guilt requires an effective action plan.
Start your healing by asking yourself these questions:

1.   **Is there something I need to forgive myself for?**

   _____

2.   **What can I do right now to rectify my situation?**

   _____

3.   **Do I need to apologize to someone?**

   _____

4.   **Do I need to tell someone the truth?**

   _____

5.   **What do I need to do to change my behavior so that this never happens again?**

   _____

**Now let the positive actions you've just taken
replace your feelings of guilt
and give yourself permission to move forward.**

THE RELATIONSHIP BETWEEN YOUR EGO AND GUILT

If you can remove your ego, you can simply drop your accumulated guilt. If you allow yourself to live in greater awareness and dampen your ego, you will no longer get unduly angry, nor will you suffer. When you do get angry, you will do so to the appropriate extent and there won't be any associated guilt. At a certain point in your spiritual evolution, you will have the realization that there is nothing you can change about your past. No one is perfect, we are human and we all make mistakes. It's important to remember to be forgiving, but also forgive yourself. Move forward in your healing journey by taking your guilt experience and turning it into a lesson that you can learn from. Guilt and regret keep you from enjoying the present moment, which is all there is.

EXERCISE #42
Affirmations To Assist You In Cleansing Guilt

Speak positive affirmations instead of negative words to express your feelings of remorse.

1. "I admit that I made a mistake."
2. "I apologize for my role."
3. "I am thankful for the lesson and the opportunity to transform my life."
4. "By choosing small positive actions everyday, I will work to improve my condition."
5. "I vow not to make the same mistake again."
6. "I forgive myself and give myself permission to move forward."
7. "I pledge to start each new day with positive thoughts and energy."

Quit beating yourself up and allow yourself to accept God's mercy. Despite everything that has happened to you and hurt you, you've still grown and you're still here. One of the best ways which that's helped me to no longer associate pain with my past choices and experiences has been to thank God for each one of them. I have developed an understanding of life through meditation, prayer, and trust that everything is as it should be. Deep down inside, guilt is merely the need for you to feel forgiveness. The most spiritual way to rid yourself of any guilt is simply to ask for forgiveness. Ask the person or people you've hurt to forgive you. Take responsibility and go to the other person and apologize. If a physical apology is not possible, then ask them from afar spiritually. At the soul level, a mental apology is just as good as a physical one. Now get rid of the guilt and shame you have been holding onto, move forward, and start to live the best life that you possibly can. Even better, ask God to forgive you. Acknowledge and confess whatever you've done and apologize for your actions. No matter what you've done or how much time has passed, you can always bring your troubles to God. Redemption is always available to you.

Self-Acceptance Mantra (say aloud)
"I acknowledge that my soul has agreed to every choice
that I've ever made. It knew that each choice would strengthen
my desire to feel, align, and respond with love. Today, I choose be
grateful for my past experiences, both good and bad. Without them,
I would be a very different being, with them I am stronger and wiser."

BLAME

For some people, everyone is to blame for their hardships except themselves. Some people point their finger at anyone close to them to avoid taking any responsibility. They believe that everyone else is the problem. It's a narcissistic trait to point fingers and constantly blame others when things go wrong. Don't blame the world for your problems, the world is not responsible for the condition of your circumstances and spirit, you are. Blame turns into bitterness. A person who constantly blames others for their own actions tends to think of themselves as "perfect," this is a flawed perspective. Blame is commonly associated with a history of childhood abuse or trauma. For example, having an abusive parent as a child who physically punished you for your mistakes would naturally cause you to adapt a kind of perfectionist approach to life. If and when you made errors, accepting the blame for them would expose you to harsh punishments. Therefore, adopting the habit of shifting blame onto others has the built-in reward of not being punished or hurt. Conversely, accepting responsibility for your questionable actions would trigger your memories of past failures to resurface. So as a result, you "learned" not to accept blame. Your choice was to shift the blame elsewhere instead of feeling hurt. It's a lot easier and less painful to blame someone else. It's not a matter of cruelty, it's a matter of psychological survival. Over time this pattern of shifting blame becomes a learned behavior with benefits.

Don't stay bitter at life. Bitterness consumes the vessel that contains it.
Try to be as joyful as you can everyday. Life is such a gift.

Choose to wear a smile over a frown. Be happy, not sad.
Choose love over hate and be peaceful, not toxic. Stay as the Self.

RECOGNIZING AND ESCAPING DENIAL

Perhaps the number one cause of human suffering is our common use of denial. When you deny your role in your failures it leads to increased resistance in your life. Denial doesn't create negative manifestations, you do. You are the great manifester of your experience. God gave you life, but it's your responsibility to learn what to do with it. When you deny what is true, you stand in resistance to both the moment and your higher self. Failure to align with the truth leads to self-inflicted suffering. You always have a choice to reside in truth or to live a lie.

A painful truth is always better than a hidden lie.
~ David Williams

YOU ARE RESPONSIBLE FOR YOUR CHOICES

Your life can only change to the degree that you accept responsibility for it, it's not always the other person. You've got to be mature enough to realize that you also have some toxic traits. It's amazing what some people are willing to go through in order to avoid facing the truth, this flawed mindset ushers in a victim mentality. Many people would rather suffer their experience than change. Once you accept your share of responsibility, you are set free.

He who blames others has a long way to go on their journey.
He who blames himself is halfway there.
He who blames no one, has arrived.
~ Chinese proverb

FORGIVENESS

Forgiving someone may seem impossible to you today, but you can do it. Forgiveness is the practice of letting go. Forgiveness releases your attachment to the anger, sadness, or resentment that you are holding onto. Think of forgiveness as an act of relaxation. From the inner state of relaxation the emotional release happens, then the spiritual state of surrender spontaneously springs forth. In simple terms, forgiveness is the commitment to show mercy to yourself and compassion to others, it's a true act of love. Compassion reduces emotional discomfort, eliminates the desire for revenge, ends separation, and elevates your mood. The forward action of amnesty has a way of releasing any stored resentment. Let go of any resentment towards anyone that has ever hurt you. When you forgive the very people that have caused you to suffer the most, you free yourself of any bitterness and contempt. In true forgiveness, you must also surrender any blame you are holding onto. Blame is a toxic emotion that only serves to weaken your spirit. One of the most beautiful things you could ever do for yourself is to let go of your painful past. Once you are empty again, love can occupy that space in your heart. Sprinkle mercy throughout your day and fill your heart with love.

> *Nothing erases the past. There is repentance,*
> *there is atonement, and there is forgiveness.*
> *That is all, but that is enough.*
> *~ Ted Chiang*

True healing is not possible without forgiveness. Forgive others, but most of all remember to forgive yourself. You are deserving of inner peace. Your spiritual healing takes place when you are finally fully loving yourself in the realm of your sacred heart.

> *Forgive others not because they deserve*
> *forgiveness but because you deserve peace.*
> *~ Johnathan Lockwood Hui*

EXERCISE #43

**Question: What have you done that is the
hardest thing to forgive yourself for
and why has it been so difficult for you to overcome it?**

_____

_____

_____

_____

BE YOUR OWN SAVIOR AND FIND GRACE

Circumstances are neutral, it's how you respond to them that determines whether they do you good or ill. We've all seen examples of people living in the harsh circumstances of poverty, war, and disease who's souls shine forth with power and grace. Be a better you everyday, for you. While it may be true that your painful past experiences can never be erased, you can choose to see it now with different optics, understand it, and grow from it. Not all storms come to disrupt your life, some come to clear your path. Nothing happens by accident, the universe is far too intelligent for that. There is always an unseen higher purpose for your hurtful experiences. Don't hold your past transgressions in your emotional body. Dig deep inside your consciousness to reconcile with whatever happened to you. Shame, blame, and guilt hold you prisoner to your past and prevent you from finding your truth. Unburden yourself by sharing your story with others that may benefit from hearing it. The past is long gone and unchangeable, the future is yours to chart. With every rising sun, you have the ability to start anew. Your story is still being written and you are the author of the chapters in your book.

Open your sacred heart and show yourself the compassion and love that you deserve. You are divinely blessed and highly favored just to wake up this morning. You have chosen to do what makes your soul happy. You are not the same person you were when trouble first found you. Along the way, you have learned not to dwell in your pain, but to follow your inner light. In your evolution, you have the tools and opportunity to live a more meaningful life; a life full of optimism, love, great joy, and divine purpose. The secret to having it all is believing that you already do. Take control over your happiness today and live love now.

CHAPTER 21

UNIVERSAL ALIGNMENT, SYNCHRONICITY, INTUITION, AND NUMEROLOGY

CENTER YOURSELF AND GET INTO
UNIVERSAL ALIGNMENT

Your most powerful healing takes place when you are in universal alignment, which is living in harmony with your mind, heart, body, and soul. Alignment has the effect of pressing a virtual reset button of your current programming. Great calm and regeneration subsequently speeds throughout your body-mind circuitry. The more frequently you come into calibration with your higher self, the further you distance yourself from your limited body-mind identity. Truth vibrates at a certain frequency. This movement, away from the world of duality and form sets you on a path to personal freedom. Don't settle for merely a small taste of freedom, give yourself permission to go all the way and transmute into your non-physical self. Your unbound soul knows the sweet fragrance of awakening coming into being. In your center is where you will find the greater you. Prove to yourself that you are capable beyond measure, deeper than your circumstances require, and giving beyond tomorrow's promise.

Yes, we see there are problems in the world.
But we believe in a universal force, that when activated by the human heart,
has the power to make all things right. Such is the divine authority of love:
to renew the heart, renew the nations, and ultimately, renew the world.
~ Marianne Williamson

FREE THE MIND AND CURE THE BODY

As a being of light, wellness naturally flows to you and through you. Proper alignment of your mind, body, heart, and soul generates feelings of happiness and joy. Disorders of your mind lead to disorders of your body. When you harbor thought patterns of resistance like fear and doubt, you block the flow of energy through the meridians of your body. No one can ever take away your freedom to decide how you feel. If you can remove the resistance which is dampening your flow, the Source Energy within you is allowed to flow freely. Pure love and joy is all that remains.

There are no accidents or coincidences in life.
Everything is synchronicity, because everything has a frequency.
~ Rhonda Byrne

BE OPEN TO THE GUIDANCE OF SYNCHRONICITY

Synchronicity is when we experience events that are seemingly random and unrelated, but on a deeper spiritual level they are actually occurring together in divine time. The ultimate idea of simultaneousness is that certain meetings or events arise like signposts or warnings. Synchronicity indicates that we are not random beings thrown out into chaos without some kind of guidance or signal. An increased frequency of serendipity happens when you are aligned with the flow of the universe. In this way, you can use synchronicity as a cosmic guidance system. There is no such thing as a coincidence, only Divine Intelligence manifesting itself.

When you become aligned with the whole, you become a conscious part
of the connectedness: spontaneous occurrences, chance encounters,
coincidences, and synchronistic events will happen much more frequently.
~ Eckhart Tolle

NUMEROLOGY

Seeing angels directly is not possible, your angels will never appear in front of you and ask what you want in your life. However, there are several other ways angels try to contact you. Many believe that the most common way angels reach out to you is through numbers. These signs appear in our lives when we least expect them. They may come in the guise of a number you notice when you suddenly take a look at your clock, see an address, watch an ad on TV, etc. Angels are sending you numbers to notice. If a certain number is following you wherever you go and you are seeing it, know that it is not a coincidence. Your guardian angels are trying to contact you. If you know the meaning of the number that comes into your life, it will be easier to understand the message. Here are some common examples that I see often.

11:11

One of the ways the universe communicates with you is through repetitive 3-digit number patterns that can often be delivered to you by angels. Let's talk about the symbolism of angel number 11:11. All the world's greatest spiritual teachers will tell you that it signifies that you are one with everything; that's what's happening when you see 11:11. You are being reminded that what you are seeking is already a part of you now. Very often, angel number 11:11 is perceived as a wake-up call. The secret meaning of its appearance is always related to new beginnings and new opportunities around you. This number has a positive symbolism and it announces that something good is about to happen. Seeing the number 11:11 means that you have the opportunity of harnessing the universe's energy to make your current ideas and projects come true. Your thoughts are always manifesting. 11:11 is the universe's way of urging us to pay attention.

The meaning of the number 11:11 stems from the angel number 1; representing individuality, unity, and new beginnings. In the spiritual significance of numbers, 11 is one of the master numbers. Number eleven is thought of as a "master" number because it is a double-digit of the same number. When this occurs, the vibrational frequency of the prime number 1, doubles in power. When we see the number one in the 11:11 sequence, the vibration of the number is quadrupled! Number 11 is the number of intuition, spiritual connection, and miraculous creation. 11:11 is the universe's way of urging us to pay attention to our heart which contains our soul's intuition. The most important significance of the 11:11 is its availability as a portal to higher consciousness. If you look at the shape of number 11, it represents two pillars, a gateway, which opens a direct portal between divine creativity and direct manifestation. When you see angel number 11:11 repeating over and over, it's a special message that an energetic gateway has opened up for you. Recognize it as a moment in time when your guardian angels can take up your offered prayers and intentions to assist their manifestation here on earth.

444

I was born at 4:44am on the southside of Chicago in Hyde Park. I was born at the University of Chicago Hospital and at the age of 23, I returned to that same institution as an intern in their General Surgery Residency program. Throughout my life I've seen the numerical sequence 444, but I always perceived and mistook this phenomenon as a mere coincidence. Over the years I must have seen this angel number over 100 times. Now, at my current level of consciousness, I know that there are no coincidences. Just last week I saw 444 twice within thirty minutes. Now, every time I see this particular sequence I feel a wave of calm inner peace that passes over me and I feel divinely supported by the universe. This is because the energy found within these three numbers provides you with divine protection against the outside world.

Number four has several symbolic meanings and is considered to be a very important number in number symbolism. Number four represents the four elements— air, water, fire, and earth. It also represents the four seasons— winter, spring, summer, and fall, and finally the four directions— north, south, east, and west. This gives number 444, four times more power, you can only imagine the wonders you can achieve when this number comes into your life. All the worldly energies combine together to guide and assist you on your quest. To activate the power behind the number, you only have to believe in it. Higher forces can't help you if you don't want to accept their help. When you keep doing the same things over and over and continue to ignore the small wonders happening for you, then you just can't rise up.

The number 444 demonstrates that there are angels presently surrounding you who are ready to aid and protect you. It's a signal that you don't have to do everything on your own. What angels offer is mental, physical, emotional, and spiritual support. Your angels will help you with anything related to hard work, endurance, safety, and stability. When you see the number 444, your angels are reminding you that you are on the right path and it's okay to accept their assistance. Angel numbers are small blessings that your guardian angels send you. When you expand your belief system to include the existence of angels, you will find yourself receiving more blessings, more signs, and greater protection in your life.

888

If you've recently been seeing the angel number 888, consider yourself fortunate. Seeing 888 means that something good is about to happen for you. The primary meaning of 888 is that you have knowledge and wisdom to share. Wisdom is the divine gift behind 888. Wisdom is knowing when to use what you've learned to make a situation better. Angel number 888 carries the vibration of your hard work paying off and abundance in all ways, especially in your finances. You can expect a windfall of prosperity, wealth, and basically winning at life! 888 may be suggesting that you will receive an unexpected reward for past good work, karma re-paid in kindness.

When this number shows up to you as a sign, get excited because you are being blessed with infinite potential. The number 8 when turned to the side is the infinity symbol, which represents where our true source of unlimited abundance comes from— Source, God, The Most High, The Divine, Prime Creator, or another name that resonates with you the most. I hold the impression that the number 8's are resonating into your conscious awareness to point at a "holy infinity" state of being within you.

You can't become more intuitive, you ARE intuitive.
Just like you ARE a human being.
~ Mastin Kipp

INTUITION

Intuition is a thing that one knows or considers, likely from an instinctive feeling rather than conscious reasoning. Most of the time your intuition is right, but it's not perfect. Clearly, not every premonition will not come to pass, but since your intuition whispers in response to something, try paying attention to it more often. Everyone has the power of intuition, but it expresses itself louder in some more than others. "Divine insight" is a form of knowing that occurs more often as your spiritual transformation advances. You can't get intuition from books, it's more complex than that. Just beyond your amazing five senses, lies an expansive intuitive inner realm which operates independently— the dimension of intuition. Your intuition loves to support your growth and success. It's an inner guidance system that works for your highest good. Emotional and physical cleansing of your body-mind improves your intuition and leads you to the best responses. Always remain open and willing to hear what your intuition says before making big decisions, then act after taking your gut feeling into consideration.

Intuition is the voice of the non-physical world.
It is the sudden answer to a question.
It is the light that comes to the darkness.
The higher self is the connecting link when
the soul speaks to its personality.
It is a dialogue between your personality
and it's immortal self.
It is the presence of the Divine.
~ Gary Zukov

YOUR HIGHEST STATE OF WELL BEING IS WHOLENESS

In life, adverse news and events will come to you to remind you that you are out of alignment with the universe. Getting into universal alignment places you into the highest state of well-being. Your mind will always see itself as suffering and in need of something. Stop blaming the messengers in your life for your discomfort, they are there to teach you the lessons you need to know. To find your truth all you have to do is align with your mind, heart, body and soul. Soul alignment is important because your soul can never become ill, this is because it's already whole and pure. When you are properly aligned, your stress levels are lowered and the opportunity to surrender to God's plan arises. In alignment, every cell in your body is in touch with everything that was, is, and will be. Today, let us declare health, healing, wholeness, wellness, and alignment for all.

CHAPTER 22

MANIFESTATION AND FLOW

DELIBERATE SPONTANEOUS MANIFESTATION, BE AN AMBASSADOR OF LIGHT

Be powerful and vibrational with your intentions and presence. Be an ambassador of goodness and a light of love. Goals are not a necessary element for the law of attraction to bring manifestation into your life. The easiest thing to do is simply be grateful as many times as possible each day. Keep in mind that if all you ever do is ask for things, you will find yourself out of balance. Locked into the state of desire is not how you should live. Try to practice daily gratitude and watch how your blessings begin to flow. Make a conscious recognition of every little thing that happens to you and take mental notes of everyone you meet. Try not to burn any bridges, you may need that very person's assistance down the road. Know that your reality is truly your creation. If you encounter resistance from a certain individual, remember that no single person can stop you from manifesting your destiny. Your journey is divinely blessed. Successful manifestations start with clear and purposeful intentions accompanied by vivid visions of how you want things to go. If what you are desiring is not currently manifesting, ask yourself: "What fears, limitations, or false beliefs am I currently believing in and holding onto?" If you're honest with yourself, you'll be able to identify the causes of your energy blocks and learn to release them.

The number one reason that people fail to reach their manifestation goals is a lack of persistence, most people never finish the race. Learn to expect and anticipate that there will always be some resistance in your journey. Stay strong and stay faithful. Remember, when you're undergoing a massive paradigm shift, things almost always get worse before they can get better. Whatever happens, don't quit. It's accepted wisdom that "quitters never win and winners never quit."

Another common reason why people fail to manifest abundance is their lack of belief in themselves. **Always believe in yourself**, you are a powerful creator and a dream catcher. **Let go** of any remaining **self-doubt** about yourself and your abilities. Limited beliefs are like viruses which build up over the years. Seeing yourself as changeful opens you up to new possibilities, new technology, and new experiences. Failure to **be flexible** enough to **adapt** to changing times, turns you into a prisoner of your past.

Identify the sources or unconscious behaviors behind your energy blocks. Once you **unblock yourself,** you will immediately become a more powerful receiver of **Source.** Learn to **let go** of whatever you are holding onto. When you release resistance, your intentions **manifest** freely into physical reality. **Trust** that the **universe** is leading you step by step to your purpose. **Create space** for your miracles through meditation and prayer. Start shooting your **rockets of desire** into the stratosphere, they won't all reach their mark, but many of them will and since **LOA** will bring more of what you are giving your **attention** to, you will start **attracting** more of what you want, rather than what you don't want. The ideal mindset for manifestation is to think of how good it will feel once you accomplish your **vision.** Let the **feeling** of already having your **dream realized** serve as the **magnet** to your manifestation. Remember that the universe schedules the **timing** of your **blessings,** not you. **Trust** that your dreams are always coming to you.

The final step of **manifestation** is the **release** of your dream. You release it out of your hands once you **get out of your own way.** Stay focused on how it will feel once it arrives. Step into your vision fully, **let it be** as if it were **already done. Stay in this mindset** for several uninterrupted minutes and practice this **manifestation exercise every day.** If the things you are trying to manifest are still not coming, you are probably giving more of your attention to the "reality" of its absence. It is this "'wanting," a feeling of separation that occurs, which diminishes your returns.

> *If you focus on the task at hand, shed all distractions*
> *and follow reason with steadfast determination, the divine spark*
> *within you will burst into flames. Nurture this inner light, keep it*
> *pure, and be ready to return it to its Source when your time is done.*
> *Expect nothing, fear nothing, speak truly, and act heroically.*
> *No one can stop you.*
> *~ Marcus Aurelius*

VISIONING

Many people I work with have trouble with manifesting because what they want is unfamiliar to them. What they need to do is to become familiar with what it is that they desire. The difficulty most have is that there is a gap between what we want and what we have. This is where visioning comes in. Visioning is the process of seeing yourself as already having what you are seeking. Know that you are a visionary, even when it seems you are lost. You are capable of creating alternate realities. What you have imagined for yourself already exists! All you have to do is become a vibrational match to it. Visioning the gap between you and your dreams shrinking, eases your manifestations into place.

In your mind's eye, visualize your highest intention.
Take mental images of your vision and use them
as points of attraction to manifest your heart's desire.

Twelve Tips For Easy Manifestation

1. **Clear your mind and relax. Do some conscious breathing and get centered. Focus on what it is that you desire. It's important to get super-duper clear on exactly what it is that you want to invite into your life.**

2. **Make a vision board with all the things you want to manifest. Start with the smaller things that lead to the bigger things that you are seeking.**

3. **Spend a few minutes every night focusing on appreciating what you have and the aspects you are trying to manifest more of.**

4. **Normalize the concept of getting what you want by using the past tense. For example: make a list of things you've created in your life in the same arena of things you want to manifest.**

5. **Announce your thoughts out loud three times before doing the actions required to create the change you desire. For example: "I am manifesting abundance in all aspects of my life right now." (repeat x 3)**

6. **Identify your feelings. What is the feeling and meaning behind what you are wanting? What feelings will accomplishing it bring to you? Is it joy, recognition, or freedom?**

7. **What is the vibrational tone that you need to display that matches your desire. Come into alignment with your future self.**

8. Write your own script as if you are the director of a movie, your movie. You get to write your role, who you meet, what happens, and how it ends.

9. Describe all the awesome feelings you will have upon the arrival of your desired manifestations. Be as emotionally involved with your dreams as possible. Passion fuels purpose.

10. Create a song, playlist, or inspirational video which describes your dream.

11. Believe it is yours and it will be yours.

12. Show active faith to the universe by doing something that shows you already have what it is, that you are wanting. This doesn't have to be something big.

13. Take action. By this I mean not just sitting around all day and expecting the things you want to come to you. You must take action in proportion to the result you are wanting and expecting.

> There's nothing you can do that's more
> important than being fulfilled.
> You become a sign, a signal,
> transparent to transcendence.
> In this way, you live and become a
> realization of your own personal myth.
> ~ Joseph Campbell

FLOW: THE OPTIMAL EXPERIENCE

Find your true place in the world, locate your grounding point. Once you are present in your center, you can head north. This forward movement places you in the proper vibrational tail wind. With the wind at your back, you glide easily into the flow state. Flow is a state of enhanced performance and intense focus. It's a concept of positive psychology regularly seen in high-performing people. Flow has been described as your most optimal mental state. Chimerinsky, the University of Chicago professor and author of "Flow," describes flow as: "The mental state of operation in which a person performing an activity is fully immersed in a feeling of energized focus, full involvement, and enjoyment in the process of the activity." One way of getting to the flow state is to focus your attention and concentrate on doing only one thing. When you do just one thing and nothing else, you give yourself permission to be fully immersed in the present moment. Another way to reach the state of flow is to find your intrinsic motivation that makes the activity incredibly joyful. This is the part that happens when you are out with friends and time just seems to fly by, or when you play your favorite sport and don't even notice that the sun has already gone down. You gain so much joy that you forget everything else around you and fully immerse yourself in your task, creating the state of flow. It's possible early on, that you may have difficulty coming into the flow state. Sometimes we block ourselves with feelings of not being enough, not being ready, or feelings that it's not the right time. Get over those distracting thoughts and you will find yourself in flow soon enough. Flow is the opposite of apathy, which is defined as "a lack of enthusiasm, interest, or concern" and it is the least productive state of mind. Achieving real flow takes time, perseverance, and talent in a particular skill. Once achieved, flow is the pinnacle of human productivity.

**The fastest route to the spiritual flow-state is
through the personal mantra "I am."
Any statement that starts with "I am" which seeks flow will do.
Use these mantras, or create your own.**

- "I am open to the flow."
- "I am fully in the flow."
- "I am full of endless flow."
- "I am in the know when I flow."
- "I am always in the flow."
- "I am in the flow, that's how I know."

When you arrive into your flow state, you naturally start to spontaneously create and manifest with ease. The flow state is the source of all creativity, intuition, insight, hunches, and great performances. When you're in the zone, you're alert but calm, confident, and motivated. You're performing at your best and do so effortlessly. Every moment comes with a divine potential and purpose. When you tap into the power of the present moment, you connect with the beauty and essence of life. Flow begets further flow. As you become more practiced and learn the habits and the triggers to self-initiate your flow state, you'll be better able to achieve it more often and more effectively.

CHAPTER 23

HEALING TOXIC MASCULINITY

PATRIARCHY

Patriarchy is the word used to describe the system that supports male dominance, misogyny, or sexist masculinity in our society. Despite recent changes in societal gender roles, ours is still a culture where sexism rules the day. Certainly all men are not misogynists, but most men have adopted and used patriarchy to their advantage. Thankfully, now is the time of historic levels of energy shifts and transformation. Dismantling the patriarchal system is what's needed for any true change in male/female dynamics. It will take a Herculean joint effort of evolved men and women to change the present course of gender dynamics, but true change is indeed possible in today's climate. Our task as visionary thinkers is to develop a holistic non-patriarchal culture where equality and freedom of expression for both men and women is valued and protected. Generational healing is what's needed to end this oppressive system and its historical dominance. Healing cleanses. When a man heals himself, he heals his father, grandfather, great grandfather, and his other great male ancestors.

No intelligent person is interested in dominating others.
His first interest is to know himself.
~ Osho

TOXIC MASCULINITY

Toxic masculinity is a collection of outdated gender-linked behaviors and standards of what it means to be a man, that either damages or hurts those who continue to uphold them. It's toxic if you believe that in order to be a real man, you have to behave a certain way, or do certain things. Toxic masculinity also speaks to the reality of the ancestral trauma of patriarchy handed down from fathers to sons and the unresolved emotional suffering and silent shame that many men feel. Unfortunately, boys and young men are taught to ignore or suppress their deep emotions instead of expressing them. Patriarchy perpetuates a culture of wounded masculinity that harms men as much as it does women. Sadly, vulnerability, surrender, and unconditional love are on the other side of that wall. Emotional suppression pushes love away, which is exactly the opposite of what your soul craves. Your soul wants you to experience spiritual love, but your ego aims to prevent you from ever being satisfied.

> *There is only one emotion that patriarchy values and is expressed by men,*
> *that emotion is anger. Real men get mad. And*
> *their madness, no matter how violent*
> *or violating, is deemed natural – a positive*
> *expression of patriarchal masculinity.*
> *The reality is that men are hurting and the whole culture responds*
> *to them by saying: "Please do not tell us what you feel."*
> *~ bell Hooks*

Toxic masculinity was originally coined by men who realized that part of their development involved learning the unofficial "masculine commandments." Characteristics of a toxic man include: holding a belief of superiority over women, being emotionless, immune to pain, never feminine, and a lack of vulnerability. The truth is that any one of these character traits, when taken to the extreme, is harmful to the male psyche. Every virtue when exaggerated, can become a vice. The behaviors traditionally associated with being masculine are no exception to that rule. Quality men do not fear equality. Misogyny encourages men to take what they want in their lives, including power over any woman. It refers to a culture that dismisses bad behaviors with rhetoric like "boys will be boys." There's absolutely nothing wrong with a man who likes carpentry, muscle cars, weight lifting, or beer pong, but there is something wrong with a culture that tells you that you're less of a man if you don't want to do these things.

Toxic "Masculine Commandments"

1. **Toxic masculinity refers to a culture that says: "Men can't express their feelings or ask for help, because doing so isn't manly."**
2. **Toxic masculinity ascribes to the idea that "real men don't cry" and "men never show emotion," which causes many men to repress their emotions, sometimes to the point of mental illness.**

3. Toxic masculinity is self-focused. It seeks to use others for personal gain, pleasure, or notoriety. Unconscious men serve their male ego and care about physical appearance and material trappings over results. This describes men that crave accolades, awards, and praise.

4. Toxic masculinity assures that some men will refuse to seek help when they're in trouble or accept help when it's offered.

5. Toxic masculinity is when assertiveness and confidence become pathological and encourage the domination of others. These men need to be seen and heard as the "alpha male."

6. Toxic masculinity is when stoicism, ambition, and competitiveness become heartless insensitivity, uncontrollable greed, and outright sociopathic aggression.

7. Toxic masculinity holds others to higher standards of appearance and behavior in comparison to themselves.

8. Toxic masculinity involves resorting to violence if something does not go their way. This is a common root cause of domestic violence.

MASCULINE SENSITIVITY AND VULNERABILITY

Patriarchal culture encourages men to deny their feelings. Male empaths are often shamed when they show their sensitive side and subsequently become reluctant to talk about them. They may feel like they are too feminine or not masculine enough. They have to fight gender stereotypes and were probably warned not to be a "crybaby" and to "act like a man." In their early years as boys, they are often told "real men don't cry." Additionally, it's commonly known that sensitive boys are often bullied at school. Consequently, men learn to repress and hide their deepest emotions. When men are not allowed to be emotional it leads to inner anger and external violence. They internalize their anger and they end up acting out on themselves, their partners, and their children. John Stoltenberg in his essay "Healing from Manhood" shares that "Loving justice more than manhood is not only a worthy pursuit, it is the future." Eventually in order to cope with their suppressed emotions, men harden their hearts. For these reasons, there are a lot of men that suffer internally because they are not comfortable enough to let their emotions flow. This belief system negatively impacts men's intimate relationships, friendships, careers and emotional health. As long as the majority of men continue to try dominating the women in their lives and also in their world, there will be separation, friction, and inequality between the sexes.

In patriarchal society, women are valued less than men. Within this narrative, the lives of men are favored over that of women. The best jobs and the best salaries are reserved for men. This system is a tool used by men to hold onto power, both in the home and also in society. Rebelling against patriarchal thinking is what's needed to march towards equality of the sexes.

> *Men have discovered their distinctive virtues and vices*
> *through grappling with the perennial dilemmas and*
> *demands of love, courage, pride, family, and country.*
> *These are the five paths whose proper ordering gives us*
> *the key to the secret of happiness for a man.*
> *~ Waller Newell*

The Awakened Man

The key to eliminating any defective mindset is self-realization. In the journey of awakening one receives many life changing gifts, Aha! moments, and blessings.

1. **An awakened man lives a conscious existence. Healthy masculinity encourages men to find purpose in their actions.**
2. **An awakened man doesn't identify with his ego, he identifies with his higher non-physical self. Healthy masculinity is when a man feels no pressure to prove anything to anyone except himself.**
3. **An awakened man is wise and secure enough with his feelings to be open and vulnerable. Healthy masculinity asks men to first feel their emotions, then heal them. You can't heal what you don't feel.**
4. **An awakened man maintains a healthy masculine energy, but is also intune with his divine feminine energy, rather than being afraid or ashamed of it. Healthy masculinity is present when a**

man accepts and owns all his imperfections and maintains the firm conviction that his manhood is still intact.

5. An awakened man is a man who practices emotional awareness and embraces the full spectrum of his emotions. Healthy masculinity encourages men to understand and control their emotions, but to never be ruled by them.

6. An awakened man has no fear of vulnerability and intimacy.

7. An awakened man believes in a higher power greater than himself.

8. An awakened man is concerned about the well-being of his family.

9. An awakened man does not fear power-sharing or equal partnerships.

10. An awakened man accepts failure and rejection without blaming others. Healthy masculinity encourages an open mindset which includes: learning, teaching, and growing.

11. An awakened man is honest, fair, trustworthy, and is comfortable having difficult conversations. Healthy masculinity celebrates men with integrity and those that speak the truth.

12. An awakened man understands the importance of service. Healthy masculinity is unselfish and seeks to help those in need with no thought to personal gain.

13. An awakened man knows the way to his sacred heart. Healthy masculinity is rooted love and kindness.

14. An awakened man doesn't have sex— he makes love. Healthy masculinity involves worshipping your body temple and upholding sexual intimacy as sacred.

15. An awakened man is visionary and comfortable deliberately manifesting.

16. An awakened man is committed to contributing positively to the transformation of society towards higher consciousness and oneness.

THE BLEND OF FEMININITY AND MASCULINITY

We were all born with both feminine and masculine energy and then at some point, some of us learned that it wasn't safe to express our feminine energy. Whether you are a boy who loved to sing or dance or you are a girl who embraced all parts of her body, or vise versa, you were most likely told to turn it off or tone it down. When divine inner feminine energy rises, masculine energy begins to awaken as well, this is the balance within us all. This relationship of male and female energy balances the yin and yang within us. We are all man and woman within. Everyone has to find their own balance of masculinity and femininity, whether it's becoming more stoic or allowing yourself to be more vulnerable when it's reasonable. Personhood is a shell that imprisons you, even the idea of being a man or woman should be discarded. The person you became at birth and will cease being upon your death is both false and temporary. You are not the body-mind that is gripped by fear and desire. You are the infinite one, love in action. Above gender identity is your timeless infinite self. Be without your ego and realize that you are pure consciousness. You are not your mind, you are the self. The more you see yourself as spirit, the further your ascension into higher consciousness. In your highest energy state you become birthless, formless, sexless, and deathless.

True love cannot exist in a culture of domination. Self-love is the key to finding love. The mission is to create a world where girls are born valued, loved, and eternally worthy. In today's world, women are transforming themselves beyond the restrictions of patriarchy to discover and embody their true divine feminine nature.

CHAPTER 24

THE EMERGENCE OF THE DIVINE FEMALE

A GIRL'S STRUGGLE

Girls today struggle against sexist defining roles in the same way that girls did before the contemporary feminist movement. In modern times, the women's liberation movement has come and delivered many gains, but the road is still rough as gender equality is still very much an issue in today's patriarchal society. Currently, women are still trapped in this male dominated environment. For example, the ERA movement of the 1970's centered on women's struggle for equal opportunity, equal pay, and equal rights. Now, fifty years later, women are still fighting to secure those very same things in the workplace. The only difference today is that many men actually are fully supportive of the feminist platform. Despite the gains of the women's movement, they are still constantly being sent daily subliminal messages of unworthiness and inequality. Women must continue to look for self-validation and love within, and stop looking for validation from a society that cares less than what they deserve. Loving the little girl within is the goal that will heal the deep wounds and lead women to stop searching for love in all the wrong places.

> *All girls continue to be taught when they're young, if not by their parents then by the culture around them, that they must earn the right to be loved, and that femaleness is not good enough. This is a female's first lesson in the school of patriarchal thinking and values, "she must earn her love." She is not entitled. She must be good enough to be loved, and good is always defined by someone else, someone on the outside. Rejection and abandonment by fathers and mothers is the space of lack that usually sets the stage for female desperation to find and know love.*
> ~ bell Hooks

WOMEN ARE NOT TOOLS, TO RESPECT HER IS TO LOVE HER

We as men need to begin to look at women beyond their physical attributes. God made women to multiply and evolve the species, but their expression is multidimensional. The Creator made women first, so for as long as men continue to obsess over women's body parts alone, they will never appreciate their incredible inner treasures. Women deserve to be valued for all of their beautiful divine gifts, every woman is deserving of being loved. If you love a certain woman, you must not only respect her mind, but you should also respect her body. Women are not the playground for the sexual gratification of men, they are the fruit and salvation of the planet. Women are the heart and soul of humanity. Salute the many women in your life by respecting them, appreciating them, and loving them. Through their divine feminine nature and motherly instincts, women have long represented the soul of nations. I have been taught that every woman, young and old, is a representative of the Divine Mother.

SUBMISSIVE FEMININE BEHAVIOR - TOXIC FEMININITY

Toxic femininity refers to traditional cultural feminine norms that can be harmful to the image of women. Conformity to traditional submissive feminine behaviors such as: meekness, deference, and conflict-avoidance are what I am speaking of. Submissive femininity is frequently a by-product of toxic masculinity. Fitting in is often easier than breaking out of patriarchy. This is how some women come to accept less than what they are worth. A "don't rock the boat" mentality, offers security over freedom from this type of oppression. Relatively recently in history, women have been integrated into occupations or social roles that were previously only for men. Worldwide, women are forming alliances and social/business networks that are shaping our world's future. They are visionary organizers who are plotting a bright new course for humanity which embraces a message of understanding, compassion, acceptance, hope, and universal love. In 2020, the fight for gender equality in the workplace is a call to acknowledge that women are perfectly capable of leading a household and becoming the primary breadwinner for their families. While the sight of women working often triggers misogynistic men, in reality, this action actually frees more men to pursue broader career options that don't bring in large salaries, but bring more satisfaction and pleasure to their lives. So in fact, working women are an asset to any household and any industry. The future of our society depends on the full acceptance of women both in the workplace and at home as equals. The centuries of past abuse and neglect of women worldwide, has contributed to much of the disorder in patriarchal society today.

GENDER NORMS

Women who don't fit the mold of standard femininity are treated the same way as men who don't fit the mold of standard masculinity. A woman who doesn't act feminine or wears unfeminine clothes is often treated as an outlier. It might be tolerated while she's a little girl, but she's expected to grow out of it by the time she's supposed to be getting married and having babies. If she doesn't live up to that expectation, she will be subject to social pressure from both women and men. Additionally, in many households, girls don't receive the love they need and then they go about seeking love and approval from boys to replace the void. Early obsession with pleasing others to affirm their worth replaces independence and self-value. In school age girls, mixed messages abound. Women are torn between adhering to patriarchal standards and seeking the fullest expression of their true selves. A woman's search to find love in a society that doesn't truly value her can lead her to acting out and exhibiting promiscuous behavior. There is a void in recognizing women for their greatness and their truth. It should be the mission of us all to knock down the barriers between men, women, and the sharing of power.

HOW TO RECOGNIZE AN AWAKENED WOMAN, WHAT IT MEANS TO BE A GODDESS

- **A goddess is empowered by her divine nature and spreads her love and light to all those around her.**
- **A goddess gives birth to Godliness, she can fill the cup of a stranger with enough love that it also fills their heart. To love her is to respect her.**
- **On her head are many crowns. She has the power and ability to help those in need if they are worried, confused, or in trouble.**
- **A goddess leads by example and practices her spirituality through prayer and meditation.**

- She has the ability to transcend darkness and the wisdom to follow her divine inner light.
- An awakened woman enjoys life more than an unawakened woman because she is free and unattached to her outcomes.
- She has no need to project to be someone important. She finds joy in everything she does. She is comfortable in any setting because she's confident in knowing her authentic true self.
- She is a beautiful balance of power and grace. She rises by setting daily intentions and she deliberately manifests her visions.
- A sacred woman knows that her lessons are her blessings.
- She maintains a healthy lifestyle which includes taking care of her mind, body temple, and spirit.
- A goddess is fully empowered by her divine nature and spreads her love and light to all those around her.
- A sacred woman smiles from her heart. She is adept at lifting the spirits of others, shifting energy, and attracting abundance to herself and her soul tribe.

EXERCISE #44
Goddess Journal

As you ascend from a wounded woman to a divine goddess, start keeping a sacred journal. Do your writing ideally after meditation or a sacred bath. At the end of your journey, your journal will serve as the record of your transformation and liberation. It will also serve to inspire all those with whom you choose to share it with. This is a movement of coming home to your higher self.

1. Give thanks to the Most High for the lessons and blessings that have come your way.
2. Write of your past struggles that have brought you to this moment.
3. Write down any positive experiences of growth and transformation.
4. Express your feelings, future goals, and aspirations.

5. Seal a vision of your future awakened self in your mind's eye.

6. Surround yourself with love and light. Love is the tonic that washes over and cleanses the spirit.

7. Go out in the world and be a living example of the sacred woman that you have become.

8. Serve as a mentor and guide for other women seeking their liberation.

THERE IS A GODDESS ARISING INSIDE YOU

A woman in her greatest place of power is pure magic. It is within the heart that everything is allowed to happen. She sees herself as a sacred woman who is fully supported by her partner's healthy masculine. When an awakened woman feels safe within, she opens her heart up to receiving unlimited abundance. A goddess rising reflects the current spiritual awakening happening amongst the mothers, daughters, and truth seekers of the world. The current shift of global consciousness is spearheaded by millions of enlightened women worldwide. A society can only be as strong as the value of its women.

> *Whether you are a man or a woman, unless*
> *the feminine becomes alive in you, you will*
> *never experience the finer aspects of life.*
> *~ Sadhguru*

EXERCISE #45
Questions To Ask Yourself:

- Do you know that it is your birthright to feel safe?
- Do you trust that your body is meant to feel pleasure?

- Do you know that you are safe no matter what happens to your body?
- Do you know that you are beautiful and unique?
- Do you know that you are divine love personified?
- Do you know that you can be healed and heal others?
- Do you know that you are a mirror and a teacher?
- Do you know that you are meant to realize your purpose?
- Do you know that you are more spiritual than physical?

CHAPTER 25

MANAGING ANGER AND RAGE

THE ORIGIN OF ANGER

The origin of anger comes from unfulfilled desires. Where there is anger, there is always pain underneath. Anger is a failed attempt at concealing one's emotional pain or disappointment. Try looking back into your past to discover when and where you were hurt. Look for times that your spirit was crushed by someone or something. Aim to identify why certain people's actions trigger and infuriate you today. Once you are able to identify the source of your anger, you can take the proper steps to analyze and process the nature of your pain. Holding onto anger is toxic, you must somehow find a way to let it go and allow it to pass. Everything that's happened in your life, both the good and the bad, has helped shape you into who you are today. You may have been victimized in the past, but you survived and you are here now. The doorway to healing your past is always open. Don't spend your life being regretful, angry, and hateful, be grateful. Every sunrise brings the possibility for new changes. There's nothing you can't do once you put your mind to it. It's our common mission to learn how to accept things as they are, not how you think it should be.

Don't let your unchecked selfish desires rule you. The "I want this" or "I want that." mentality forms anger from your discontent. Desire is capable of delivering either joy or disappointment, but winning in life doesn't always deliver what you need. Winning is also having experiences which redirect, change, and shape you. The task is to activate your awareness and turn your attention to your deepest feelings of disappointment and failure. Focus your attention inward and live in the Now instead of living in the past. When the roots of anger are exposed, it dissolves. If you must be mad, be mad for God and be filled with the spirit of divine love.

Anger is a paralyzing emotion, you can't get anything done.
People think it's an interesting, passionate, and igniting
feeling. I don't think it's any of that, it's helplessness.
It's absence of control, but I need all of my skills
and all of my powers, all the time.
Anger doesn't provide any of that, I have no use for it whatsoever.
~ Don Swaim

Much about anger stems from past injustice and victimization. Perhaps you were good to someone and you got burned, or maybe you were kind to someone, but that person was unkind back to you. There's always a degree of underlying social-political forces behind a display of fury. Other common societal sources of anger are: cultural differences, bias, access to education, discrimination, systemic racism, economic disparity, poverty, lack of opportunity, religious differences, poor access to healthcare, and the divisions of politics and war.

ANGER IS AN ENERGY FIELD

Any person that angers you becomes your master. Learn to walk away from negative discussions and people that threaten your peace. Note that your encounters don't have to be fueled with negativity and fighting. Sure, anger needs to be felt, but then it needs to be extinguished from inside by recognizing what it truly is, disappointment. Reframing the situation as your life lesson, rather than finger-pointing and blaming results in a positive shift. The true nature of anger is that it is a negative energy field. Energy fields project both visible and invisible vibrations that you have the ability to detect before they rise up and affect you. Use your keen awareness of anger as a spiritual practice. Anger is toxic to your mood and also toxic to other people that witness it. If you learn to recognize it as it starts building in you, you can let it pass and avoid becoming hostile. On the other hand, if you become aware of your arising anger too late, you will be unable to prevent it from erupting in you.

Many sages have said: "You can't see your reflection in boiling water." Similarly, you can't see truth in a state of rage. Rage is unchecked anger. Activation of your sympathetic fight or flight nervous system ignites the fire of anger. You are the first victim of your own wrath. Awareness of irritation in your energy field can be used as a spiritual practice. You always have the choice to avoid becoming outraged, but the window of observation is very narrow. You can either feel anger coming and bypass it, or become the anger. In other words, try to catch anger before anger catches up with you. Always respond to heated situations with a calm demeanor and try to remain cool, calm, and collected. Your inner power is regulated by the presence of love and hate. Anger and hatred flourish whenever you are lacking in self-control and self-love. Love is the ultimate medicine for hate and fury. It's been said that one minute of anger robs you of sixty seconds of happiness. When you practice love, you expand your sacred heart consciousness. The energy form of anger finds the response of love absolutely intolerable.

Most people find anger addictive because it makes their ego seem righteous. Anger is just another emotion. Rage let's a person know how out of control they feel about certain situations. An emotion becomes a problem when there's no self-regulation or control over it. For example, let's take road rage incidents. What is it about driving that pisses people off so much? It's commonplace to see otherwise normal people honking their horns, yelling, or flipping someone off out of anger.

> *Whenever you were upset about an event, a person, or a situation,*
> *the real cause it's not the event, person, or situation but a loss of true perspective*
> *that only space can provide. You are trapped in object consciousness,*
> *unaware of the timeless inner space of consciousness itself.*
> *~ Erkhart Tolle*

THE CONSEQUENCES OF ANGER

Anger will have you making decisions from your shifting emotional state instead of from the steady place of love. Anger pushes the line between sanity and insanity. If you make a habit of practicing anger, you will be at risk of losing everything you value, including yourself. You literally risk making yourself physically ill from exercising a faulty mindset. Worse still, you may even do something reckless or regretful in the midst of a fit of rage. As a result of your anger, you could one day end up in a hospital where you are strapped to a bed, or find yourself in jail lying in deep regret from your unconscious actions.

> *Whenever you're feeling an extreme emotion, whether it be anger,*
> *hurt, despair, or even bliss, and you act on that feeling, there can be*
> *no clarity. The feelings are here to be felt. True action or inaction has*
> *to come from what lies beneath all feelings. At the core of any matter,*
> *in the core of any emotion, however horrendous, there is peace.*
> *~ Gangji*

DEALING WITH ANGER

Angry people often act out and exhibit dangerous and regretful behavior. When a person fails to control their emotions, it can lead to an episode of rage. Every violent crime ever committed was preceded by some form of rage. Unchecked stress and anger can also lead to physical and mental illness because anger lowers your vibration and decreases the effectiveness of your natural immune system. When you encounter unpleasantness, why not try to keep pleasantness about you? Remember to be kind to others when they're stressed out instead of matching their negativity. Last but not least, the most important thing to balance your inner power is to seek higher consciousness. Seeking restraint is how I survived as a young man. When I was put into violent situations, I managed to master my emotions, maintain my sanity, and not to become filled with hate and resentment. Seeking God saved me, protected my integrity, healed my broken heart, and saved my soul. Once you find your truth and remain in alignment with your mind, body, heart, and soul, it makes it easy to love yourself and to remain peaceful and joyful.

EXERCISE #46

- **Make a list of what anger rewards you with, for example: not to be taken advantage of, speaking your mind, defending your ground, etc.**
- **Make another list of what anger stops you from having, for example: sincere relationships, a stress free life, the ability to relax, etc. You need to see both sides, too many people only see one side. Investigation and clarity will inspire you to set anger down and embrace inner peace.**

CALMING RAGE

The best way to exit from rage is to not go there in the first place. Know that for every action there is an equal and opposite reaction. Unfortunately, millions of people have suffered unspeakable tragedies, all victims of someone else's rage. Rage is a problem because it can get so quickly triggered and escalate like a wildfire. Unlike ordinary anger, rage is hard to catch before it's out of control. Breathing is probably the best way to calm your nerves when you're being triggered and provoked. Turn inward to your heart center. Take a moment to pause and witness the negative expression of your emotions. In your moment of observation and reflection, notice that you can self-modulate. You are the controller of your speech and your actions. Take three slow deep breaths and try focusing on anything pleasant in your field. Notice that you have options on how to react to your circumstances. Choose wisely and always choose love over fear.

What To Do When Faced With A Threat Of Rage

Just Follow These Five Simple Steps:

1. **If you are sure that you are not in any physical danger, don't do anything.**
2. **When the person is done ranting, ask them if they are finished. If they say yes, ask them: "Do you feel better now?" Then continue on as if they said nothing.**
3. **Don't move and don't say anything. Don't nod and don't break eye contact. Wait it out and just look at them while they shout. Remember that you are dealing with a triggered person, it's about them, not you.**
4. **Don't engage with them, it makes them look silly because they will realize that they are out there alone. Sooner or later the person will realize that he or she is getting nowhere and they will say something like: "'Well, aren't you going to say anything?" Your response at this point should be "'Not until you are calm." If the shouting resumes, simply remain passive until it ends, no matter how long it takes.**

5. **Refusing to feed or fuel someone's anger will result in them deflating a lot sooner than if you attempt to rebut or appease. I like this method because without your reaction, it puts the angry person out on a limb by themselves.**

REPLACE YOUR HURT AND ANGER WITH LOVE

The world is sick from several viruses linked to anger which are in need of healing: scarcity, fear, ignorance, racism, rejection, shame, hurt, hatred, worthlessness, hopelessness, etc. Anger exists in you because at the moment, you are lacking in self-love. When you go inside your heart to heal the source of your pain and disappointment, you discover your true nature which transmutes any existing anger into love and light.

CHAPTER 26

DARK EMOTIONS AND THE SHADOW SELF

WE DECLARE HOLISTIC HEALTH

Together we declare holistic health, healing, wholeness, and wellness among us all. We are here to advance the healing of our past emotional trauma. People don't respect health, they respect healing. Most people take their health for granted, especially the youth. We are attracted to what we want because we believe our desires to be attainable. We are attracted to healing because we don't have it. We need healing because over time our bodies accumulate stress and emotional damage that prevents us from performing at our highest capability. Healing is the medicine for all souls.

DARK EMOTIONS AND SHADOW WORK

The presence of darkness in our lives is a complicated issue and because of its mystical nature, darkness is frequently misunderstood. Darkness is the contrast necessary for your light to reveal itself. Without darkness there would be no light. Certain memories, limiting beliefs, and untruths are what form your dark emotions. The accumulation of dark emotions weigh heavily on the spirit. Finding and healing inner darkness can be difficult. The issues of your past will continue to break through and affect your psyche as long as they are allowed to remain unrecognized and untreated. Shadow work is complex. Most people never approach or analyze the darkness within themselves. Facing your shadow self can be scary and disturbing, but it is essential to your healing journey. Everything in need of healing must eventually be brought to light and into your conscious awareness.

Knowing your own darkness is the best method to deal with
the darkness of other people. The most dangerous psychological mistake is the
projection of the shadow onto others. This is the root of almost all conflicts.
~ Carl Jung

HEALING INNER DARKNESS

The first step of healing inner darkness is to accept and embrace all aspects of yourself including the darkest corners of your mind. You must recognize yourself as both sad and happy, and dark and light. Attempting to control or suppress your dark emotions through conscious willpower simply doesn't work. This is because darkness is a part of human nature. It is through the gaps between your imperfections that your true nature shines. If you try to numb all of your dark emotions, you will also numb your positive emotions. Don't pretend to be happy while wanting to cry. Be authentic, be real, and take the time to get to know and love your shadow self. Every part of yourself, dark or light, is deserving of your loving attention.

Make it your practice to sit in solitude regularly to process your buried emotions, memories, and limiting beliefs. This action will illuminate any darkness hiding amongst your divine light. Knowing and accepting all aspects of who you are is the essence of the healing journey. Deep healing cures fragmentation and makes you feel whole again. Wholeness then allows you to release what no longer serves you.

IDENTIFYING YOUR SHADOW SELF

In 1930, psychiatrist Carl Jung presented the shadow self— the dark side of human nature. It's not called a shadow because of its darkness, it's called a shadow self because everyone has one. There's no point in fighting it because you can't get rid of it. You can only manage your shadow self. The only thing you can do is accept it and manage it by befriending it. It's your choice to deny the dark aspect of yourself, but you will have to live with the unknown consequences of doing so. Your shadow self is the dark place in your subconscious mind that contains every taboo, thought, feeling, desire, or personality trait that you've ever rejected, buried, or suppressed. It consists of everything you don't know about yourself, the light, the dark, and everything in between. The easiest way to identify your shadow self is to examine what annoys you about other people. The things that annoy you the most in them are likely the very things that you can't face in yourself. At some point in our lives, we all need to initiate the process of self-examination. If we don't acknowledge our darkness, then we cannot fully appreciate the experience of bathing in the light of unconditional love.

Darkness may hide the trees and flowers from the eyes,
but it cannot hide love from the soul.
~Rumi

DOWNLOAD THE PROGRAM OF LOVE FOR FREE

Your childhood emotional trauma has deeply affected and shaped you into who you are today. Faulty programming, like shame and guilt, behave like viruses that seep into your subconscious and pollute your mind and body. Enter the space where you can download the program called "Love" for free. Love is a beautiful space of non-judgement filled with the presence and unlimited potential of: acceptance, compassion, forgiveness, and transformational change. People often hide things in their subconscious minds to deal with the pain that they are feeling inside. It is important to face your past trauma in order to heal yourself. When you work through your painful memories, you will come to the realization that past trauma can no longer hurt you. When you reconcile with your past, you are transported into present moment awareness. At that very moment, you are free from the past and ready for a limitless future. Everyone deserves to be happy. Bad things may have happened to you, but it's your choice to hold onto these memories or learn to let them go. The past no longer has a hold on you. The past is the past because it's no longer present. You are free to heal today, now and forevermore. Life is for the living. Move forward, choose life, and always choose love.

EXERCISE #47
Know Yourself

1. What is your life's biggest disappointment?
2. Have you identified the source of your pain and moved beyond it, or are you still stuck in the past?
3. In what identifiable ways has your past trauma affected your life? The greater your pain, the deeper you bury it, the longer it takes to recover from it.
4. Be honest in search of your truth; "I don't know" is an unacceptable answer.
5. Identify the factors you need to heal successfully.
6. Who are your sources of strength? Identify those individuals that comprise your support system.

7. **Write an action plan for your healing.**
8. **Visualize your healed whole future self and keep this image of yourself in your mind's eye.**
9. **Work your plan everyday, persistence yields results.**

CRACKING THE CODE OF YOUR FEELINGS

What stops the spell of the mind is to become the witnessing presence of your feelings. Seek liberation, liberation of what? Liberation from the manipulation of your feelings. Mostly you are a human being feeling your feelings. Every time you have happy thoughts your brain makes chemicals called neurotransmitters that make you feel happy and the same is true for sadness. You are largely being guided by your feelings. Have you ever reacted emotionally to a situation without thinking things through first? Practice lessening the fluctuations that accompany your feeling. Reach for emotional stability. Masters often teach egolessness. To be egoless means that you are no longer dominated by your feelings.

EXERCISE #48

The Release Exercise
My asks for you in this exercise are:

1. **Place yourself in a private and safe space where you won't be disturbed.**
2. **Identify a time and experience that still brings up a strong negative emotion in you.**
3. **Tap into that deep emotion by visualizing yourself in the time and place of your life when the emotionally damaging event took place.**

4. **Bring forth your painful memories of the past and see them in your mind as a slideshow.**

5. **Remain calm and breathe deeply and consciously.**

6. **State the negative emotions that you felt and still feel.**

7. **Release those emotions through an interpretive acting or dance performance, or create a short play surrounding your emotions and perform it in the mirror.**

8. **Record your performance and play it back for yourself. Analyze and state aloud what you learned from performing and watching this experience.**

9. **Reframe your past. Write your feelings into a journal. List the positive ways that your past has helped you to grow and list your future goals.**

10. **Close this exercise by coming back into the Now. Take a nature walk, remain in the present moment, and come into the spirit of gratitude.**

THE CHEAT CODE FOR HEALING ANY SITUATION IS UNCONDITIONAL LOVE

All healing requires the realization that you have suffered emotional wounds in your past, it also requires you to accept the responsibility for healing it. All learning experiences create the opportunity for us to love ourselves more. There is a divine plan in place for all souls. If you choose to live in your mind, your soul sleeps. Your soul will awaken when it has endured enough suffering from living a mind-based identity, or whenever it decides to wake up in order to be free.

ELASTICITY AND PLASTICITY

Know that you are capable of enduring and adapting to any situation, past or present. Stay grounded in your center, this is how we recharge ourselves.

A strong force from the north will soon attempt to knock you off course. Be ready to withstand these uncertain winds of change. At a challenging time in your life, you will feel weak and vulnerable. There will be no escape, no place to hide, and nowhere to run from your situation. You will have to face it and walk through it, the best you know how. It's time to get ready for your future. Life pulls you from your center every time. By the mighty strength of your inner power, you will prevail. Remember that there is a force of good which always surrounds you and protects you. Be grateful for your existence. May God bless both you and your endeavors.

EXERCISE #49
Create a Time Capsule

The purpose of this exercise is to locate, identify, process, and bury your identification with your body-mind. Like a snake that sheds its skin, you are always evolving into a more awakened version of yourself. Detaching from physical trappings and old ineffective beliefs allows you to create a lighter identity. Make a time capsule as a dedication to transformation. Place in it symbols and remembrances of your hurtful past. Make a list of the qualities of your present self and your future self. Put the list inside the capsule as a wish list. Place inside your time capsule: a book, a poem, photos, old letters, or a piece of jewelry that you are willing to part with. Thank each item for serving you in your old identity. Say this mantra: "I hereby let go of all that no longer serves me. I release all forms of attachment into the universe. I declare my freedom from any and all trappings and I acknowledge the sacred space in my heart that's filled with unconditional love.

ESTABLISHING A STRONG SUPPORT SYSTEM IS CRITICAL FOR YOUR RECOVERY

One of the most important factors in healing from anything is the quality of your support system. Compassionate ears often result in a faster healing time. In times of need, everyone could use someone to listen to their feelings, a hand to hold, a shoulder to cry on, a compassionate hug, and a place to live that feels safe. It's important to find and surround yourself with other souls that comfort you. If you are alone or don't have a best friend to help you in your healing, seek professional assistance. Every successful recovery is a team effort. You don't recover by yourself, you recover with the assistance of earth angels.

Ten Steps to a Greater Version of You

1. **Get in alignment with love. Love is the light. You get into alignment with love by thinking loving thoughts and by practicing kindness and gratitude.**
2. **Set the intention to be a greater version of you everyday.**
3. **Spend at least one hour working on your passion everyday, this is self-expression.**
4. **Stop blaming others for your own shortcomings, be accountable to yourself.**
5. **Pledge not to procrastinate anymore. Don't speak about it, be about it.**
6. **Wake up early and work harder in your endeavours. Make each day count.**
7. **Verbalize your goals and future plans in front of a mirror and also in front of others. Speak your dreams into existence.**
8. **Expect some resistance to your plan. Stay focused and stay the course.**
9. **If you fall (and you will), get back up. Never give up, success is effort driven.**
10. **Remember that you are buoyant and resilient. Nothing can stop you from creating your future except yourself.**

CHAPTER 27

HEALING FROM GRIEF

YOU CAN GRIEVE THE LOSS OF ANYTHING

When one first thinks of grief, we think of the loss of a loved one but earnestly, human beings can grieve the loss of anything: a relationship, car, job, apartment, house, parent, relative, boyfriend, childhood idol or money. We grieve whatever we've lost and traditionally we suffer from our loss of attachment in a self-centered way. Attachments are all your hopes, beliefs, and possessions. Belonging is beautiful, until it isn't anymore. Humans can't seem to resist attachment, especially to other beings, that's what makes us human. We can't seem to control the extent to which our attachment affects us, but we can learn to see the attachment and loosen it over time. The answer to our suffering is detachment, but the road is long and has many detours and turns. Grief is just another opportunity of life to practice detachment.

GRIEF

I am very sorry for your loss. I am sending you healing thoughts and strength in your difficult time. Grief comes from losing someone you love and missing them. Remember them at their best and imagine them in eternal peace. There is no perfect way to cope with death, everyone grieves differently. I have come to the understanding that all relationships eventually come to an end whether in time or by death. You can't flip a switch on grief and tears. Your emotions will flow until your mourning is over. People will grieve until they release all the grief from inside of them and in many cases the grief is always there under the surface of life. Grief is not linear. I have a friend who recently lost her teenage son to gun violence, she states that, "Grief is like the movement of ocean waters, it comes in tides and waves." In the acute stage of your grief, I advise you to share your pain and suffering with your friends and family. This allows your emotions to be shared and heard. You can't overcome grief until you bring your pain to the surface, process it, grow from it, and release it.

> *Each person's grief is as unique as their own fingerprint.*
> *However, there are some basic tenets. When we lose our*
> *parents, we lose our past. When we lose our spouse,*
> *we lose our present, and if we lose a child, we lose our future.*
> *~ Laurie Schlangen Traub*

DON'T BE AFRAID OF DARKNESS AND
DON'T BECOME TRAPPED IN YOUR GRIEF

When darkness comes to you, fear not. The darkness comes, but it will also leave. Sorrow settles and then leaves whenever you cease paying attention to it. Brent Brown says, "Only when we are brave enough to explore the darkness, will we discover the infinite power of our light." Take all the time you need to heal your grief, everyone processes grief differently. The key to freedom from suffering is to not let the darkness of grief swallow you up. We all know someone who has never recovered from their unfortunate loss. Some people are unable to accept the loss of a loved one and they put themselves in a pattern of profound grief for years or even decades of their lives. Their inability to see the loss of their relative or friend as a natural event independent of themselves keeps them trapped in grief. Acceptance of death with an even perspective with the same balance that we welcome new life is our challenge, to one day process the departure of a dear soul with acceptance and deep appreciation for their time here.

Everyone has a soul contract with the Creator. Each soul will outlive its body, that's the nature of life and that's the nature of death. When you come into alignment with the natural flow of the universe, all resistance to change is lost. Be the one who can endure your losses and you will find the one who thrives in acceptance. Let go of your suffering and let unconditional love dance and play once again inside your heart.

GRIEF IS AN AGENT OF CHANGE

The moment we lose someone intrinsic to our lives, grief ensues and begins to change us. That's what grief is, an agent of change, and it affects us all differently. Words cannot possibly describe the impact of the loss of a parent or child. We don't choose grief, grief chooses us. It takes us from a stage of hopelessness and despair to eventual hope and happiness. Acceptance is the lesson of loss. The sooner we accept the loss of someone dear and stop resisting their departure, inner peace arrives.

HONOR YOUR DEAD AND PRAY FOR THEM

The best way to handle grief is not to move on from your dearly departed, but to move forward with them. Carry them with you in your heart through all your endeavors. Honor them and treasure them. Grieve for them but don't suffer, they wouldn't want that. Your dear ones would want you to live a productive life, a life filled with abundance and joy. Remember them, speak of them often, tell stories of them, and share your brightest memories with others. Your loved one is not dead, but alive in each one of the people whose lives they touched. Honor your dearly departed by finding yourself. Be inspired by all the great human beings you meet in life. Be inspired to go all the way to complete the journey of self-realization.

EXERCISE #50
Choose a Healing Partner:

Don't be afraid to lean on friends and family when you are distraught. Choose one or two healing partners to accompany you on your healing journey. Healing partners can be a friend or family member, but choose wisely. The people that are best able to help you heal your grief, should have a similar loss or experience to draw from in order to support and advise you. Choose someone with wisdom and clarity. Sit with those that cultivate inner peace within themselves. When you choose this individual, you must ask them for their permission to assist you. It will require that person to commit both their time and patience to you, which is a lot to ask of anyone. Be mindful of who you choose and what they are capable of. If you cannot think of someone today, that is perfectly fine. Trust that you will find or meet someone along your journey who is capable of supporting you through your grieving process. Perhaps it will take days, weeks, months, or even years to find the person you want to be your healing partner, but the wait will be worthwhile. Ideally choose someone who you have a spiritual connection with. Your

healing partner is similar to a prayer partner. This soul contract requires a spiritual connection between both souls. If you are in deep emotional pain or thinking of harming yourself, tell your partner or a friend. Too many lives have been lost when people are isolated, quiet, afraid, hopeless, and fail to communicate their suffering to others.

CRYING IS A USEFUL TOOL FOR HEALING

The way laughing is good for our health, crying can also be good for our health. A good cry is something everyone needs in this stressful world. Emotions are what reminds us that we are alive. The elderly often say that after crying, the mind becomes soft. Recently scientists have verified that crying removes stress. Dr. William Frey, a biochemist, found that tears actually wash out chemicals that cause cortisol (the stress hormone) levels in your body to rise. Tears are normal and are a healthy way to express your emotions. Cry but do not despair, nothing that you see in this world is permanent, everything is always changing. Big transformations happen with the destruction of the old. Crying can show what your words can't express. What flows is alive. Each time that you feel sad, weak, or confused, release those emotions and know that you are transforming on the cellular level. Crying is a natural detox tool and it mentally cleanses you. Crying is like a thundershower for the soul. The action of crying doesn't make you weak, it makes you stronger. Studies at the University of South Florida have found that crying actually elevates the mood of criers 90% of the time. When you are healing from the loss of a loved one, have a good cry. Chances are that you will feel relieved, cleansed, and uplifted.

EXERCISE #51

Honor your loss and grief by bringing life to a plant and
nurturing it through its life cycle. Plant the seed of a tree.
Plant the seed in rich black soil and cultivate the soil.
Water the seed everyday. Talk to your plant.
Place it in sunlight for it to
undergo photosynthesis and transformation.
Plants are a reminder of the cycle of life.
What no longer grows is dead. A plant will not
beg, plead, or cry for your attention.
You must commit to nurturing it and shower it with
love and attention each day. Otherwise, if the plant is
neglected, it will die. Honor the commitment that
you are making to your plant and promise to
attend to her as best you know how.
It is when we see things to the end that we can
truly find peace and contentment.

LIFE IS FOR THE LIVING

Don't think of death as wrong because it happened to you and changed your
experience. When your day of loss comes and you have to face the death of
a loved one, let grief take you. Try to experience a pure grief, let it take you
wherever it goes. Do whatever you need to do to survive. Be free to grieve
your own way without deadlines or boundaries to express your love and loss.
Realize that grief has its own time schedule and timeframe, nothing is set in
stone. Grief is the natural and normal response to the death of a loved one,
don't try to numb it or run from it. It's impossible to prepare yourself for the
loss of a loved one. Even when someone's death is expected, their departure
is still quite shocking. Life has its own way of teaching you. No matter how

unwelcome or unfair death seems, life must go on. As many sages have said: "Life is for the living."

21 WAYS TO ASSIST YOUR RECOVERY FROM GRIEF

1. Remember that death is inevitable for all living things. No one escapes death. This acceptance will build your fortitude and calmness.
2. Remember that you are not the body but the eternal soul that lies within.
3. Remember that it's okay to share your emotions and cry. Crying releases overwhelming emotional currents and reduces stress.
4. Take good care of yourself personally. Drink plenty of water and eat healthy. Get your daily allotment of sleep. Push yourself to exercise and don't let yourself go downhill.
5. Don't practice anger, practice acceptance and gratitude instead.
6. Take long walks in nature and practice mindfulness.
7. Join a grief support group.
8. Maintain job excellence at work.
9. Invest in consciousness so that when your turn comes to die, you will not fear the loss of your wealth or material things. Your spiritual consciousness is yours to keep.
10. Celebrate your departed loved ones life by remembering them always. Speak of them often and see their life as a blessing to you.
11. Write a letter to the person you've lost and pour your heart out to them. Journaling through your grief will bring you perspective on your circumstances and promote healing.
12. Keep your chin up and focus your gaze upon the sky.
13. Imagine and begin to dream again. Visualize how you plan to live your new life without your loved one. Visualize with clarity your new life coming into being.
14. Heed the call of adventure, get out of your comfort zone, and try new things to divert your attention away from your loss.
15. Honor your departed one with a life remembrance ceremony of your own design.
16. Remember and believe that the veil of grief lessens over time.

17. **When you have fond remembrances of your loved one, smile.**
18. **See their loss as God calling them home.**
19. **See yourself as adaptable and able to endure the rollercoaster of life.**
20. **Be brave, you can do this.**
21. **Remember that it's not "goodbye", it's "I'll see you later."**

A THANK YOU LETTER TO MY MOM

Mom, I want to thank you for giving me life. Thank you for conceiving me. I feel so blessed to be your son now and forever. Our relationship didn't end with your departure, it's just getting started. Bodies disintegrate but souls never perish. I pray for your everlasting peace in whatever form you are presently. Thank you for teaching me how to love. Thank you for teaching me how to live. Thank you for teaching me what true unconditional love feels like. Thank you for building me up when I was down and for filling me with the belief that I could do anything. I continue to feel blessed by the strong current of your soul. Your eternal wisdom impacts me every single day. I still recognize and feel your spiritual existence and a part of your spirit in myself. Thank you.
I love you and I always will.
Your loving son,
Russell

CHAPTER 28

ADDICTION AND RECOVERY

ADDICTION

E ven if they don't recognize it, most people who abuse drugs or alcohol and become addicted, do so to escape their personal circumstances. Others start their use to enhance their experience or party. At the root, it's often an effort to soothe unresolved trauma from the past or present, or it can be a form of self-medication for an undiagnosed physical or mental imbalance. The reason for alcohol or drug abuse can be traced to anything that causes great stress, loneliness, fear, depression, dis-ease and trauma. Simply put, the most common reason that people become addicted to substances is because there is a void in their lives they are trying to fill. When I say void, I mean there is something very important that's missing in their lives. Usually what is missing is rooted in a history of neglect or abuse, fear of failure, emotional pain, or lack of confidence or direction. These conditions often result in the desire to escape reality. Drugs and alcohol are excellent choices for someone looking to escape the realness of life. If you don't confront the core issues of what's triggering your addictions, more addictions will accumulate and come to haunt you. If you go inside with the intention to heal, you will eventually find the realm of stillness and peace. Tranquility is a place that needs no pill or elixir.

Drug and alcohol dependence isn't a problem that few people face, it's a global issue that needs more awareness and attention. The consequences of substance dependence affect all demographics and has a far-reaching impact on individuals and families around the world. Please remember that addiction is not a personal choice, nor does it mean the user is a bad person, it's a disease which is caused by an underlying issue. There is no simple cure for anyone. Every addiction is different because so is every person. The primary reason some people become addicted while others do not, comes down to personal differences, genetics, and circumstances. There are simply far too many different situations to wrap them all into one bag. This is one of the reasons why substance abuse is such a difficult and complicated issue to understand. Persistent drug usage and other long term addictions result in chemical dependency, organ damage, rapid aging, and disastrous consequences to the relationships with the very people that love them. Addictive behaviors are the outer result of one's inner struggles. Each human being is experiencing the cause-and-effect of his or her desires and choices to fill in the empty powerless places within themselves.

Substance abuse is a form of body-mind illness that requires some sort of therapy or treatment. What festers inside the body eventually makes its way to the outside. Addiction largely stems from a void somewhere in the human spirit. A sense of diminished self-worth that reveals itself via a physical craving from the body that is manipulated by an undisciplined mind. Dependence is largely based on patterned conditional responses to one's feelings of isolation and unhappiness that are counterproductive to one's existence. When a person resists the natural joy that is available in the world and also in the present moment, they're standing in the way of the flow of the universe. Resisting (or in extreme cases rejecting) the natural flow of life causes pain and dis-ease. Another aspect of addiction is the environment. When people are surrounded by poverty, hopelessness, or struggle, they become vulnerable to the temporary feeling of ecstasy and false courage that drugs and alcohol provide. Scientific evidence shows that when "what is" is not enough, people turn to excessive consumption of food, alcohol, tobacco, sex, or drugs in an attempt to block and numb their inner pain and to fill the void of what's lacking. While these temporary pleasures can briefly distract one's attention from their painful reality, they do little to positively change one's larger circumstances. What is missing is a long term method to supply the user with positive long term structure and routines that can positively affect their lives and change their circumstances. This is why drug rehabilitation is so important and why rehab must include addressing the issues with what's really going on beneath the addiction, personal development therapy, access to jobs, affordable housing, and resources to elevate one's daily life.

> *Lameness may strike your leg. but not your resolve.*
> *Sickness may weaken your body, but not your determination.*
> *Nothing can steal your peace of mind unless you let it.*
> *Each time an obstacle arises, remind yourself of this truth.*
> *When you understand that outside events do not touch your deepest self,*
> *you can use any circumstance to your benefit.*
> *Trust fate and trust yourself.*
> *~ Epictetus*

THE ROOTS OF ADDICTION

Addiction starts as a choice, but if a habit forms, it can become a disease. Substance abuse consumes a person physically, emotionally, and spiritually. Feelings of guilt, shame, remorse, and regret, are common emotions that addicts feel. The choice they are making to use drugs is made to suppress and cope with their dark feelings. It's important to recognize that we all have addictions, some are just more serious than others. It might be sugar, shopping, social media, gambling, pornography, sex, etc. Recognizing your own addictions requires inner work. More importantly, if you are seeking a cure for your substance abuse, your healing journey first requires you to acknowledge your dependence. Accepting that you have an addiction is acknowledgement that a part of you is out of control. In general, we don't want to do that because it's our nature to avoid pain and resist change. Your addiction is not stronger than you. It's also not stronger than who you want to be. Though it may feel that way, it can only win if you let it. Like any weakness, it's not stronger than your soul or will power. The greater the desire of your soul to help you heal your dependency, the greater will be the cost of keeping it. By the magnitude of the costs of your habit, you can measure the importance of healing it to your soul. Whenever you feel in yourself the addictive attraction of sex, alcohol, or drugs, remember these words:

You stand between the two worlds of your lesser self and your higher self.
Your lower self is aligned with temptation while your higher self desires nothing.
~ Gary Zukov

The first time someone uses drugs or alcohol they are making a choice, but what people don't have is a choice about how drugs change their brain. They also didn't choose to be genetically predisposed to certain addictions, like alcoholism. When a person uses alcohol or drugs, their brain changes and it affects and disrupts regions of the brain that are responsible for learning, judgment, motor skills, performance, and memory. Addiction makes the brain "think" that the use of its drug use is just as important as eating, sleeping, sex, love, money, shelter, and security. Some people can drink or use drugs and stop whenever they want, but other individuals lack the self-control to resist temptation. In many instances, certain individual's brains make them feel incomplete without the drug. Being close to many who have lost themselves in addiction, I feel that substance abuse is an unhealthy coping mechanism for one's struggles.

THE ROLE OF NEGLECT AND ABUSE IN CAUSING ADDICTION

Prolonged neglect and abuse results in a person feeling unworthy. In the absence of love, there is room for addiction and codependency. Until you fill the inadequacies within you, you will always have your addiction. When there is unworthiness in your mind, you may begin to doubt your reason for living. Ultimately, it is your task to take the higher path. Ask yourself: "Is today the right time for me to release my pattern learning the hard way?" Ask yourself if it's time to accept the fullness of who you are? Even if your answers to these questions are "no," you will eventually come to the place of higher learning, forgiveness, clarity, and divine love. Know that there is space in you for your evolution. Never stop believing in yourself and your ability to change. You are love temporarily hidden from itself. Everything in the universe evolves, including you. If you choose to challenge your addiction, move consciously towards wellness and wholeness. Choose to learn through wisdom and understanding instead of through first hand suffering. Heal your mind first, your heart second, and your body will follow. Self-analysis is an important first step before choosing sobriety and recovery. Acknowledging your addiction includes accepting the notion that a part of you is out of control. Until you admit that you have an addiction, it's not possible to diminish its power or receive the help that you need.

The personality tends to rationalize it's addictions.
It paints the behavior as acceptable and dresses it up in attractive clothing.
It presents the addiction to you as something
desirable and beneficial when it is not.
~ Gary Zukov

DEPRESSION AND ADDICTION

Substance abuse is an expression of a disturbed mind and it often goes hand in hand with undiagnosed or untreated mental health issues. Depression is often an underlying condition of addicts. People who are depressed may drink or abuse drugs to lift their mood or shake feelings of guilt or despair. In reality, substances like alcohol are really depressants which actually increase sadness and fatigue. Additionally, some people suffer depression from the withdrawal of a prescription drug. Depression occurs when a person is repeatedly suffocating their emotions. Suffering stems from blocking the emotional memories of one's past. Depression and addiction can happen whenever a person suffers the full impact of their negative emotions repeatedly. Addiction is often the result of not being able to deal with someone or something. An addict must create separation away from their emotions in order to heal their emotional pain. If a person is unable to find stillness and peace in a realm beyond their emotions, suffering will soon follow. I am not suggesting that one cease to experience their emotions, I am merely pointing to the need to be the witnessing presence of one's emotions. The position of the witness is the altitude of the higher self. When you are able to view life from the position of the self, there are no more desires, wants, or needs— only wholeness and oneness with God. When divine bliss is attained from unity with Source, one becomes filled with it and the urge for unhealthy substances disappears.

It is ten years since I used drugs or drank alcohol,
and my life has improved immeasurably. I have a job, a house, a cat,
good friendships and generally a bright outlook. The price of this is
constant vigilance, because the disease of addiction is not rational.
~ Russell Brand

EXERCISE #52

Pet Therapy
Visit an animal shelter.

See the suffering of the abandoned animals.
See that it is not their fault.
Show compassion and empathy to the unloved.
Play with them. Feed them. Bathe them. Groom them.
Shower them with unconditional love.

SPEAK UP

If you feel something is off with a loved one or you suspect substance dependence, talk to them about it. By opening a dialogue with your loved one, it allows them to come forward. Some people ignore warning signs for the same reason people hide or lie about needing help. Approaching them in a loving, supporting, and caring way shows them that you care about what's happening to them. Speaking from the heart about the impact of their addiction on you will help them shed the stigmas of shame, blame, and guilt.

Being in recovery has given me everything of value that I have
in my life. Integrity, honesty, fearlessness, faith, a relationship
with God, and most of all, gratitude. It's given me a beautiful
family and an amazing career. I'm under no illusions where
I would be without the gift of alcoholism and the chance to recover from it.
~ Rob Lowe

RECOVERY: THE POWER OF CHOICE
THE CURE FOR ADDICTION

There are many discreet ways to get the help you need. Stay focused on the solution of treatment rather than continuing to justify and cover up your problem. Denial of your condition blocks healing and recovery. It's important to put all your cards on the table. Be truthful and honest with yourself and with your situation. Viewing your addiction as changeable will not only help you to fully accept your current condition, but it also will help medical professionals be more successful at understanding your issues and implementing your personal treatment plan. Reach out and talk to someone close to you and ask them for help. Contact local mental health services and focus on finding a solution for your problem.

In recovery, the biggest issue you will first face will be finding positive things to utilize your free time. It will be very important to find new engaging things to do in a constructive light, whether that be more meetings or activities. AA and NA typically organize activities such as picnics, trips to the beach, movies, church, etc. Another thing to increase your chance at a successful recovery will be to stay away from the people and places you frequented when you were using. Please remember that recovery is not just quitting the drug, it's getting to the root of what caused your addiction. Go deep inside to discover why you continue to mask your emotions and then examine how you deal with them. Most addicts spend so much time with their addiction that it becomes a part of them. The key to recovery is to fight for your sobriety as hard as you fight for your addiction. That's why people call them baby steps and encourage you to take life one day at a time, because your brain is actually learning how to live and survive all over again. Even in the moments when you feel that all is lost, just try to understand that whatever you are experiencing is just part of your larger process of recovery.

The curious paradox is that when I accept myself
just as I am, then I can change.
~ Carl Rogers

Many people get help with substance dependence, but never share their stories. Some entire families perform interventions and help to save their loved one, but never talk about it. I encourage you to share your story and your struggles. You never know who's listening. When you share and tell your story, it could very well be saving someone's life. Rather than focus on what happened with your addiction, focus your story on what helped you and what methods you used to overcome your struggles.

To sober up seems to many like making life "so serious,"
as if seriousness precluded joy, warmth, spontaneity and fun.
But there can be a delusional, blind quality to non-sober festivities.
To have our eyes open soberly with all our senses and memory

intact allows some of the most rewarding, soul-nourishing,
and long-lasting pleasures possible.
~ Alexandra Katehakis

EXERCISE #53

Restore a Previous Friendship.
Call or contact someone from your past who supported you.
Reconnect - Forgive - Replenish - Restore

SOBRIETY

The struggle of addiction is lifelong and the rewards of sobriety are many, yet sobriety wouldn't be so hard if reality wasn't so difficult. Motivation to change varies from person to person, from one situation to another, and of course, over time. Some are willing to change, some are unwilling, and others are not ready to change. You have to find your own reasons for staying sober. If those reasons are more powerful than your desire to drink or use, you'll fare well with sobriety. Be present enough to know that just because your brain says something, you don't have to do it. To pick up your habit again is not accepting the wisdom of your inner being. But how do we learn to resist our urges? The only way to beat an urge is to be completely present in the Now. You find freedom from your past trauma by turning your attention to the timeless, thoughtless, and emotionless dimension of Presence. Present moment awareness stresses that the moment itself is enough. Urges are pulsations in the universe which hope to catch your attention in the hopes of attracting you to follow. The late great poet William Shakespere once said, "Temptation is the fire that brings up the scum of the heart." You must find a way to believe that your self-destructive habits of the past can no longer touch you. I pray that you allow your innate blessings of determination, conviction, and faith to flood your beingness, wash over you, and dissolve any remaining temptation to use.

The vibrational distance between hope and fear
is the same distance between recovery or not.
~ Abraham

RELAPSE

Relapse is part of the process of recovery, it happens. If you can look at it as part of the process, it's easier to get back on the wagon. Addicts may relapse five times, ten times, or not at all, everyone is different. It sucks to fall off the wagon and for some, there is the very real danger that the next time could be the time the drug kills them. The best teacher in life is experience, sometimes you have to fail before you succeed. I want to emphasize that no addict wants to relapse. Relapsing after a long period of sobriety usually results from personal angst like a romantic breakup, depression, grief, or a financial crisis. The people at Alcoholics Anonymous help one another to stop drinking and stay sober. One of their slogans is, "The one in this room with the longest sobriety is the one who got up the earliest today." An addict knows how easy it is to fall back into substance abuse unless they work their program everyday. "One day at a time" is their mantra. If one specific treatment did not work out for you, don't give up, try a different treatment modality. The first part of rehab is focused on getting the addict past the withdrawal. Next is to teach you how to avoid the low, by avoiding the high. There are many secular treatments backed by good evidence of efficacy that you can try, they include AA, SMART recovery, LifeRing, contingency management, community reinforcement, medication assisted recovery, motivational interviewing, cognitive behavioral therapy, and many more.

People are better persuaded by the reasons they themselves discover,
rather than those that come into their minds by way of others.
~ Blaise Pascal

THE CURE FOR ALL ADDICTIONS

Will you continue to act out in an unconscious way or will you give yourself permission to act consciously? Look towards the light of spirit deep inside of you and you'll find the way that only awakened spirits take. The greater the desire of your soul to heal your addictions, the less the cost of keeping them. It's the compassionate universe saying to you that although your inadequacies may run deep, you are capable of accomplishing anything you set your mind to. You are stronger than you think.

CHAPTER 29

SURVIVING SEXUAL ABUSE, PHYSICAL ABUSE, AND PTSD

DARK SECRETS

D ark secrets are a part of everyone's history. Are you tired of holding onto a secret from your past? Don't cry alone in silence anymore, everyone has a dark chapter in their story they are suppressing. Your circumstances won't begin to change until you start looking at things differently. Stop filling your mind with stories of shame and guilt. You are worthy of being free of the weight of yesterday's sad memories. Even the darkest corners of who you deserve to be loved. I am sending love to everyone reading these words who's trying to heal from a painful secret in their past. The key to healing lies in changing your thought patterns and shifting your attention to the present moment, the place where things are always working out for you. From this sacred place, you can turn back to your past and see that you are not the identity of an abused victim anymore. From the elevation of your infinite higher self, you are free of your past. Now, you can face your past trauma with nothing but love and forgiveness for yourself. Be compassionate for those that have harmed you, otherwise you will be stuck with the shame of their actions. It is from this higher elevation that forgiveness can take place. True forgiveness is when you can finally take your attention off someone else, because you have overcome the addiction to the emotion they remind you of. This action gives that person permission to show up differently in your life and allows you to move on.

SEXUAL ABUSE AND SEXUAL PREDATORS

Many people have suffered sexual abuse and have lingering damage from it. Sexual trauma can affect every aspect of your life, mentally, physically, and spiritually. Trauma is like a mountain in your subconscious that many souls never get over. The worst aspect of sexual trauma is that if it's not dealt with, it can sabotage and threaten the intimacy in your future relationships.

Sex predators largely act to fulfill their own desires with no regard for their victims. Many sex crimes are committed by habitual offenders who have lost their souls. The act itself is horrible and worse than that, it leaves crippling wounds on the spirit of the victim. Human predators who commit violent acts against innocent victims are also guilty of committing a supreme violation against all mankind. Sex criminals tend to be simplistic in their pursuit of control over both the experience and their victims. At the root of their sexual deviance is a selfish desire for attention, recognition, and domination. Survivors of any form of sexual abuse are victims who are forced to carry the memories of their trauma and often suffer from post traumatic stress disorder.

> *Your boundary need not be an angry electric*
> *fence that shocks those that touch it.*
> *It can be a consistent light around you that*
> *announces: "I will be treated sacredly."*
> *~ Jaiya John*

Part of your recovery is understanding the psychological profile of most sexual abusers. It's important to remember that hurt people hurt people and healed people heal people. Mental illness is often a part of a sexual predator's psychological profile and they usually have one theme in common, most have been traumatized in their own past. Violence is indeed a learned behavior. Because they were once traumatized and victimized, they are prone to doing that same learned behavior to someone else. Something in their past allows them to violate another human being in the absence of guilt. Placing yourself in the heart and mind of your attacker is awkward, but it's helpful to activate the powers of empathy and forgiveness inside you. You will never climb over your "trauma mountain," until you take a moment to see things from the abuser's perspective. This exercise is very difficult, but an important and necessary step in your healing. In no way am I minimizing the ugliness of their actions, but I am asking you to remove judgement on their soul. One never knows the sadness and struggle of someone else's story. This step opens up the opportunity for you to develop compassion for them as a sick, struggling, traumatized human being. See them as victims themselves. This removes the "personalization factor" of your trauma. It answers the question of "Why me?" Your traumatic experience was not your fault and you need not carry the burden of guilt for something that was out of your control. You are pure loving awareness. Know that your ego doesn't have to take the "hit" so personally. As disgusting and violent as your suffering may have been, your full recovery is dependent on the reclassification of your suffering and your ability to find the compassion to ultimately forgive your attacker. The default mindset of victims is victimhood. Remaining a victim allows you to settle for far less than you deserve. Your thoughts and emotions about what happened is a function of your ego. The good news is that you can transcend your ego. What I mean by that is you are pure love and light. If you can find a way to step into your identity as your higher self, you can exercise your inner power to edit the narrative of your past suffering. This "depersonalization exercise," is a very helpful step in your healing journey. Depersonalization helps to end victimhood by seeing yourself in a brand new light and by creating the opportunity to release any hidden shame, blame, and guilt that you've been holding onto.

> *Empowerment is something that happens throughout your healing,*
> *as courage and success in facing your memories builds your self-esteem.*
> *Some of the strengths you get from taking on your buried memories does not*
> *show up in your life until long after the resolution has been achieved.*
> *~ Renee Fredrickson*

DOMESTIC ABUSE

Spousal abuse has many forms. You don't have to physically assault someone to be guilty of abuse. Many abuse victims are bombarded verbally. The most common act of domestic abuse is spousal abuse. The abuser holds the key to the abused person's feeling of well-being. The abuser delivers the high highs that bookend the low lows. The worse the bad times get, the better the good times are in contrast. Although leaving their abuser is the best response to violence, it's in trying to leave that many women are harmed. The best advice I can provide to a woman who thinks she might be harmed is to seek shelter elsewhere and apply evasive strategies that make you unavailable and inaccessible to your threatening partner. If you really believe that you're at risk for being harmed, battered women shelters provide the best way to remain safe. Shelters are where your physical safety lies. Support is what you need to overcome your situation. Guidance is what your spirit is seeking. Understanding is the key to your emotional healing. Peace of mind is your objective. Freedom is your gift at the end.

So often survivors have had their experiences denied, trivialized, or distorted. Writing is an important avenue for healing because it gives you the opportunity to define your own reality. You can say: This did happen to me. It was that bad. It was the fault & responsibility of the adult. I was—and am—innocent.
~ *Ellen Bass & Laura Davis*

VICTIM MENTALITY

In extreme cases, victimhood has some people believing that they somehow deserved to be abused. Only a compromised spirit can fall victim to unworthiness as their mantra. Don't be fooled. In every case of disrespect, no act of love can be found. Without respect there can be no love. Victim mentality is when you allow other people to control your mood, which means you are giving away your power to someone else. Don't sell yourself short, you were not born a victim. The way to get your power back is to understand that you have the innate power to create your reality. You were born a great manifester. You may have lost some confidence, but you still have the ability to shape your outcomes.

When a trauma victim becomes too used to living that role, a victim identity sets in. They've been treated as a helpless victim for so long and have been showered with attention by so many, that they actually convince themselves of their identity as a victim. Once the attention they receive for this passive behavior fades, they are left feeling empty, lonely, and just floating around in life. Unfortunately, many people try to deal with it by further embracing the role of the victim. They find it safer to take orders rather than give them. They'll obey even if they don't agree with the order they've been given. They feel much safer this way and adapt to a meek existence. Exiting within this passive mindset is complicated. First, one must accept their circumstances and reality. When we are not well, we can't afford to waste energy and suppress the immune system with fear and resistance. We must accept our circumstances and trust that it brings a valuable message, take responsibility for our health, find our support team, and go through the difficult process of changing our lives for the better.

YOU WERE NOT BORN A VICTIM: SURVIVAL DEFENSE MECHANISMS

The greatest story seldom told is the story of your life. Not to be confused with a list of your stumbles and falls. Tell me a story of your survival. Tell me tales of your adventures, treasures, revelations, and awakenings. Be a storyteller from the position of your divine soul slowly remembering its own divinity. Speak from the position of a survivor. You are a divine light and you are worthy of peace and joy. When you share your story, tell of your courageous fights to persevere in the presence of overwhelming adversity. Tell why you believe you were placed here on the planet and share the keys to your bravest victories.

> *Instead of saying, "I'm damaged, I'm broken, I have trust issues"*
> *say "I'm healing, I'm rediscovering myself, I'm starting over."*
> ~ Horacio Jones

Our survival defense mechanisms keep us feeling safe and insulated from our emotional trauma. Denial, shame, and guilt are lower vibrational energies that form an emotional umbrella that keeps us sheltered, functional, and safe until we learn different coping mechanisms that allow us to step away from our trauma and heal.

THE PRACTICE OF SETTING BOUNDARIES

You disrespect yourself every time you say yes when you really mean no. No one deserves to be controlled or abused. Find your voice and speak up for yourself when you sense that someone is taking advantage of you. Don't remain silent when your intuition alarm is ringing. Abusers are always showing their unresolved issues. When physical abuse shows up in any of your relationships, get out the first time it happens. Physical or sexual abuse are actions that terminate any soul contract. From that point on, there is nothing to learn from that person, only hard times will follow. Gather yourself and your belongings and get out. Give them more space than they need to reflect and heal. They are subconsciously intending to transfer to you whatever violence they experienced in their own past. People often show you where they are from and what they have endured through their actions. Pay attention to the road signs and respond accordingly. Choose to save yourself, that's how you teach them, by choosing yourself over them.

> *The difference between shame and guilt is the same as*
> *"I am bad" in comparison to "I did something bad."*
> *~ Brene Brown*

POST-TRAUMATIC STRESS DISORDER (PTSD)

PTSD is a result of a traumatic past event. In most cases of PTSD, the consequences are similar: social, professional, and psychological impairments. Trauma is defined as, "An experience that limits your ability to cope with daily life, without referencing your trauma." One way to heal is to educate yourself, seek to learn more about the integration of the mind. Hypnotherapy is an effective way to influence your greater subconscious. It's a method that's seeing great success in treating PTSD patients. "Hypnotherapy works to build walls of support and encouragement around the patient and develops a lens to see the world in a less threatening light," says psychotherapist Paul Hokemeyer, PhD. While there are several modalities of hypnotherapy, most involve a combination of deep relaxation and cognitive restructuring.

> *PTSD is a whole-body tragedy, an integral human event*
> *of enormous proportions with massive repercussions.*
> *~ Susan Pease Banitt*

"Through breath work, guided meditation, or yoga practice, the clinician gains access to the patient's subconscious thoughts," Dr. Hokemeyer explains. For example, meditating can help you relax by forcing you to focus on your breath. It can also help you to see your fears and anxieties not as threats, but as opportunities to overcome and make you stronger. "The work would also enable them to re-evaluate their own perceptions, correcting any distortions and strengthening their agency and resilience," Dr. Hokemeyer says. Hypnotherapy generally takes at least four sessions, or a month of preliminary work with your therapist. That preliminary work involves finding a therapist you can trust, undergoing the hypnosis treatments, and implementing your desired changes into your everyday life.

CHAPTER 30

SEVEN MANTRAS FOR SEVEN DAYS

MONDAY MANTRA
I Shall Not Be Moved (say aloud)
"Despite my circumstances, I shall not be moved.
I will remain where I am, deeply present in the stillness
where I reside. I shall not be moved because I am the
witness to all that is. I am the receiver of
all that I see, sense, and feel. I am Presence.
I accept all this moment has to offer
and hold no resistance to it coming or going.
Let it be, because this moment too shall pass."

TUESDAY MANTRA
The Acceptance Mantra (say aloud)
"Today I choose to fully accept myself in the world.
I have decided to move beyond any mindset that is limiting me.
I release all actions and past experiences that caused me to suffer.
I release all that no longer serves me.
I recognize that my true self is pure love.
My truth is luminous and real.
Today I accept the truth of who I am— a soul,
an expression of love and a vital piece of the universe."

WEDNESDAY MANTRA
Gratitude Mantra (say aloud)
"I am always filled with gratitude and I am blessed to be alive.
I am drawing inspiration today from the power of Mother Earth herself.
I can feel her boundless natural electricity resonating underneath me.
I feel rejuvenated as the energy waves of the planet surge into my body
through the soles of my feet. As the earth's vitality flows through
my veins towards my heart, I reconnect with Source.
I am grateful for this day, this moment, this love, and this life.
There is no such thing as impossible and
no greater opportunity than right now."

THURSDAY MANTRA
Manifestation Mantra (say aloud)
"What I see before me today was created from
a single thought that I turned into a belief.
I am aware that intention is pure purpose.
I believe that intention is the God of dreams.
I realize that whatever effort I put into my dreams
is what I will get back out.
I vow to practice my intentions daily.
Divine momentum will be added by the law of attraction.
I realize that each of my experiences has a hidden meaning.
I have the ability to see the outcomes of my desires in mental pictures.
I will not worry about how or when my visions will manifest.
I will trust the universe to deliver the people, circumstances,
climate, and experiences to manifest my dreams."

FRIDAY MANTRA
I Am Mantra (say aloud)
"Life is spiritual, nothing more and nothing less.
My path is illuminated by the divine light of the Creator.
What others see in me is only a fraction of my true power.
I have the capacity to accomplish anything that
I set my mind to. The only limitations that I have are
the ones that I am currently believing."

SATURDAY MANTRA
The Love Mantra (say aloud)
"I am not my past experiences.
I am not my broken heart.
I am open to healing my deep emotional wounds.
In my healing, I welcome pure love into my sacred heart.
I am both resilient and strong.
I am deserving of greater love.
My heart is open and ready to receive.
I will share my love with the world.
I am energy and I am love.

Every morning I will rise.
Every day I will sing.
Every moment I will appreciate.
Every second I will love."

SUNDAY MANTRA
Mantra For The Soul (say aloud)
"I give myself permission to let go of any
memory or mindset that no longer serves me.
I surrender to what's happening for me right now.
From now on, I pledge to get out of my own way.
I realize that every being must walk their own path.
I believe that love is the highest power.
Indeed, love is the answer to all life's questions.
My mission is Oneness inside myself,
Oneness in mankind, and Oneness with the Creator.
My inner light of divine energy is my soul.
My soul's direction is always home.
Like a river that runs into an ocean,
a soul always returns to Source.
My home is Oneness with God."

Final Statement
Join me in this affirmation: (say aloud)
"Today is the beginning of the rest of my life.
I am the author of my story and the co-creator of my experience.
I am strong. I am capable. I am willing to change.
I am willing to grow. I will lead with my heart.
I will bypass my mind and reach inside my soul
to access my inner greatness."

CHAPTER 31

HEALING ANCESTRAL TRAUMA

ANCESTRAL TRAUMA

Mindsets and emotional patterns are transferred by DNA to sons, daughters, and generations beyond. This inherited, emotional trauma can only be cured by addressing it with forgiveness and love. Shadows, ancestral trauma, and emotional wounds will continue to be passed down from generation to generation until someone in the family has the courage to take on the journey to heal themselves. If something bad happens to your parents, it gets locked into their DNA and you inherit that trauma into your genes. The way to break free out of bondage is by shifting out of your old mindsets, emotional attachments, and patterned behaviors and getting into alignment with Pure Divine Light. Divine Light heals. What you heal in yourself, you heal in your family line. Be the one who breaks the cycle. Simply decide that these corrosive patterns end with you, so that they are no longer passed onto future generations.

Healing Mantra (say aloud)
"I am good enough. I am not my past.
My existence is not defined by
my past nor my circumstances.
I open my sacred heart to heal my past.
In my healing, I welcome abundant
love into my heart and soul.
I believe that love is medicine and
I vow to share my love with the world."

Forgive your parents, they too had a childhood they didn't heal from. They didn't know what they were doing to you because they didn't get to experience unconditional love. Don't try to change them. Now that you've become aware of the repetitive pattern, you can break the cycle. When you go inside of your heart and practice forgiveness, you can heal the source of your suffering. Inside of your sacred heart, you will find your true nature which has healing powers beyond your current ability to understand. Your divine truth is capable of replacing your pain and suffering with understanding and love. Trauma is healed by sharing your experiences and exposing them to Light. Healing your ancestral trauma raises your consciousness and allows you to expand into realms that your ancestors couldn't.

Intergenerational trauma is carried from one generation into the next. It can be thought of as a cycle of dysfunctional behavior that causes trauma from generation to generation to generation. Trauma is shaped and flavored by the psychosocial, contextual, political, and cultural milieus in which it occurs. Slavery, extreme poverty, and forced relocation are horrific experiences shared by diverse tribes, that have resulted in cumulative emotional and psychological wounds carried across generations. Now is the opportunity to heal your family's struggle. It's crucial to be aware of intergenerational trauma in your family so that you can be the one to break the energy of the past.

Admitting trauma means that you have to take a look inside of yourself. Be careful not to deny your past suffering. Know that if you can heal your ancestral trauma, then you can be the one to heal the trauma of your sons, daughters, grandchildren, and great-grandchildren. It all starts with you right now. You are the first one in the precious position to heal your family's ancestral trauma. Just because you had it rough as a kid, it doesn't mean that your children have to go through what you did. One of the greatest acts of redemption that anyone can do is to love their children and not abuse them, even if you were abused yourself. One common example is child abuse. A child who was beaten by their parent is much more likely to physically assault their own children. Abusers are often children of abusers who abuse their own children. Your DNA, conditioning, and social-economic status are the main factors which shape your behavior. Ancestral trauma can persist through generations until the chain is broken. Once in a generation, an individual arrives with enough passion, insight, determination, and the wisdom needed to escape the pattern and stop the cycle. People with similar intergenerational trauma tend to flock together. If you grew up believing that you are a victim because your parents believed that they were victims, then you may be suffering from a victim mentality. If that is your case, you will attract other victims to you, it's a vicious cycle.

LEVEL UP YOUR DNA

Your DNA is constantly being upgraded. Leveling up is raising your level of consciousness, so that your newly formed DNA is manufactured from a higher vibration. In effect, your new DNA is supercharged. This new genetic wiring is superior to the old you and your old DNA. It's time to heal and replace your traumatized DNA with new and more highly evolved genes of love. DNA replication happens every minute of your existence. Your old and damaged cells are constantly being destroyed, while simultaneously, new cells are being born at various locations in your body to replace them. The DNA within each new cell is being manufactured on a nanosecond basis and is influenced by the emotional environment that you produce and maintain. In addition to DNA, cellular memory is also passed down from one generation to the next.

VIBRATIONAL DNA

You can raise your energy by shifting your awareness to the present moment which contains pure infinite potential, this simple conscious action increases your inner vibration. Your DNA is being created every single day and it is stamped with the history of your current emotions. The DNA that you create today can be no more vibrant than the power of its source. Joy is your highest energetic state. The secret to being joyful is to shift your energy into the state of joy and freedom. Free of mind, free of body, and free of any negative emotion— pure positive vibes.

CHANGE YOUR INNER WORLD; HEAL AND REPLACE YOUR SUFFERING WITH LOVE

One of the deep purposes of life is to heal your emotional self. By healing your own inner pain and suffering, you contribute to the healing of your ancestral past and global human consciousness. The more you explore, discover, and heal the damaged emotional aspects of your spirit, the closer you get to the living identity of your true self. This ongoing healing process allows you to reflect out more of your inner light. Once you learn how to use the power of vibration to change your inner world, you begin to see evidence of change in your outer world. Be patient with yourself, you are love in motion. Your greatness is starting to shine through.

CHAPTER 32

HEALING YOUR INNER CHILD

WHY IS IT CALLED YOUR INNER CHILD?

A person's inner child is that part of themselves that remains child-like with features such as innocence, naiveté, or gullibility, but also with more curiosity, creativity, and spontaneity. Learning to care for your inner-child is a psychological method of recovery from childhood conflict and trauma. Your inner child is often scared, hurt, angry, and full of doubt. In other words, a deep part of your ego-self thinks like a child and is indirectly asking you to hear them, comfort them, and heal them. It's important to understand that one's inner child is simply an inner mental energy structure. A construct based on past history which does not and can not exist on its own.

Your inner child is an unconscious aspect of your mind, a place where you lament your unmet needs. It is an image of yourself that you have crafted, chosen, adopted, and held onto. Ultimately your inner child is not real, but it doesn't know that. The aim of the journey of healing is to identify and listen to the feelings of your inner child— understand her, nurture her, accept her, and simply love her. Your inner child needs to be gently guided through the process of unlearning and learning. Connecting with and healing your inner child is an important part of your spiritual journey. Whatever questions you have, whatever you don't understand about yourself, you should pursue. We see the world through the lens of our inner child. Eventually, everyone should attempt to uncover and deal with the various mental formations and content of their minds. Even after some people have the ultimate experience of enlightenment, they too still have to integrate their ego and their inner child.

THE IMPORTANCE OF INNER CHILD HEALING WORK

In the effort to raise your vibration, it's essential to lift the energy of your inner child. Your inner child is the part of you that takes things to heart and feels overwhelmed when things aren't going well. The little you is still inside. Many of us were traumatized as children and still carry the burden of our pain decades later. Trauma happens to a child when they feel that they are not being seen, heard, respected, or validated. Childhood wounds are carried into adulthood and are buried under layers of shame, blame, guilt, and denial. Childhood trauma shapes how you react to stress as an adult. Know that you no longer need to shoulder the weight of your past alone, God has already forgiven you and your past.

After a traumatic experience, the human system of self-preservation seems to go into permanent alert, as if the danger might return at any moment.
~ Judith Lewis Herman

YOU'VE GOT TO DO THE INNER WORK TO FIND THE SOURCE OF YOUR ISSUES

Subconsciously, we actively seek out relationships and experiences which continue to support the messages we absorbed as a child. That's why it's important to study your childhood history and search deep inside for the sources of your emotional issues. Inner child work helps you to discover the roots of your long term problems. The childhood events that caused you deep suffering in the past will continue to resurface until you understand why those experiences came to you. Once you learn the lesson behind your pain, the suffering will lessen and the repetitive patterns die out.

Most self-help books fail to help you uncover exactly how your unfavorable conditions developed. *Love And Healing* offers a systematic and open approach to walk you through the process of your Inner Restorative Healing. Like other programs and tasks, "What you put in is what you get back." Hard work, focus, determination, practice, and commitment always pays off. You are the lead designer of your healing journey. Once you are able to identify your deep seated emotional issues, the rest is up to you. You decide how hard and how often you want to work at this. Reading this book is not a coincidence. *Love And Healing* is a calling to everyone to heal the damage of your emotional trauma. Learn how to heal and replace the pain of your past with forgiveness and love. Together let's spend some time working with your inner child and lifting the energy of your spirit. It's never too late to start your inner child work, no matter how old you are. Your inner child is still there inside you, it never leaves. Today is a great opportunity to improve your relationship with yourself.

EXERCISE #54

Questions to Ask Yourself About Your Childhood
The purpose of asking these questions is to help you take a better
and more realistic viewpoint of yourself. You've undoubtedly
been exaggerating your weaknesses and overlooking many
of your assets. Your poor opinion of yourself is overstretched
and you've been seeing yourself through the wrong lens.
Reviewing your answers to these questions will point you to
the remaining inner child work that you need to complete.

1. How were you treated as a child?

    _____ __ ____

2. What are the things that happened in your childhood that led
    you to the image you hold of yourself now?

    _____ __ ____

3. Were you over-protected by your parents?

    _____ __ ____

4. Were you belittled, ignored, or abandoned by your parents?

    _____ __ ____

5. Were you mentally, physically, or sexually abused?

    _____ __ ____

6. What was the quality of your relationship with your sisters and
    brothers, particularly the ones older than you?

    _____ __ ____

7. As a child, did you suffer from having a poor self-image?
    Insecurity?

    _____ __ ____

8. Did you grow up feeling that you were inferior to anyone else?

    _____ __ ____

9. Did you suffer from poverty, discrimination, or racism?

    _____ __ ____

10. Were you raised in a loving home?

    _____ __ ____

11. Did you feel safe in your living environment as a child? If the answer is no, what made you feel unsafe?

_____ _____

12. Are you a positive or negative person? If you answered "negative," when and where did these feelings of negativity arise?

_____ _____

Your childhood attachment patterns will continue to bleed into and affect your current and potential relationships until you take the time to understand them and heal them.

POVERTY AND INFERIORITY COMPLEXES

A "complex" is an emotionally charged group of related ideas, feelings, memories, and impulses working together mainly in the subconscious mind. Inferiority and poverty often act together to hold one back from success. Andrew Salter in his book *Condition Reflex Therapy*, recommends these wonderful exercises which aim to overcome any inferiority ideas. Practicing these exercises act to gradually build up your ego and self-confidence. All these points can be practiced and carried out in an acceptable way. They will be found to be very valuable in helping you to overcome any feelings of inadequacy.

Self-Empowerment Exercises by Andrew Salter

- Say what you feel. Utter any spontaneous felt emotion. If you're angry, say so in an acceptable way. If your feelings are hurt, don't withdraw— express your feelings.
- Contradict and attack. When you disagree with someone about something, say so instead of remaining silent or agreeing. This should be done aggressively, but also politely.
- Use the word "I" frequently and with emphasis. "I think this." Capitalize and emphasize the "I" by saying it louder and with

feeling. **Using the word "I" is empowering and increases ownership of your conditions.**

- **When someone praises you, agree with them instead of deprecating yourself with some phrase like "Oh it's nothing." Simply admit that you did well.**
- **Improvise more often and live more in the moment. Live spontaneously, don't plan ahead to an extent. Salter calls this "the development of excitatory conditioned reflexes," to counteract inhibitory ones.**

CHILDHOOD BRUISES

Most of our emotional wounds are from our childhood. Getting unstuck sometimes involves doing the self-analysis of our childhood pain to determine what parts of us were damaged from certain encounters. The wounds to your spirit that you thought were scars are merely bruises. The only good thing about bruises is that they are temporary. Bruises heal in time, but your greatest pains often get buried underneath profound shame and misplaced guilt. You heal yourself by shifting your focus and attention, away from your past pain and into the energies of acceptance, forgiveness, and love. Take the time to identify the main painful memories and events that negatively changed your trajectory. Eventually, you must create separation from your painful memories and emotional suffering in order to heal your addiction to replaying the past.

FEAR IS CONNECTED TO YOUR INNER CHILD

Fear is your crying baby, don't run from it, pick up your inner child and nurture it. Your inner child is only worried and concerned because it seeks your love and attention. Once you acknowledge the aspect of yourself that's seeking your love and attention, you can shift your narrative and align with your higher self. The choice is yours: love or fear, consciousness or unconsciousness, growth or stagnation. Eliminate fear by aligning with your higher self, residing in gratitude, and by surrendering to love. When you reside in gratitude and love, fear and anger disappear.

THE ROOTS OF OUR FEARS OF INTIMACY

We fear intimacy because we have fears of abandonment, betrayal, and rejection. We have these fears because many of us were wounded or abandoned in our early childhood. As children we experienced abuse and betrayal at the hands of adults, because they too were wounded by their past experiences. The unconscious behavior of others caused us to feel unworthy, unloved, and unsafe. As a result, our egos were so traumatized that we adapted defensive programming to try to protect us from experiencing any further pain. Growing up, good parents place their children in virtual bubbles to protect them from harm. They carefully surround their kids with friends and family that they love and trust. Unfortunately, many trauma victims are often violated by the very elders who should have been protecting them. The people we love and trust are the ones capable of hurting us the most.

SEEK AND CONNECT WITH YOUR INNER CHILD

If you peel back the decades of social conditioning, you will find her, she is there. Your inner child wants from the world what it did not receive as a child. If you step outside of yourself, you can see your inner child. Connect with your inner child, she is invariably repressed. Talk to your inner child. Tell her, "It's okay to be lonely, to feel hurt, and not to understand." Tell her it's okay to feel scared. Tell her that what happened to her was not her fault. Remind her that no one is perfect. Tell her that it's okay to be scared yet strong at the same time. "Be strong, little one, you are a spark of the divine and nothing else matters." Make her feel safe and loved. Tell her no one can hurt her or leave her anymore. Tell her it's okay to come out and play again.

A wounded inner child often has rage inside at her core. At the root, this rage is born from a history of undeserved injustice and emotional suffering. After years of blocking the source of your pain, it eventually comes out. Misplaced anger and rage are commonly seen from people who have suffered damage to their DNA as a result of repeated neglect or abuse. Abused people have the tendency to repeat the same harmful words that were harmfully spoken to them and they also tend to repeat the same violent behavior that they once experienced. This misguided anger is the will of the inner child attempting to take back its power by whatever means necessary.

Try to apply the middle path of compassion. Your subconscious memories are constantly signaling and influencing your emotional self. The response is to purify your subconscious mind. Your inner child stores your childhood memories, and ultimately it calls for its own purification. Be grateful for your emotional body, as its calling is to activate the greater you. Connectivity to your inner child connects you to Source Energy. Always find time to be playful, this childlike energy is your core. When you strengthen your core, you strengthen your inner power. Healing your inner child helps to heal your childhood wounds and make you unstoppable. Let the healing begin.

No one saves us but ourselves, no one can and no one will.
We ourselves must walk the path.
~ Buddha

EXERCISE #55

Ten Steps To Awaken Your Inner Child

1. **To address your inner child, first create a peaceful atmosphere.**
2. **Set your intention for your healing session.**
3. **Lay down, get comfortable, relax your body, and be still. Close your eyes and focus on your breathing.**
4. **Picture yourself as a child, hold this image in your mind. Keep your message to your inner child brief and simple.**
5. **Address your inner child with love from your sacred heart.**
6. **Once you feel the presence of your inner child, silently speak your truth; you may also speak aloud if that feels better.**
7. **Give her comfort and compassion. Your wounded inner child often doesn't feel deserving. You can validate her feelings and just sit with her.**
8. **Apologize for ignoring her all this time and affirm that you hear her now. Reassure her that you are here for her from now on.**

9. Nurture your inner child, hold her close and dear to your heart and simply love the shame away. Make her feel safe to join you in deep compassion.

10. Love your inner child and never leave her again.

HEALING YOUR INNER CHILD TAKES PLACE AT THE LEVEL OF YOUR SUBCONSCIOUS MIND

The healing process begins with the intention to heal yourself. The act of healing involves making strong but gentle suggestions to your subconscious mind. Your subconscious is the place where acceptable mindsets are stored and the useless ones are deleted. Try connecting and making some suggestions to your subconscious, so some of its ideas can change. Affirm to yourself that you are a pretty good person after all, with lots of good points and abilities, and that in the future you will be correcting some of your shortcomings. Gradually, your subconscious will accept your suggestions as your new truth. Observe the shift as it begins to influence your attitudes, beliefs, and behaviors.

EXERCISE #56
Write a Letter to Your Inner Child

"To the inner child that lies inside of me,
Know that I am sorry for your pain and your struggle.
I am sorry that you were hurt and had to hide in the dark.
I am sorry for neglecting you for so long.
I am here now and I will support you.
There is nothing wrong with you.
You are alone no more. I will never leave you again.
You can trust me. Please come out and play.

299

I will listen to you, I will honor you,
I will protect you, and I will love you.
You are safe with me now and forever.
You are loved and now you are free.
With Love,
Your Adult Self"

CHAPTER 33

MANAGING STRESS, OVERCOMING BURNOUT, HOW TO GET UNSTUCK AND UNLOCKING HAPPINESS

STRESS

I dedicate this chapter to those who are currently feeling overwhelmed by their circumstances. Stress, fear, and doubt are major factors which can potentially cause disruption in your mental and physical health. Most stress comes from the way you respond to things, not from the way life is. When too much stress accumulates, people are driven to the limit of their capacity to cope. The danger of prolonged stress is that it can lead to a mental health crisis. A "nervous breakdown" happens when a person's psyche becomes overloaded, they temporarily become unable to deal with life and need immediate intervention or hospitalization. A nervous breakdown can be viewed as an emotional crisis that makes a person dysfunctional. An interesting note is that usually a person doesn't know they're having a breakdown until after it happens.

Daily stress is ubiquitous in our lives. As beings of light, we must find ways to stop the flow of negative thoughts, overthinking, and worrying. The task in today's world is to learn how to balance work, stress, and a personal life. When stress begins to affect your relationships it's a warning sign to relax, do some self-care, and unplug for a while. Whenever I need to recharge, I take what I call a "golden-hour break" to decompress. I go to the beach, spread out a blanket, soak up the rays of the sun, walk barefoot in the sand, experience the ocean, and absorb the energy of the universe. This formula never fails. The goal is to learn how to self-motivate and condition ourselves to reflect positivity, wellness, personal growth, and love in the presence of omnipresent adversity.

The Prescription To Lower Your Work Stress Level

In 2020, work stress is a common diagnosis in my patient group. These patients are hard to manage within the time constraints of my daily schedule, but I typically prescribe the following things:

1. **Aim to reduce your job stress. Establish your boundaries, don't take your work home with you.**
2. **Take 2 ten minute "time outs" to relax and recharge— one in the morning and one in your afternoon.**
3. **Don't forget to take time out just for yourself for self-care.**

4. Count your blessings and be grateful.

5. Spend as much time working outdoors as you can.

6. When seeking inner peace, practice conscious breathing. Breathe in through your nose and out of your mouth. Repeat this three times. This simple exercise recenters you.

7. Lighten your load by seeing yourself as an extension of the infinite universe, not just a worker at a job to make money.

8. Schedule an occasional vacation day on Monday or Friday to create long weekends. If possible, take well deserved 7-14 day vacations at least once a year to rest, recenter, and rejuvenate.

9. Remind yourself that with every tomorrow comes the opportunity to improve yourself.

10. If your stress levels continue to rise, consider a different career path or a move.

RECOGNIZING NEGATIVITY

Negativity is a downward spiral. The more you focus on your problems instead of solutions, the more negativity you will attract. As hard as you may try to avoid it, negative thinking happens to everybody from time to time. Negative thinking occurs most frequently whenever you are not monitoring your thoughts. Be a watcher of your words, ideas, and speech. Some become so distanced from their truth that they speak without any self-awareness. Catch yourself anytime before you finish any sentence that begins with "I can't..." Negative thinking reinforces neural pathways that are intimately associated with your negative emotions. Whenever you feel overwhelming negativity, it's important to ventilate. Whenever you recognize a recurring pattern of negativity in your attitude, speech, or behavior, quickly upshift to a solution-based mindset and adjust your behavior accordingly. All effective changes start with a single bold intention to change. Have the intention to keep positive thoughts on your mind and loving feelings in your heart, this is the way of higher consciousness. Self-acceptance, self-awareness, self-discipline, and self-love, lead to self-realization.

EXERCISE #57

Inner Work

1. Name three specific ways that you can make yourself happy.
2. Name three things that you may not be giving yourself.
3. Name three genuine ways that you are not loving yourself unconditionally.
4. Name three things that you can do for yourself to practice self-love.

ARE YOU FEELING BURNED OUT?

Are you feeling exhausted and meaningless lately? Life events can sometimes leave you feeling drained emotionally, financially, mentally, and physically. Burnout is when you fall out of alignment and get stuck in a mundane low energy routine. A low personal vibration blocks your soul's reality. Your individual frequency is yours, but your vibration can also be influenced by others and events. Remember that whatever or whoever you surround yourself with becomes a part of your overall consciousness. Whenever you find yourself stuck, a change of scenery always does your mind and body good.

Free yourself of negative vibrations through solitude, silence, and stillness. You are not running away from your problems, you are merely creating the physical space needed to achieve a different perspective on things. If you don't have the luxury of taking a few days of vacation, then take a few hours off just for yourself. Breaking away from your daily routine to recharge and get some self-care can make a world of difference.

IDENTIFY YOUR LIMITING BELIEFS

Limiting beliefs are generated in your mind. Don't feel bad, there are "belief skeletons" in everyone's mental closet. Know that you can clear any limiting belief that you are holding. These falsehoods are essentially lies about yourself that you've long believed to be true. The process of getting rid of these beliefs is more complicated than you think. This is because the extent to which these beliefs are attached to your psyche is related to the amount of time you have associated yourself with these beliefs.

The first step of getting rid of your limiting beliefs is to identify them. Once you identify them, you can address them. Ask yourself, "How much has it cost you to believe these falsehoods?" Soon thereafter, they simply lose their power. At some point, you have to be willing to let go of what is not serving you. Learn not to place any limitations on yourself. God Almighty is limitless and you are created in His image, therefore nothing is impossible. Life is always about moving beyond your limits.

Be willing to see and do things differently. Take this opportunity to identify your limiting beliefs. As you identify each one of them, write them down on a piece of paper. Address each issue internally, take time to analyze and process them, then edit those ideas out of your programming. Hold a release ritual and ceremoniously burn your notes in a symbolic release of the beliefs that no longer serve you. The idea is to develop and maintain a growth mindset free of your past failures.

EXERCISE #58
Eliminating Limiting Beliefs

Anytime you use one of the following statements,
it's a clue that you have limited yourself.
Fill in the blanks to these questions:

1. I am not really good with _____
   (eg: computers, people, cleaning, getting up early, etc.)

2. I could never _____

3. I can't _____

4. If I meditate, I will feel better about this problem: _____
5. The reason success has not found me is because: _____

MOOD SWINGS AND HOW TO CURE THE BLUES

You can always improve your mood by becoming more aware of your higher self. You alone are responsible for your happiness. If you are suffering your emotions, shift your awareness to your five senses. Feel the vitality that comprises your inner energy field. It is all about your ability and willingness to remain in complete loving awareness. When you are tuned in and tapped into your divine stream of consciousness, you no longer need other people, possessions, places, or things to make you happy.

Bypass the programming of your mind by focusing on how you feel. Your vibration is the result of your thoughts, emotions, and actions. When you focus on your desired results, your thoughts and emotions will fall in line. The path of life is not a straight line, it's a spiral. There are many twists and turns that can occur which can affect your vibration. You can be experiencing the most incredible day, yet a single phone call or event can destroy your mood set-point. Balance is the key to emotional intelligence. Try to maintain an even keel, especially when things don't go your way. When you remain stable, you can prevent yourself from overreacting, which is a key component of imbalance. Remember that you are an infinite being derived from Source Energy. Attitude is everything and improving your mood is always within your reach.

THE INGREDIENTS OF DEPRESSION

People who are depressed tend to be more focused on themselves and less connected with others. Many suffer from concrete thinking and are less flexible with their worldview. They often see themselves as outsiders and victims of a cruel world. Most people can generally spot when they see a depressed person, they are quiet, subdued, dull, they look heavy, maybe even deflated. Their eyes lack light, their body lacks energy, and they tend to contribute very little to conversations.

Sadness always points to an area of yourself in need of healing. Depression is your internal braking system which slows your momentum down from going in the wrong direction. In severe cases, your mood might become flat and disinterested. When you are in the grip of depression, you might feel that you don't love your partner anymore or that they are not the one for you, like you once thought they were. You might start to focus on all the things you don't like about them and you might even verbalize this directly to them. You might find yourself pulling away and not wanting to spend time with them, causing them to feel rejected while they don't really understand what's happening. Be careful not to externalize your depression by shifting the blame onto innocent bystanders in your life. This is why you should never make any decisions about your relationship when you are in the depths of depression. You might do something that causes irreversible damage to your union.

Sometimes you may feel nothing at all. Your ability to feel anything can seem to disappear in depression, all you might feel is a numbness or nothingness. No joy, no sadness, no anger, and no empathy for anyone else. A depressed person can have mental or physical fatigue or both. Disturbances in sleep and appetite are common. In severe depression, a feeling of hopelessness is common, a person can feel worthless and fall into despair. If you are depressed or you know someone who is depressed, the first thing to do is to reach out for professional help. The treatment for depression is multi-layered, but should include psychotherapy.

People who aren't interested in seeing why everything is good, get to be right. But that apparent rightness comes with disgruntlement, depression, and often separation. Depression can feel serious. So counting the genuine ways that this unexpected event happened "for" me, rather than "to" me, isn't a game— it's an exercise in observing the nature of life. It's a way of putting yourself back into reality, into the kindness of the nature of things.
~ Byron Katie

GETTING UNSTUCK

Why do we sometimes feel like we are stuck in a loop? It literally feels like we are stuck in a recurring movie. In these times, we seem to be attracting the same kind of people and circumstances to our lives. We do everything to heal our present, but what we don't realize is that what we really need to do is heal our past. Feeling stuck is a key sign of underlying trauma. The key to getting unstuck is to commit to get started. Start taking baby steps every day. There is no future in remaining stuck because the world never stops evolving. There is a pace and rhythm to life. Whenever you stand still and do nothing, you fall behind. First, identify your motivation for living and commit to moving out of your current position. Start by making affirmations that are more positive than you are used to, not "I am old," "I am dying," "This is killing me," etc. Look past any drama going on around you and just be grateful. Focus on what you can do today to improve your circumstances. If you never take any action to step forward, you will always remain in the same place. If you fall down while trying your best, then you deserve a second chance at redemption. Get back up and try again. Learn from your past mistakes and make the necessary adjustments. If you must fall, make sure that you fall forward. Your stumbles are not in vain, every time you fail, there is an aspect of you that becomes wiser, stronger, and more adept at life.

A mighty tree grows from a tiny seed.
A pagoda of nine stories is built from small bricks.
A journey of three thousand miles begins with one step.
~ Lao Tzu

THE END OF SUFFERING

Suffering and happiness are interconnected. The suffering in our lives is needed to grow our happiness. A beautiful lotus flower grows in a muddy pond; the lotus cannot grow on marble. Likewise, out of human suffering comes growth, resilience, wisdom, and understanding. Lotus flowers blossom on long stalks, which float above the muddy waters of attachment and desire. This is great symbolism for human life as well, that difficult situations can ultimately lead us to our most beautiful outcomes and help us grow into greater human beings.

SELF-CARE

Learning to love yourself unconditionally is one of the greatest lessons of your spiritual journey. Treat yourself with compassion and forgive your shortcomings and past failures. Love each and every part of yourself, even your dark emotions that you don't currently understand. You are one magnificent miracle in the process of a spiritual awakening. Wisdom and understanding are gifts of your transformation. You are an expression of love born from consciousness itself. You are worthy of receiving real love and living a peaceful existence. Get unstuck through the practice of self-care.

Self-care is self-appreciation and self-love. Make it a point to love yourself today. It's time to start pleasing yourself. Start by putting yourself first, it's not ego, it's survival. Some people don't make it through life because they are pleasers and give away too much of their energy. Learn to take care of yourself first and give love to others from your overflow. Self-care is the key to the recovery of your body and restoration of your spirit.

HAPPINESS ATTRACTS ABUNDANCE INTO YOUR LIFE

Build a life of happiness. Your natural state is happiness— not happy about this or that, just happy for no reason at all. Try to keep a peaceful mind and be joyful. Happiness is an inside job. Being happy is effortless, being sad takes work. Don't try to seek happiness, just be the happiness. Happiness is a compass, not a destination. True happiness is not conditional on your circumstances. It's important to take responsibility for your bliss.

Occasionally, I get asked the question:
What's the difference between the notions of happiness, joy, and bliss.
In my opinion, the differences are that happiness is mentally
sustained and is personal. Joy is psychologically stimulated and

> *socially driven. Lastly, bliss encompasses mental, psychological,*
> *and physical, and is cosmically and/or divinely driven.*
> ~Robert Gerard

We are programmed to seek happiness. We try to avoid unpleasant emotions and we seek experiences that make us feel good. In general, the motto is, "What makes me happy must be good for me and what makes me sad I choose to avoid." The trouble with this approach is that sadness is the very emotion we use to measure our happiness against. In truth, we need both emotions. Happiness and sadness both have the power to accelerate our spiritual growth. All profound change has a pivot point and these two emotions certainly qualify as game changers.

> *You need nothing to be happy.*
> *You need something to be sad.*
> ~ *The Master*

THE SCIENCE OF HAPPINESS

In today's world, there is a tremendous amount of scientific research focused on pleasure chemicals known as Neurotransmitters (NT's) which are polypeptides that relay messages from the brain, neuron-to-neuron. These NT's are extremely important in brain functionality, without them you could not think or feel. Neurotransmitters are a chain of amino acids linked together which are very important in bringing forth your emotions. Psychiatric medications work by altering these chemical compounds in your body-mind. When a thought is activated in your brain, it is spontaneously attached to an emotion. It then colors your emotion with a feeling: unpleasant, pleasant or indifferent. You tend to avoid what is unpleasant and seek to approach what is pleasant. What you are neutral to, you are unmoved.

> *If abundance is essential to happiness,*
> *then happiness is essential for abundance.*
> *Happiness is your true nature.*
> ~ *Ramana Maharishi*

HAPPINESS IS YOURS TO BE HAD

You likely didn't get to where you are today in a day or even a year. Similarly, you won't heal in one moment in time. Healing is a cumulative process. The more time you spend recognizing and savoring the good things happening in your life, the better you will feel. The more you choose to focus on gratitude and living in the moment, the more aligned with spirit you are and the more joyful you will become. Choose happiness over history, it's always been up to you. When you come into alignment and remain in your center, negative mind noise fades away. Inner peace will promptly arrive and stay with you for longer periods of time.

EXERCISE #59

Play Time!
Greet today with the incredibly happy enthusiasm of a child.
Plan something simple and joyful, and then do it.
Invite friends over for a game night, attend a paint
& sip, or perhaps take a cooking class.
From the wave to the particle, make it happen.
Exercise your power as the creator and curator of your fun reality.

THE PURSUIT OF HAPPINESS

Pursuing your happiness is the most worthwhile and rewarding thing you can do. Find the things that help you find joy in life and do more of that. Don't lay around wishing for a happy tomorrow, live out your happiness today. No one is responsible for your happiness except for you. If you're unhappy, set out to make a new road for yourself. Happiness is yours to be had. Your reality is a combination of your thoughts, emotions, morals, beliefs, feelings, and dreams. Your mood matters. When you are joyful, joy will follow you. Meet others with a smile. When you smile, others will find a reason to smile as well. Be someone who lifts the vibration of any room you enter. Dish out compliments, not bitterness. Bitterness consumes the vessel that contains it. Whenever you bring joy into the lives of others, your joy is multiplied. Don't seek happiness, just be happy. I hope that you become so full of happiness that it heals every cell in your body, as well as all those whose lives you touch.

CHAPTER 34

SURVIVING DEPRESSION AND SUICIDAL THOUGHTS, INSPIRATION, MOTIVATION, AND ACTIVATION

THE STIGMA OF DEPRESSION: WHAT DEPRESSION REALLY LOOKS LIKE

On the outside it's tough to see the magnitude of how debilitating depression can really be. Below are a few descriptions of former patients over the years. Jessica described depression as: "My mind and body are completely exhausted and it feels like I'm wearing a thousand pound weight." Low self-esteem and self-hate are not easily willed away or removed. Other common ways that people describe feeling depressed are: "I feel like I'm drowning, everytime I come up for air, I get hit with another wave," "Everything seems to have slowed down and I have extremely low energy," "I am doing less and eating more," "It's almost impossible to just get up and go to work," and "I've lost my hopes and dreams." Maria, another patient suffering from depression, described her condition to me as a black cloud moving towards her and hovering over her head until she had the strength to get up and get on with it. Depression literally blocked these people's happiness. Stress adds to depression and many times causes it. If a person has a history of stress stemming back to their childhood, it can cause depression later in life. Depression is the emotion of apathy. Depression is like any other emotion, it can be felt on a small or severe level. Severe depression is nothing to play with and requires immediate professional help, intervention, analysis, and treatment.

EXERCISE #60

Damaged But Not Broken
If you are down, know that you won't always remain down.
Have faith for a better tomorrow and continue to believe
in miracles. It helps to focus on your objectives in
healing your depression. Complete the following exercise:

1. For whom do you do all of this for? Bring the images of all those who inspire you on your journey into your mind's eye.

2. **What is your motivation for living? Make a commitment to continue to grow and evolve.**

3. **Name three short term goals for this week.**

4. **Now, smile from within with immense gratitude, humility, and grace, because you are alive.**
5. **Say aloud: "I am feeling better every single day. Everything is as it should be and all is well."**

GETTING OUT OF A DEPRESSED STATE

You have the ability to rise up from anything. You can accomplish whatever you set your mind to do. Everything starts with an intention. Believe that you can alter your life trajectory by completely changing your current mindset, habits, and routines. Don't be afraid to mix things up. Develop action plans and activities that elevate your mood. Make sure to follow your joy. Plan activities that bring happiness into your life. Be disciplined and hold yourself accountable to manifest your dreams. Aim to take daily baby steps towards achieving your goals.

One method that I use to improve my mood is to allow my emotions to come up and out of my body. I focus on breathing consciously, in and out, deep and slow, calm and easy. Emotions are tiny yet powerful vibrations in the universe. Vibration is pure energy and energy naturally flows through both you and the universe. Use the universe as the foundation of your recovery. Trust the universe to deliver your desired outcomes. Many spiritual masters say, "You have to feel it to heal it." At our core, we are emotional creatures. Whenever you feel sad, angry, stressed, or frustrated, acknowledge them as genuine feelings. Your feelings matter, so remember to validate them, especially with what's happening in the world right now. In light of the current COVID-19 pandemic, societal stress is at an all time high. Anxiety, depression, mental illness, and overall death rates are increasing worldwide.

Don't let your sadness linger. If you are feeling depressed, pick an activity of self-expression to assist in releasing your energy blocks. Typically your blocks are located inside your body. Blocked energy can lead to "stasis" of your blood flow which slows and damages the circulation to your vital organs. This is why movement and exercise are so important. Exercise raises your heart rate which increases your cardiac output and blood flow. Enhanced cerebral blood flow is nourishing to your brain, clears away negative energy, and stimulates the neurons in your brain to grow. Knowing this, be mindful of your thoughts, your thoughts determine the quality of your existence. Good ideas lead to good decisions, which largely determines your fate.

ALLOW YOUR EMOTIONS TO RISE AND LEAVE

Processing your emotions helps you to achieve balance. Try this: allow your 3 most dominant emotions to rise in you. If you feel that you must cry or scream in frustration, do it! Don't be tempted to suppress the way you feel by numbing your emotions with drugs or alcohol. Millions of people never take the time to analyze themselves. Self-analysis is one of the main healing methods available to you. Examine your situation and your role in it. Contemplate the actions you took or didn't take that brought you to this moment. Being true to yourself and separation from your emotional-self allows you to implement your action plan in the most divine way.

SADNESS ON A PERSONAL LEVEL

Whenever I have the blues, I find it extremely helpful and healthy to change my environment by going out in nature. I have come to the conclusion that whenever I am feeling the blues, it's largely the rising symptoms of living out of alignment. The negative thoughts and emotions stem from being distanced from my vortex of happiness. Personally, my go-to action plan for instant elevation back into positivity and happiness is to go to the beach. Once there, I walk barefoot in the warm sand to connect directly to earth's magnificent power. Once I see the beauty of the beach, it doesn't take long for me to feel lighter and free. Along my walk I ceremoniously release my deepest feelings into the ocean air. I repeat this mantra aloud: "I am standing on the leading edge of the universe. My energy is rising. I am free. I am blessed. I am filled with gratitude. I feel amazing and I am connected with Source. I am pure love and light. I am a great manifestor. If I can conceive it, I can believe it, and I can be it." A purposeful mind-body connection with the four elements of the wind, sun, water, and sand always centers me and makes me feel whole again.

THE SHELTER OF YOUR SACRED INNER SPACE

Seek silence and stillness in your times of turbulence; this simple action connects you to your sacred inner space and allows remote viewing of your condition from the seat of your soul. Be the witness of your rising thoughts and emotions. From this spiritual perspective and elevation, you will see all your problems from a higher plane and with greater insight and power. You can't solve a problem by remaining in it. Alignment with Source Energy instantly elevates your mood and stimulates spontaneous healing of your body-mind.

DEPRESSION THERAPY

1. Take an honest hard look in the mirror at yourself. Ask yourself how and why you have chosen to embrace sadness instead of happiness.
2. Seek to understand the specific biological factors that are fueling your sadness. Is your depressed mood tied to any physical illness? A lack of rest? Poor nutrition? Or poor mindset?
3. Don't allow your inner critic to determine how you feel. Understand how self-criticism and poor self-esteem have roots in your lower mind, but manifest in your body.
4. Notice that to heal from your depression, you have to work through your anger. Ask yourself, "What about my current condition makes me angry and wanting to fight?"
5. Imagine in your mind's eye an emotion that you prefer to feel. Shoot rockets of intention towards your target experience. Set

your goals high and just out of reach, so that if you fall short you stumble upon a star.

6. Identify and address the root causes of your feelings of inadequacy. If you feel disappointed, unworthy, neglected, abandoned, or rejected— what is your target outlook for tomorrow?

7. How did you get yourself into this position? Do you need to call a member of your family or a close friend? Do you need professional help to assist you in lifting your depression? If so, contact a professional therapist. Resist the idea of going through your depression alone in silence.

8. Crying is an effective action that releases pent up emotions. It's okay to cry because crying is said to wash the soul.

9. Initiate daily morning conscious breathing exercises which helps to lighten your load and recenter yourself. Meditation and physical exercise are always helpful.

10. Ground yourself in gratitude. Give thanks and blessings for your breath of life and for your blessed heart.

11. Drink plenty of water, it is your essence. Maintain a well-balanced diet, which largely means natural foods grown from the earth.

12. Take minerals to strengthen your core. It's well known that iron increases your red blood cell count and vibration. Minerals strengthen your body and promote clarity and critical thinking.

13. Lastly, strive to become a better person and visualize yourself constantly improving your mindset, health, and body each and every day.

HERBAL TREATMENTS FOR DEPRESSION

Take herbs to boost your immunity and improve your wellness. St. John's wort, Ginkgo Biloba, and Elderberry help people to live as their best self. Omega-3 supplements are currently being studied as a treatment for depression patients and for depressive symptoms in people with bipolar disorder. Interestingly, it has been found that people who have depression have lower levels of omega-3's and countries with high levels of fish consumption have lower

levels of depression. Get your omega-3's through supplements or by eating fatty fish twice a week. Several studies have shown improvement in depression symptoms when taking DHEA as a dietary supplement. Cannabis also serves as a mood stabilizer and effective stress reducer for millions of people worldwide.

MOTIVATION AND ACTIVATION: EVERY VALLEY HAS A PEAK THAT FOLLOWS

The treatment for depression requires a breakthrough. Something that creates a spark has to resonate with you deep inside your core. This new thought, motivation, or inspiration is what has the power to crush your current blockages and transform your energy molecules. A spark can be a bright idea, the realization that you love someone, an unexpected financial boost, a stroke of luck, or an unexpected miracle. Any of these things could spark a revolution in your life. Know that you are worthy of achieving all your dreams and that you deserve to be happy. Now bring a smile to your face.

Every change in the physiological state is accompanied by an appropriate change in the mental-emotional state, conscious or unconscious. Conversely, every change in the mental-emotional state, conscious or unconscious, is accompanied by an appropriate change in the physiological state.
~ Elmer Green

HOPELESSNESS AND SUICIDAL THINKING: A CRY FROM THE DARK

Despair sometimes appears as though it's the truth, that's the deceptive power of the mind. A mindset of unworthiness forms from a longstanding pattern of suffering, doubt, fear, abuse, or neglect. This quote is from Sarah, a homeless patient that I counselled who was experiencing depression: "I am only a shell of the person I once was. I spend most days feeling anxious, insecure, paranoid, hyper-vigilant, and angry. I've been accused of being negative, controlling, and worthless. My physical appearance isn't good.

I've started to age rapidly, my hair is falling out and I'm far too thin. I don't even know how to relax and enjoy life anymore." Like Sarah, many suicidal patients develop a sense of helplessness and hopelessness that is beyond despair. This helplessness is not the ordinary sense of helplessness, but the sense of feeling collapsed, immobilized, and helpless. Suicidal thinking makes a person feel on the verge of collapsing from the overwhelming burden of a lifetime of pain and suffering. In some instances, people contemplate suicide when they are suffering from chronic disabling physical pain related to a past injury. They simply cannot bear to live another day in their body. In their brokenness, they see no other viable alternative but to end their life.

Unfortunately, most people that commit suicide never contact anyone before they commit their act. The family and friends often wish that they would have had the opportunity to talk to them before they died. What must be gleaned from the current rising suicide rate is that there is a need for more expansive mental healthcare services. There is a need to develop more outreach programs that identify and treat conditions such as: self-harm, chronic pain, depression, cutting, bipolar disease, and schizophrenia.

Reclaiming Your Joy Mantra (say aloud)
"I am not a burden, I am worthwhile.
If I can persist, things will get better.
I will take life one day at a time and live in the moment.
I know that faith is the power of evidence unseen.
Help is always close by and I will reach out to
a loved one on my most difficult days.
My family needs me and loves me.
I occupy a very important place in this world of mine.
I am special, unique, and valued by many— the world needs my presence.
I believe in my heart that I am not finished yet."

SUICIDE

Long after frustration has crept in, a person can get fed up with trying and feel like a failure in life. It might be failure in a relationship, business, health, or family matter. A moment of reckoning arrives when a person's misguided limit has been reached. No other way is seen other than to end their life and leave everything behind. Suicide rates around the world are increasing every year. Many families have been touched by suicide or will one day be touched by it. In 2017, my father in law, Michael "Micky" Fischa committed suicide. The event was a surprise to everyone who knew him. Mickey was always the life of the party. He was a famous Hollywood director who lived life passionately at every turn. He was in a lovely relationship with his beloved Silvie. Retrospectively, he likely received bad news from his physician of metastatic cancer in his lungs, a result of decades of smoking cigarettes. Mickey had developed a hoarse cough that plagued him day and night, he had difficulty sleeping. Evidently, his rapidly declining health was too much for him to bear. He hated the idea of becoming a burden to anyone but himself. On an early Sunday morning, just outside the city of Vienna, Mickey walked into a lake fully clothed and never returned to shore. His body was discovered a few days later and he was pronounced dead. His story is sad, but it is a tragedy that many families have and will experience. If there's a silver lining to the suicide of a loved one, know that it's not a final goodbye, it's only goodbye for now.

There is growing evidence from around the world that prime-age adults
are struggling, and especially so if they have low levels of education.
This is particularly apparent in the United States that has seen a rapid rise in
deaths of despair, principally down to drug poisonings and suicide.
Studies suggest that optimistic people live longer.
~David Blanchflower

DON'T DESPAIR IN YOUR STRUGGLE: LIFE IS TRYING TO BRING OUT YOUR HIGHEST WISDOM

There is a hidden purpose behind the struggles that you've endured. Every time that you suffer, a window of opportunity opens for you to choose acceptance and grace. Behind your suffering there is an opportunity to accept the changes that the winds of life bring and to deepen your faith in the Divine. Trust your journey. Your challenges are not here to weaken you, but to strengthen your resolve.

The very same things that make you uncomfortable,
also take you to the edge of your fears.
You are the real one who resides beyond fear,
the one who walks by faith and resides inside the realm of love.
You are the very one who allows love to take over.

EXERCISE #61
Life Is Like An Echo

What you send out into the world reverberates and comes back to you.
Ask yourself today: "What am I sending out into the world,
that's coming back to me?"

INSPIRATION FUELS PURPOSE, DON'T SETTLE FOR SADNESS, TAKE ACTION TO HEAL YOURSELF

Your present circumstances don't define your reality, your actions do. Let's take a moment to key in on what inspires you. I invite you to discover what ignites you. Motivation is a vital component of all successful healings. Try this simple exercise: Start to bring new creative images forward from your subconscious into your conscious. Imagine that your project or goal already exists somewhere out there in the universe. All you have to do is align with the exact feeling and vibration of that manifestation. Begin picturing in your mind's eye, the miracle that you're asking for actually taking place. All successful manifestations require your focus and loving attention. Take this opportunity to rededicate yourself to your dream mission. Be passionate about what you hope to achieve and always give your best effort. State your current dominant intention or desire, say it aloud three times with clarity and conviction. Believe that it is already done. And so it is.

The best way to predict the future is to create it.
~ Dr. Joe Dispenza

YOU ARE INFINITE POTENTIAL ITSELF: YOU HAVE THE ABILITY TO TRANSFORM YOURSELF

There is a space inside you where greatness lies which answers to no name, it's a dynamic space of pure potential. This space is not a new happening, it's been there your whole life. It was you before you were born and it shall remain as you for all time. Your essence is infinite potential itself. Infinite means you are not limited by anything, including the current state of your mind.

Self-realization is what triggers the acceleration of your full potential. Your final destination is the full activation of your highest self. The reason why this step in your evolution is so important is because it is the key to finding your purpose. Whenever you become activated and aligned with your greater purpose, your consciousness rises to higher heights. Commit to doing your inner work everyday. Be self-motivated, tuned in, turned on, and tapped in, and live as the best version of yourself. What's happening on the spiritual level of awakening is pure love coming alive in you. You can't believe what treasures await you once you begin to live consistently at the speed of love.

CHAPTER 35

RELATIONSHIP DYNAMICS: THE STORY OF THE RUNNER AND THE CHASER

Love is one of the deepest mysteries shared by all humanity.
Almost everyone wants to be in love and yet it can be the most
subtle, elusive, and frustrating thing to find and sustain.
When both souls are pure in their commitment to love,
everything aligns to ensure its success.

INCESSANT ARGUING IS WHY
MANY RELATIONSHIPS FAIL

D o you know why so many relationships fail? It's arguing. We yell,
scream, shout, and degrade our partners until they are bloodied and
ripe for surrender. Then we stand on top of a fake mountain banging and
sticking out our chest saying, "I'm better than you." It's all ego-driven. We
must all find a way to lose our ego's and surrender to love. Don't let the
negativity of yesterday's argument control your vibration of today. Love
holds no grudges. Be quick to forgive, forget, and move on. The longer
you take to make up, the steeper the price to pay. If a relationship can't
provide you with joy and peace, then it's not true love. Send love, light, and
forgiveness to your partner on a daily basis. Support them when they are
weak and love them enough to say, "I'm sorry."

NO RELATIONSHIP CAN PROSPER
WITHOUT GOOD COMMUNICATION

Vulnerability and openness bridge the gaps of separation and frustration.
It's our challenge to communicate effectively by speaking from the heart
to those we love, even when it's difficult to do so. Communication is
like oxygen to any relationship. We all want somebody to speak good
natured words to us. When you speak positive words every day, it elevates
your mood, as well as the mood of those around you. Open and honest
communication is essential to any successful union. It's never about who's
right or wrong, it's about who is willing to drop the beef and apologize
for temporarily forgetting that togetherness requires accountability,
sacrifice, vulnerability, humility, and surrender. Whenever you fail
to communicate positively or effectively with your partner, it erodes

shared intimacy and trust and signals the beginning of the end of your relationship.

> *Don't look to your relationship for your own salvation,*
> *you will only be disappointed. Your partner is not your savior.*
> *Relationships are not meant to save you from yourself.*
> *Relationships exist to mirror your current emotional state and*
> *push your evolution towards higher consciousness and unconditional love.*

INSECURITY KILLS ALL THAT IS BEAUTIFUL

A man who is intimidated by a strong woman who knows what she wants, needs to be far more open-minded and much less insecure. Insecurity and jealousy in relationships is often rooted in the insecurity of the partner that projects it onto the other. Insecurity and jealousy are low vibrational energies. What is meant for you will be yours. You can't make anyone love you or be with you if they don't want to. If you find yourself insecure about your relationship, perhaps it's not the right relationship for you. True love strengthens you, it will never weaken you.

THE RUNNER DYNAMIC

Most romantic relationships don't make it to the altar. In fact, even of couples that do marry, more than fifty percent end in divorce. It's time we look into the human relationship dynamics which influence our choices. In a typical romantic relationship, one person usually becomes the runner and the other the chaser. The runner is the one that runs away because consciously or subconsciously they become afraid of the intense emotions they are feeling or receiving. As a result, they feel overwhelmed or in some cases undeserving. I admit that I was a runaway lover. Before I met my soulmate, I ran from every relationship I ever had. I ran from my relationships thinking I was running away from the person I was with, but I was really running away from love and commitment. When a runner is fearful of love, they will go to great lengths to run, including sabotaging their union. Cheating is definitely one way to run. Runners will run away from their love connection, only to try to find it again in another person and in another relationship. In reality the runner is not running away from anyone, they are running away from the condition that they refuse to accept in themselves.

THE CHASER DYNAMIC

Chasers chase because they believe that uniting with someone else will end their suffering and make them feel whole again. Don't ever mistake your obsession for someone with love. Real love never runs away from you, it's always coming towards you. Until a chaser learns this valuable lesson, they will continue to manifest other lovers that run from them. What chasers feel is that they may never find a love so passionate again. In extreme cases, chasers turn to alcohol, drugs, and other relationships to overcome their feelings of rejection and abandonment. If you have identified yourself as a chaser, then stop chasing. In a breakup, it's healthy to give each other space to reflect on your feelings. Once you're apart from one another, observe if you really miss them or if you have more peace without them. If a relationship is divinely meant for you, you won't lose it. It's difficult to let go of someone that you still love, but spiritual transformation is also learning to love yourself enough to let them go. Rejection from anyone is painful, but try to remember that everything is happening to you for a reason and also for your soul's evolution. Don't sulk in your loneliness, being alone creates more opportunity for reflection and personal growth. Heartbreak and loss, while temporarily painful, are deep emotions that eventually create an upshift in your consciousness, which releases your soulmate energy and begins to magnetically attract your life partner.

TOXIC RELATIONSHIPS

Toxic relationships can sink a person's life trajectory. Relationships riddled by incessant arguments, neglect, or abuse can ruin a person's life. Most people stay in toxic relationships too long because they're afraid they are unable to love themselves enough without seeing love reflected back to them by the presence of a partner. Self-preservation is essential to self-realization. Know your value, never let anyone get comfortable disrespecting you. The more chances you give someone, the less they will respect you. The one who broke you cannot fix you, sometimes you just have to walk away with a hard lesson. In the end, no relationship is a wasted experience. Each relationship or experience in your life guides you closer to your truth.

STOP WATERING DEAD PLANTS

Relationships are much like plants, they need attention, light, nurturing, and love. If a plant is not properly cared for, it will shrivel up and die. To help a flower grow, you must understand the nature of how much water and sunshine it needs. No relationship survives neglect. People thrive with time spent, attention, and love. The idea is to water your partner's garden and don't bring them more garbage. If you can see your partner as a flower, you can take care of them well and they will grow beautifully. If you take care of them poorly, they will wither. Treasure each relationship that you experience and don't hold onto them too tightly, relationships require oxygen and space to grow.

EXERCISE #62

**Love Lessons by Relationship Expert, Tracy McMillan
She states that the end of a relationship is
not a fail, it's a lesson on love.
She targets four questions to ask yourself when
your relationship ends prematurely.
Ms. McMillan asks you to answer these four important
questions honestly from your heart:**

1. **Can you identify the areas where you need to love yourself more?**

   _____ __ ____

2. **What lessons do you feel that you still need to learn?**

   _____ __ ____

3. **What do you believe about yourself that this situation is showing you?**

    _____

4. **What can you do about it going forward?**

    _____

CHAPTER 36

SOULMATES AND TWIN FLAMES

SOULMATES

The vasana of meeting a mate or a partner is perhaps the most common vasana in all of humanity. It is commonly said that every romantic relationship that has ever failed you, was because of the magnetism, presence, and calling of your soul mate. Your soulmate is calling you. It may be a whisper today, but soon it will become a roar. You are worthy and deserving of a higher love. Whatever relationship woes you have suffered in the past, happened to prepare you for your greatest love. With soulmates there is very little suffering to work through, words are often not even necessary. A soulmate intuitively knows your needs and their presence pleases you effortlessly. Your soulmate is someone who inspires you to be your best self and is a tonic to your soul. Your soulmate is your emotional counterpart, romantic counterpart, spiritual counterpart, and the perfect complement to your higher self.

You don't need another human being to make your life
complete but let's be honest. Having your wounds kissed by
someone who doesn't see them as disasters in your soul,
but cracks to put their love into, is the most calming thing in the world.
~ Emery Allen

BEFORE YOU MEET YOUR SOULMATE

A wise man once said, "If you look at her and don't feel anything, then she is not yours to keep, she is another man's blessing." Be real about how you feel about your partner and if you don't have serious intentions, stop wasting his or her time. We all need to stop messing with other people's soulmates.

There are many people that desire true love, but for so many reasons they are unable to find a partner. Some have failed to find love for so long that they have given up hope on finding love. In love's journey, it's important that you never give up on love. Love is always available to you if you continue to believe in it. If you have aspirations for love, keep faith that you are someone's soulmate. Somewhere in the world someone is craving the idea of being with you. Your face may be unfamiliar and they may not know your name yet, but somewhere, someone is imagining the idea of being with you.

Meanwhile, live as a person worthy of an epic love and allow the universe to play matchmaker. Before you meet your soulmate you must become a vibrational match to them. When you finally find the formula to your highest vibration, they will soon appear. Your soulmate doesn't arrive to complete you, you are already complete, he or she arrives to compliment you.

LOVE YOURSELF FROM THE INSIDE OUT

Until you become your own soulmate by loving yourself from the inside out, you are going to manifest more relationships that end in failure. If you question how to act in the absence of your soulmate, act as if they were right there beside you at all times. Love is the heart's expression of your very truth revealed. Love radiates from the center of all beings. Everyone is capable of having a soulmate and sharing a great love, but first you must learn how to love yourself.

SOULMATE ENERGY

Everyone is important to your spiritual growth, everyone is a mirror for you. Every interpersonal interaction you have, shows you what inner work you have left to do. Soulmates are people with whom we have soul contracts to learn from and grow. Soulmates complete one another and their unions are capable of lasting a lifetime. Soulmate energy is very powerful and uplifting; it encompasses the body, mind, heart, and soul. Because your soulmate has such a deep love for you, their presence gives you great balance and comfort. They seem extremely familiar to you and it often seems as if you know them from a past life. Don't claim someone as your soulmate too soon, true soulmates withstand the tests of time. A unique quality of soulmates is that they inspire each other to become the greatest versions of themselves. They also inspire their soul group and serve as a reminder to all, that love is real and within reach for everyone.

LOVE IS NOT A COINCIDENCE

Soulmates reincarnate at the precise time and place in synchronicity to fulfill their soul contract. Love is not a coincidence, it's a divine connection.

Soulmates are members of your "soul group," usually ten to twenty souls with whom you reincarnate together. In most past lives, the members of your soul group play different roles: family members, best friends, lovers, students, and teachers. Soulmates wake up each day and say, "Today is a new incarnation and I choose you over and over again."

TWIN FLAMES

Many experts believe that twin flames are halves that make up one soul, however if they break up, they become their own soul. If finding a soulmate is like finding "the one," then discovering your twin flame is the discovery of "oneness," being that your twin flame is the other half of your soul. Twin flames make soulmates look and feel totally small in comparison, since they're like soulmates on steroids. You may have more than one soulmate, but there can be only one twin flame. Your twin flame arrives to help you face and resolve the very emotional issues that you are here to transcend. A twin flame is someone who enters your reality to fast track your consciousness in a relatively short amount of time. Twin flames mirror each other energetically and have a strong attraction to each other. As your mirror, your twin points out aspects of yourself that need healing. Everything that we have spent our lives running from or denying is suddenly in front of us via our mirror. This mirrorlike quality is also responsible for some of the drama you will likely encounter with your twin flame.

TWIN FLAME RELATIONSHIPS ARE TRANSFORMATIVE

The real purpose of a twin flame connection is to unearth all the unhealed trauma that you've been carrying, both consciously and unconsciously that has kept you from becoming who you are meant to be. The greater purpose behind a twin flame relationship is to strengthen your heart, to let go of your old self, to learn new life lessons, and ultimately to spark and speed up your inner transformation to become a more awakened version of yourself. A twin flame is supposed to cause you pain to a certain degree. Without a certain amount of struggle, you're probably not going to go through any real impactful transformation. Indeed a spiritual awakening often follows for the participants in a twin flame relationship. Silently and watchfully, the universe counts on your twin flame union to raise the level of consciousness and awareness of both participants. The highest purpose of a twin flame is to help mold you into the type of person who is capable of embodying divine unconditional love for yourself, your partner, your family, and for all humanity.

CHAPTER 37

HEALING FROM HEARTBREAK, SEPARATION, AND DIVORCE

A BROKEN HEART CREATES AN OPENING FOR A NEW BEGINNING

Falling in love more often than not comes along with the possibility of heartbreak. Most of the time it happens, especially if you are in your teens or in your twenties. This generation is the generation of broken hearts. We are smiling on the outside, but we are broken on the inside— this is the bitter truth that too many of us share. The pursuit of happiness is rocky by nature, there are many peaks and valleys to life and in relationships. Many people who have loved and lost are wondering if they will ever love again. Heartbreak can be devastating and is capable of leaving you feeling lost, insecure, damaged, and alone. It's amazing how someone can break your heart open and you can still love them with every broken piece of it. The universe wants you to know that your heart can never truly be broken, but your ego can convince you otherwise. Know that your pure heart cannot break. The feeling of heartbreak is created when we feel separated from someone we love. Although this may feel very real, it's only an illusion because it contradicts everything we know to be true on a soul level. The word heartbreak is only a word used to reflect the emotional suffering which accompanies the loss of a romantic love.

The purpose of a crisis that leads to a fractured heart is actually to crack your heart wide open. When your heart breaks, there's an opportunity for you to surrender. In surrender, the unhealthy wanting aspect of a devastated mind all but disappears. Surrender is the shift from no to yes. Say yes to the present moment and whatever form it takes. The action of surrender leads to vulnerability, which opens and ultimately heals the heart. Heartbreak changes people and devastation is fertile ground for spiritual transformation. Some romantic breakups are good for you. Being alone is how you come into alignment with your higher self. Sometimes heartbreak can be devastating and many people never recover from a difficult breakup. The tragedy of love is not in the separation of lovers, but in the separation of people from love. Many people lament the loss of their ex for the rest of their lives. A person can literally die of a broken heart. Resist any temptation to remain in your sorrow, there is no time for self-pity. It's time to let go of the hurtful memories of your past that are taking up valuable space in your mind and numbing your emotions.

If you are broken-hearted, let your pain remain in the past and live love now. Lift yourself in song, dance, and in celebration of life itself. Remind yourself that you are blessed to have opened your eyes this morning. Make the choice to be seen as a survivor of your loss, not as a victim. Choose to focus on the astounding beauty of life and know that when the sun rises tomorrow, you'll be presented with new opportunities for growth, awakening, romance, and true love. Heartbreak is not the end of the word, it's actually an opening for a new beginning.

EXERCISE #63

Sage Burning (smudging)
The end of a relationship is a calling for change.
Cleanse the energy in your home
by burning sage or jasmine, passing through
and purifying every room.
Ask pure intentions to come and cast out old energy.
Invite new positive energy into your living space.
Chant: "Out with the old, in with the new." (repeat x 3)

HEARTBREAK AND HOPE

May you never lose hope that you will love with all of your heart once again. I pray that you find a love that endures the test of time. I ask that you keep romantic stories of true love burning in your heart. When you stay in alignment with your higher self, you can believe that your dreams will still one day manifest. Everyone ends up with the person they are meant to be with, your destiny is in the hands of your soul. Believe that life is always working out for you and that true love will always find its way to you. I pray that your current heartbreak subsides and that you heal your pain.

COURAGE COMES FROM WITHIN

Courage is a virtue that enables us to withstand our suffering, combat our fears, and offers us hope for a better tomorrow. Courage is a state of mind that allows you to morph into myths and legends. Courage doesn't imply the absence of fear, but the willingness to act despite fear and the determination to surmount it.

Whenever a loving relationship of yours comes to an end, make sure to hold the other aspects of your life together. Focus on your job, physical fitness, mental health, life goals, and dream projects. Keep it together. Find the strength to overcome any obstacles in your life and stay the course. Courage asks much of you, but it is always within your reach. Bravery is not inherited, it's a learned belief. The more you believe in yourself, the more your inner power and courage expands. If you're feeling powerless today, remember that you are capable of making favorable changes to your life. You are a mighty infinite being in a human body capable of mastering your thoughts, emotions, and circumstances.

LOVE AND FAITH, THE POWER OF FAITH CAN SUSTAIN YOU

Never lose faith in your ability to love. You are worthy and deserving of a mutually beneficial loving relationship in your life. We all need love in our lives to grow and thrive. It's time to refocus, move on, and open your heart again for another chance at love. Our capacity to love is ultimately a function of our ability to forgive, forget, and be vulnerable enough to risk our heart being broken. The steady practice of kindness and love gives one new life. Faith happens when you go beyond your mind and it lies just beyond reason. Though your beliefs may run out of steam, your faith will still be there for you. Faith is eternal hope and it's presence is crucial to your survival. Supreme faith is when you believe in something so strong that you are willing to die for it.

If you ever become spiritually lost, one way you can find your way back home is by faith. Belief is the name of the strong tailwind that flows under the wings of the victorious. Step out on faith and never stop believing in yourself. You are never not on your path. You are simply in the process of remembering that you are a masterful creator who can manifest your subconscious dreams. You are on the way towards reaching your greater self. You are always marching forward along the superhighway of higher consciousness.

Faith is taking the first step even
when you can't see the whole staircase.
~ Martin Luther King Jr.

YOU ARE DESERVING OF AN EPIC LOVE

Sometimes deep down in your ego-self, you can feel undeserving of a great love. You may have already begun to doubt whether true love will ever come your way. Many people live their whole life without finding a partner. The question is, was it a lack of effort or a lack of belief? Both questions are valid and carry truth. Many heartbroken people trash their ex and claim that they're better off when that couldn't be further from their truth. Deeper still, some people renounce love in an attempt to heal faster. Never doubt the divine power and presence of love. Know that your setbacks and failures sometimes take center stage and can block your ability to see visual evidence of love in your life. Know that love surrounds you and will always be present in your life. You are destined for a great love which will show up in your life when you are a vibrational match to it. You deserve a soulmate to share your life with. Remember that real work is done in pairs.

THE BRIDGE FROM ROMANCE TO FINDING YOUR SOULMATE

Most romantic relationships break up and never make it to the altar. When the eventual breakup and separation of your ex does occur, great pain ensues. In the aftermath, there is hurt, heartbreak, sadness, and sometimes betrayal, which in some cases can lead to clinical depression. Depression always points to an area of yourself in greatest need of attention, love, and healing. This chaos and breakdown are the exact conditions to bring on your spiritual transformation. A lack of insight into your failed relationship increases the chances of repeating similar mistakes. Take time out for self-analysis. Even though you may experience great pain in separating from your ex, you will also be shown the way to healing and that's where the magic lies. What's being mirrored to you by your ex is most important for you to heal in yourself. This heartbreak and grief cycle actually brings forward your higher soulmate energy to attract your kindred spirit.

RECONNECT WITH YOUR SUPPORT TEAM TO ASSIST IN PROCESSING YOUR EMOTIONS

Most people are very afraid of negative feelings and will do anything possible to avoid them. Remember that your emotions can't hurt you, they are simply an energy that needs to move through you and move on. Unfortunately, some wounds to the heart are so deep that time alone cannot heal them. In that light, breakups are a natural part of our lives, only most people are not very practiced in healing from them and letting go of the ensuing pain. You have to have faith and understanding that things happen for a reason, even though you may not know the reason at this time. A part of the recovery from an emotional breakup is to identify and start leaning on your support group. Reconnect with the friends and family members that took a backseat during your relationship. Find in them what you are missing in your breakup. Your loved ones are here for you to utilize them. Reach out to them to ventilate and cope with your crisis. Sometimes just straight up tell them that you just want to vent and ask them to withhold their advice. Let yourself cry. Remember that you're not crying for the other person, you're crying for yourself. In breakups, you cry tears to release the grief of the lost future that you once saw with this person.

EXERCISE #64
Group Healing Session

**Invite 3-4 friends together who are willing to commit to an evening
of sharing stories, processing emotions, supporting one another,
healing from heartbreak, and self-discovery. Use the elements
of the earth, sun, fire, water, and air to assist your healing.**

Earth: Open the gathering with a grounding exercise to center yourselves.

Sun: The sun rises in the east. Honor the sun and its rising energy by facing east.

Fire: Light candles for ambience. Take turns speaking words of encouragement and truth to one another.

Water: Drink natural and essential water from the earth in dedication to new life.

Air: A simple breathing exercise is a natural beginning and end to the evening.

REVIVE YOURSELF

Solitude and stillness are essential in self-examination and the repair of your spirit. Spend some quality time alone with yourself, journal your recovery, and make mental notes of your progress. Reset and restate your goals for the future. Be patient with yourself, healing doesn't happen overnight, it takes time to recover. I know that it hurts, but keep in mind that you are not broken, rather you've been cracked open to feel your deepest feelings. From your profound hurt, you can create a new connection with yourself and others that wasn't possible before. In time, I hope you realize that your breakup was really a blessing in disguise.

HEARTBREAK AND REBUILDING YOUR LIFE

Schedule an experience that you've never had before. Be adventurous and daring in your return from heartbreak. It's also the best time to figure out who you are and what you truly want out of life. Set ambitious new goals for the next phase of your journey. Is there something out there that you always wanted to do or be? Focus on your goals and start chasing your dreams. If you always wanted to travel and live in a foreign country, but you couldn't because you were in a committed relationship, now is the perfect opportunity to do so. You are no longer tethered by anyone, you are free to fly away. Repair of your spirit is not only possible, it's your new reality. Make it your mission to recover, move forward, and never look back.

CHAPTER 38

NARCISSISTIC PERSONALITY DISORDER TRAUMA BONDS AND HOW TO BREAK THEM

NARCISSISTIC PERSONALITY DISORDER (NPD)

A healthy ego is a valuable asset. However, when an ego fails to control itself and goes into the depths of self-absorption, it enters into the world of narcissism. According to The Mayo Clinic, narcissism is defined as: "A mental condition in which people have an inflated sense of their own importance, a need for excessive attention and admiration, troubled relationships, and a lack of empathy for others." A narcissists' (narc) primary focus is on themselves, thus there is a lack of compassion and concern for the welfare of others. It is expected that all humans have mercy for one another, but alas, a typical narc lacks compassion for others and only cares about themselves. The attachment system of a narcissist is highly dysfunctional, thus they don't usually form healthy bonds in their relationships. This is because narcs have an exaggerated sense of self, hence they only have a one-way flow. Most narcissists have big and bold personalities, they know how to charm you, distract you, lie to you, and exploit you. Be forewarned, a narc can appear to be seamlessly coexisting with you on loving and equal terms at the beginning of a relationship, but they usually fail to live up to your early expectations. A narcissist's sense of entitlement and disregard for other people spoils the harvest of their lives and further erodes the trust inside their relationships. Narcissists are energy vampires, they prey on the energy of others to deal with their own internal emptiness. Narcs thrive by upsetting people and robbing them of their energy. The key to surviving a relationship with a narcissist is to understand their "taker" energy-dynamic and to protect yourself from allowing them to "steal" your energy and self-worth.

Once a person with a permeable energy system bonds with a narcissist, it's hard to break it off. Narcs go through cycles of abusing and rewarding their romantic partners which confuses their victims even further. This on/off pattern of abuse followed by rewards is why it's so difficult for victims to leave. This is how abuse victims are weakened and become emotionally dependent on their partners. A narc will reward your good behavior, but they will become abusive towards you when you disobey. On any given day, a narcissist may tell you how amazing you are and how much they treasure you in their life. They might even do random things that they don't usually do; for instance, they might buy you gifts, be incredibly loving, or do chores that they've never done before. This behavior is known as "love bombing," which is essentially a manipulative tool to draw you closer, so that you will stay with them. After being love bombed, you may end up feeling a sense of relief, hope, and temporary happiness. Then suddenly, the narcissist sociopath will tell you that you are worthless, stupid, and can't get anything right, which makes you feel betrayed, neglected, and disrespected. In this way, they take control of your emotional state of being. Love bombing, devaluing, and discarding is the typical pattern of behavior of a narcissist.

Shielding is a basic skill I recommend to prevent empathic overload. Shielding is a quick way to protect yourself. You can rely on it to block out toxic energy while still allowing for the free flow of parties' positive energies. Use your virtual energy shield at a crowded airport, at a party if you're talking to an energy vampire, or in a doctors packed waiting room. Shielding puts you in a safe bubble where you won't be drained.
~ Judith Orloff, M.D.

A hyper-activated attachment system is the main reason that you may find yourself in a toxic relationship with a narcissist. You can address your attachment issues and your role as "the pleaser," but it is advisable that you do so with the help of a trained trauma therapist. You run the risk of shrinking your persona if you don't act with your own self-interest in mind. Being a people pleaser makes you a target for a lot of unwarranted abuse and manipulation from someone who takes your kindness for weakness, so they attempt to exploit you. If you recognize that you've been dealing with a pathological narcissist and you evaluate your mistakes and process your emotional trauma, you can get out of it. No doubt you've fought many battles and come a long way, you are a trauma survivor. You deserve high praise for your long struggle to get free. Now that you are aware of the traits of NPD, you can properly process your past, move forward, and begin to plan your optimistic future.

Never argue with anyone who
believes their own lies.
~ Buddha

Symptoms of Narcissistic Personality Disorder

1. Has a grandiose sense of self-importance and exaggerates their talents and achievements. They tend to be fake and are expert liars.
2. Dreams of unlimited power, success, brilliance, beauty, or ideal love. They have a preoccupation with fantasies of unlimited success.
3. Lacks empathy for the feelings and needs of others. They only do what's in their own personal interest. They have little emotional memory and can't see beyond the moment they are in.
4. A need for excessive admiration and a sense of entitlement to special treatment. They have difficulty tolerating criticism or admitting defeat.
5. Believes that they are special and unique and can only be understood by, or should only associate with other special or high-status people.
6. Expects favorable or special treatment and compliance with their wishes.
7. Exploits and takes advantage of others to achieve their personal ends.
8. Envious of others and they also hold the belief that they are envied by others.
9. An attitude of arrogance is common.
10. They purposely bond to you by inflicting pain onto you, so that they can dominate you and gain control over your body and mind.

TRAUMA BONDS

A trauma bond is, "A strong emotional attachment between an abused person and his or her abuser, formed as a result of the cycle of violence." When humans have close contact over a prolonged period of time, they start to bond. Sadly, many people unknowingly bond to an abuser. They commonly justify staying and putting up with the abuse because of the fear of losing them. Trauma bonding is the unhealthy emotional attachment or connection that a victim of abuse has for their abuser. Trauma bonds are hard to break free of, they are a vicious cycle which are capable of causing serious psychological damage. Trauma bonding is one of the reasons people continue to stay in abusive relationships, it's being loyal to a person who is self-centered and exploitative. It's a subconscious survival strategy and a way of coping with prolonged, severe, and repetitive abuse. In trauma bonding, the attachment bond is so strong that it stops the victim from seeing the abuse, confusing it for love. This "toxic-love" is quite similar to *Stockholm's Syndrome* where a hostage bonds with their violent captor during captivity.

If you experienced abuse in childhood, the way you seek love can become a familiar pattern, being drawn to abusive partners in ways that feel familiar to you. This traumatic attachment bond allows you to become hooked on the toxic relationship by finding ways to get the love you long for. The bond is so strong that you fear losing it and you will try hard to fix your partner. You normalize attracting abusive partners with the wish to be good enough for them, so that you can get the love and approval you're looking for and avoid abandonment. While a trauma bond can be very emotionally and spiritually painful, try to remember that you have the control to change it if you want to. The more you understand about how your abuser got you into this, the easier it will be to get out.

BREAKING A TRAUMA BOND

End your denial about the abuse you are suffering. First recognize it's abuse, not love. Your task is to let go of the fantasy that you are being loved. Take a deep-dive look into yourself. Examine your past, present, and future visions for yourself. Your self-analysis will help you to understand how it happened. It's likely that you will end up very angry at them for doing this to you and betraying your trust, but also angry at yourself for ignoring so many signs and letting it go on for so long. Stop blaming yourself for the abuse you are suffering. Forgive yourself for what you may perceive as your mistakes. You will eventually gain clarity and see how he or she did it, methodically by a thousand cuts. Trauma bonding means that it will never feel right to leave. Separate facts from feelings. Make a list of all the times you were lied to and faked out. Once you recognize their deceptive patterns and sociopathic behavior, you can use your rational mind to finally leave and stay away for good, because it's the right thing to do for you and your well-being. Lastly, every moment of weakness, every time you feel like reaching out to them, similar to an addict experiencing a relapse, remember that you are the lucky one who dodged a bullet. Save yourself further pain and suffering in the future by remembering to put yourself first.

Traumatic bonding can have a terrible effect on not only yourself but also on other relationships you have with family and friends. By understanding what trauma bonding is, who is most at risk of doing it, and what the common signs are, you will learn to recognize any red flags, narcissistic traits, and ways to prevent selecting future abusive partners. If you think you are currently experiencing trauma bonding, know that it's a complex issue. For this reason, it's important to seek immediate help so you can move forward swiftly and safely. When we meet and fall into the gravitational pull of a narcissist, we are entering a significant life lesson that involves learning how to create boundaries, self-respect, and resilience. Through trial and error (and a lot of pain), our connection with narcissists teaches us the necessary lessons we need to become mature empaths.
~ *Mateo Sol*

EXERCISE #65
Creating a Freedom Mindset

1. Think about all of the reasons that you don't want to be trauma bonded with your ex. Imagine how you would feel, how your life would look, and what would be different for you if you were single and free.
2. Write your abuser's negative traits and abusive behaviors on index cards. Once you can see them in black and white, it will finally sink into your subconscious. Use the cards and read them every time you have the urge to contact them or go back.
3. Educate yourself on NPD, trauma bonding, and love bombing, so that this never happens to you again.

4. Pinpoint the red flags that you'd like to be aware of before choosing a future partner.

5. Believe that you deserve better. You are capable of experiencing a real love.

Relationship with a narcissist in a nutshell: You will go from being the perfect love of their life to nothing you do is ever good enough. You will give everything and they will take it all and give you less and less in return. You will end up depleted, emotionally, mentally, spiritually, and probably financially, and then get blamed for it.
~ Bree Bonchay

Dr. Clayton's Twelve Step Recovery Plan For Healing Trauma Bonds

You were intentionally isolated from your friends and family. You received little to no appreciation or praise. You were constantly undermined. You endured gaslighting. Your self-confidence was systematically eroded. It's time to heal.

- The First Challenge: Getting over them. You have to be strong enough to start doing things by yourself. At first you may feel that you aren't strong enough to be alone, that's normal. Your number one priority is to protect yourself from any further abuse. Go "no contact." Block their phone number and their social media.

- The Second Challenge: Identify and heal your inner wounds. Be kind and compassionate toward yourself. You cannot heal without having a compassionate look at yourself and by embracing constructive inner dialogue.

- The Third Challenge: Come to terms with the fact that you somehow managed to lose yourself in the process. Find yourself again by redefining and rebuilding yourself. Face up to the reality of having to pick up the shattered pieces of your broken heart and begin to put yourself back together again.

- **The Fourth Challenge:** Completely let go of the dreams that you might have had about the future with your ex. Sadly, these dreams were all unfeasible fantasies. Understand that you were lied to and abused.

- **The Fifth Challenge:** Free yourself of as many stressors as possible. Frequently, this means downsizing and possibly even moving away from your old neighborhood completely.

- **The Sixth Challenge:** Set personal goals regarding your physical health. Work on your appearance to be the best physical embodiment of yourself, this alone can boost your self-esteem dramatically. Get plenty of exercise, ideally in fresh air.

- **The Seventh Challenge:** Replace your hate with pity because even though they may have come close to destroying your life, you got away from them. On the other hand, they are stuck with their enormous toxic ego that will follow them for the rest of their lives.

- **The Eighth Challenge:** Work on your mindset towards your ex. Hate is the incorrect mindset. Not only does plotting revenge take up precious mental bandwidth, but narcissists derive energy from the attention behind anything you do. Your reactions are the very fuel and motivation for their misbehavior.

- **The Ninth Challenge:** Take some time out to analyze and better understand why you are trauma bonded. What was this relationship actually about? How did you end up bonded to this person? What lesson did you learn from the time you spent with them?

- **The Tenth Challenge:** Work through the loss of unmet love and get therapy to overcome your feelings of diminished self-worth. You literally have to take yourself through deprogramming to get yourself healed. Get professional counseling.

- **The Eleventh Challenge:** Make it a priority to build healthy new relationships. Make new friends. Hang out with a different crew of people who are fun to be around. Seek friendships with those that lift you up and make you feel good. Get out from under your "pain cycle" and get going independently. That's the only way to break free.

- **The Twelfth Challenge: Don't give up. Don't rush your healing. Hold on to the belief that you will get over your pain in due time. Along the way, you will learn some amazing life lessons, discover a lot about yourself, and live out your destiny. In the end, you will emerge stronger and wiser than ever before.**

CHAPTER 39

ROMANTIC RELATIONSHIPS, SPIRITUAL PARTNERSHIPS, AND UNCONDITIONAL LOVE

ROMANTIC LOVE AND SEXUAL RELATIONSHIPS

R omantic love is the story of how you need another person to complete you. The beginning of most romantic relationships starts with a "honeymoon phase" of pure bliss. Couples often describe feeling better about themselves than ever before. They feel more confident, happier, livelier, sexier, and have a more optimistic sense of self. This period is largely adrenaline-based and is not long-lasting. The honeymoon period is known for very few arguments or conflicts because at the start, each person puts their best foot forward. You could say that both parties temporarily reside as their false selves. The honeymoon phase of the relationship ends once couples begin to let their guards down. Soon, they start to see a more realistic version of their partner and see each other as they really are. Eventually, people's preferences, strange beliefs, and prejudices leak out. Discovering boundaries are growing pains that all new couples experience. Each person has to find their tolerance levels for their partner's limitations and curious habits. True selves cannot be hidden for long. Many couples don't survive the challenges of everyday domestic life. Particularly at this time, the COVID-19 pandemic has placed additional stress on live-in couples. In the most unnatural way, the "work from home" paradigm places couples face-to-face in close confinement, forced to co-exist for much longer periods of time than ever before.

Statistically, the majority of unions end in their first year of existence. The truth is that most relationships that are centered on sex and romance don't endure the test of time. When the curtains rise, reality emerges and the illusion begins to fall apart. This is when relationships become unsteady and vulnerable to failure. Romantic relationships initially serve to distract people from their emotional pain, but the soul knows what it wants and needs. Sexual hookups only serve our most superficial needs. Most of the time what is highly desired is not what's needed or fulfilling in the long term. In comparison, spiritual unions are unconditional and unlimited in potential. No one can come between you and your soulmate. Every relationship in your life can be seen as a mirror for your current level of consciousness. The deeper you go inside with someone, the more beauty and truth you will experience.

TRUST

One of the most important aspects of any relationship is trust, an unwritten contract based on safety, reliability, and love. Trust evolves over time and is proven by deeds, not words. Trust is achieved through lasting honesty and sincerity, it takes years to build and only seconds to break. When trust is present in a relationship, it allows both participants the personal freedom to expand and grow as individuals and also as a couple. To love is not possessing the other person or trying to consume them. To love is to offer one another an open heart and a tonic for their suffering. This extended capacity is what we must learn in order to create and cultivate a deeper love for ourselves and for our partners.

INTIMACY

People think that intimacy is about sex, but that's not true. Many dating relationships end soon after their first sexual encounter. Having sex feels great, but it doesn't reveal your true worth to someone. The best way to create intimacy is to be open and vulnerable. Romance is mainly based on fantasy. By gaining intimacy with someone, you start to see more of the real person and less of your idealized projection. Real intimacy is about sharing your heart and soul with someone, facing your fears, speaking your truth, and shedding your inhibitions in the absence of judgment. Revealing your true self is what empowers you from your core. When you share your deepest feelings, you truly allow someone to see all of you, not just your body-mind.

People think that intimacy is about sex. But intimacy is about truth.
When you realize you can tell someone your truth,
when you can show yourself to them, when you stand in front of them bare
and their response is, "You are safe with me"— that's intimacy.
~ Taylor Reid

Physical and emotional intimacy stimulates the production of the neurohormones vasopressin and oxytocin, which both act to increase your feelings of trust and bonding. The neurotransmitters dopamine, norepinephrine, and serotonin bind to receptors in the brain that bring excitement and pleasure, while adrenaline gets us pumped. Intimacy stimulates our brain's pleasure center which makes us feel vibrant, energetic, and alive.

The highest form of intimacy is honesty, the enemy of intimacy is secrecy. When you fail to communicate your true feelings and intentions, your relationships will lack trust. The consequences of being dishonest is that you will find yourself in and out of meaningless sexual "hook ups." The potential harm of casual sex are unintended consequences like dettachment, accidental pregnancies, and the risk of contracting sexual transmitted diseases. Fear not, deep intimacy is on your evolutionary path, trust your higher self. We are all here to connect and grow.

HARMONY

There are three kinds of intimacy: physical, emotional, and spiritual. When a relationship has all three elements, it becomes harmonious. Harmony is both nourishing and healing to all souls. As individuals, it's natural to desire harmony with someone. One of the main reasons why people feel like they are in a one-sided relationship is that they don't feel appreciated. When you express what you appreciate most about your partner, you make them feel valued and cared for. The stronger the bond with your partner the more harmony you create. Common elements of successful relationships are cooperation, teamwork, and shared goals. This fusion is similar to how a number of different musical notes are blended into a beautiful chord. A blessed union can be described as two people blending their signature subconscious beliefs into one beautiful harmonic frequency. Let nothing hinder the harmony of the whole. Harmony's beautiful vibration stimulates people to become better human beings and more joyful spirits. Let harmony and love reign supreme.

I believe in the immeasurable power of love— that true love can endure any circumstance and reach across any distance.
~ Steve Maraboli

COMMITMENT

For absolute healthy love to flow and be a healing experience, there must be commitment. Too many couples give up too soon on their relationships when things begin to get hard. The close proximity of partnership often triggers you to react to one another. Each time you are triggered, it presents an opportunity to respond with either love or fear. By choosing love over and over again, you win at life. You grow as a couple by choosing higher awareness over low-level unconscious behaviors and arguments. Learn to support each other's choices. Admit to your mistakes and be unafraid to apologize when you are wrong. Start to recognize your frightened personality when it arises and take time to comfort it. Spiritual love emanates from your heart and soul. When you open the door to your spiritual heart, it transforms your personal interpretation of love into impersonal love, the love of all beings.

A genuine relationship is one that is not dominated by the ego with its image-making and self-seeking. In a genuine relationship, there is an outflow of open, alert attention towards the other person in which there is no wanting whatsoever. That alert attention is Presence. It is the prerequisite for any authentic relationship.
~ Eckart Tolle

EXERCISE #66
Make A Couples List of Important Shared Values

This exercise gives you and your partner a chance to talk about where your romance is headed and what common values, beliefs, and goals you share. You can even make a date night out of it. Sit down with your partner and come up with an individual list of 10-15 of the most important areas that you value in a successful relationship.

Here are some examples of areas that you may want to address:

1. Communication
2. Spirituality
3. Fun Activities and Games
4. Honesty, Truth, Support, and Trust
5. Creativity and Shared Projects
6. Passion, Sensuality, and Sexuality
7. Love Building
8. Family Planning/Children
9. Individual Life Goals
10. Wealth Planning and Financial Freedom
11. Health Goals, Exercise, and Weight Loss
12. Charity and Service
13. Travel
14. Your 3 Year Plan As A Couple

Once you have both come up with your individual
lists, have a discussion and share
what you came up with. Discuss each item on
your list and why it's important to you.
Make sure to listen to your partner and be supportive of their ideas
as if they were yours. The goal of this exercise is a combination of
honesty, trust building, couples therapy, and shared vision building.

DON'T SETTLE FOR LESS THAN TRUE LOVE

Most people settle for a love far less than what they deserve. Some romantic breakups are good for you. Indeed, it's truly better to be alone than with the wrong person, even if being with that person made you feel as comfortable as an old pair of shoes. Being alone has many benefits, the best part of being alone is that you have more moments of solitude and opportunity to explore your own spirituality. It is through moments of solitude and stillness, that you discover your divine truth.

> *Use "I statements" instead of using "you statements,"*
> *The basic idea is that saying, "I feel*
> *hurt when you say that" is much less aggressive and much*
> *more likely to lead to productive dialogue than saying, "You*
> *are such a jerk for saying that," or, "It's your fault."*
> *Talk to your partner using requests instead of*
> *lashing out at them and attacking their character.*
> *Couples should complain instead of criticize.*
> *~ Marshall Rosenberg*

THE QUEST FOR UNCONDITIONAL LOVE THE DIFFERENCE BETWEEN ATTACHMENT AND LOVE

Some couples' idea of love is to remain bound to one another permanently, even in the absence of love. If your love ever becomes a sad story of events happening to you instead of for you, it's a warning to take notice and action. Relationships with weak spiritual bonds are vulnerable to feelings of unhappiness, insecurity, and codependency. Sadly, some people feel trapped by their circumstances, yet they remain attached to their partner for an entire lifetime without ever truly loving them. Everyone is deserving of a deeply loving relationship. If you haven't found your soulmate yet, it's not too late. There is still time for you to discover real love. The road to love is paved by acts of kindness, gratitude, respect, truth, and peace. Real love is authentic, honest, liberating, and thrives in a spiritual partnership.

Love is always a choice. Two people truly love each other only when they are quite capable of living without each other, but choose to live with each other. The highest level of love is unconditional love, it's the practice of loving another without the expectation of receiving anything in return. Unconditional love is synonymous with unconditional acceptance. It's love with no strings attached, a love that persists regardless of what the other person does. The kind of love that you can see someone at their worst, yet still believe there's something inside them that's worth all the trouble. It's something that many people talk about, but few come away with. It's possible that you can love someone unconditionally and still have expectations for them. The difference is, if your expectations aren't met, your love won't diminish. The highest level of love is the type of love that transforms the receiver and makes them feel and believe that they can and will, change the world.

The potential for unconditional love exists in us all, but it's buried deep inside. The first time that you feel unconditional love as an adult, it will melt you and you'll never see or define love the same, it is truly an opening of the heart. Spiritually, we are transported from our ego level to our soul level by unconditional love. When your ego dissolves, your heart arrives and catches you. This is the path of surrender, out of a mind-based identity and into a heart-based identity. Once you come to this point in your journey, you will begin to emanate love and be able to teach those around you to do the same. Know that your spiritual relationship will need to be cared for and attended to. Nothing in life is promised, everything is earned. Successful spiritual partnerships are constantly evolving and growing. Stagnation in any relationship is a precursor to its death. Spiritual relationships are ones that move along with the times and value the importance of imagination, spontaneity, and romance. If you sprinkle love on your relationship everyday, it's sure to blossom into a reflection of your loving heart.

EXERCISE #67
Eleven Sacred Breaths And Soul Gazing

This close breathing exercise will put you and your partner into an intimate, timeless, and connected space. Practice it whenever you feel the need to come together, bond, and refocus on one another.

- **To begin the session, lie down on your side facing your partner or sit upright and face your partner.**
- **Gently put your foreheads together.**
- **Make sure that your chins are tilted downward so you're not bumping noses.**

- Breathe in and out together. Take eleven slow, even, deep breaths in sync with your partner.
- Connected breathing is spiritual, no words are required.
- Place your palm on your partner's heart center and have them place their palm over yours.
- Surrender to the intimate experience of appreciating both your own and your partner's heartbeat.
- Gaze into each other's eyes, but allow yourself to blink. One suggestion is to only look at their left eye. I believe both methods work equally.
- As you stare softly into each other's eyes without looking away, each of your souls is revealed to the other.
- Take a moment to fully appreciate the amazing person you've chosen to be with.
- Close this connection exercise with a kiss and a compliment.

SPIRITUAL PARTNERSHIPS

Spiritual partnerships are not a struggle for power but a surrender to love and togetherness. Author Gary Zukov defines spiritual partnership as, "a relationship between two equals for the purpose of mutual spiritual growth." Zukov adds that spiritual partnerships are vehicles that multi-sensory individuals use to create authentic power and support one another in realizing their authentic power. Spiritual relationships have authentic substance and depth that fuels the development of higher consciousness. They trust one another enough to explore the deeper levels of love together. Physical relationships only skim the surface of the heart. Physicality does not satisfy the appetite of the soul. These old style relationships have outlived their usefulness. The stress of these uncertain times calls for a new type of partnership, one with teamwork, higher accountability, quality emotional support, and immeasurable depth.

Instead of blaming one another for painful experiences, such as anger,
sadness, and feelings of inadequacy, spiritual partners see one another
as colleagues and spiritual growth partners, who
activate frightened and loving parts
of one another's personalities so that each can heal the frightened
parts of his or her own personality and cultivate the loving parts.
~ Gary Zukov

Spiritual partners recognize the importance of stating their intentions and practicing deliberate manifestation. Spiritual partnerships magnetically attract other couples that value and build love the same way. Kindred spirits understand how to use the law of attraction to obtain more of what they want and less of what they don't want. Spiritual partners don't threaten, deride, or abuse one another. Spiritual partnerships are resilient in the long run and provide strong emotional shelter to survive a crisis and to facilitate growth and recovery. True lovers support each other and embody the principles of kindness, compassion, and empathy as they explore the source of their pain. They make sure they end each day by checking in on each other's feelings. A spiritual partner is indeed an asset. Spiritual evolution is as important to us as sunlight is to a flower.

Resilient trees can weather a violent storm because their roots are deep and strong. The roots of a lasting relationship are: mindfulness, deep listening, loving speech, and a strong surrounding community of family and friends to support you both. To have a shot at a spiritual love, it helps to feel already complete in yourself, not looking for or needing someone else to complete you. Spiritual love is like the sun shining in its own light, accompanied by the gift of brightening each other's worlds.

Top 11 Keys to a Successful Relationship

1. **Effective Communication:** Idea sharing, intimate conversations, compliments, sharing personal feelings, goal sharing, honesty, constructive disagreement, and rapid conflict resolution.
2. **Positive Attitude:** Maintain an attitude of caring, respect, awareness, honesty, empathy, and commitment.

3. Connection: Togetherness, non-physical interaction, spending time together, meaningful eye contact, sharing tasks and activities, imagination, spontaneity, and adventure.

4. Honesty, Trust, and Commitment: Relationships prosper when people feel safe and secure, insecurity is shaky ground. Integrity opens the door to meaningful intimacy. First you have to discover what is really true for you. A dishonest "yes" answer is a "no" and is disrespectful to yourself.

5. Vulnerability: People connect with each other at the heart level through vulnerability. You can't get someone to open up to you if you're not willing to be vulnerable yourself.

6. Power Sharing: Spiritual partners share and promote equal power. Focus on creating a life of purpose and harmony together.

7. Nesting: Cohabitation, building a life together. Survival strategies for living together include effective communication, super sweet compliments, and loving collaborations.

8. Affection: Romance, hand-holding, touching, hugging, kissing, loving, and sexual intimacy.

9. Spirituality: Mindfulness, meditation, faith, ceremonies, family time, family meetings, and prayer.

10. Bonding: Get to know your partner's true self. People often seek superficial relationships to avoid going inward. Be different. Seek a soul-to-soul connection and don't settle for anything less.

11. Love over fear: Lasting life partners support one another in choosing love-based thoughts over fear-based thoughts.

CHAPTER 40

OPENING YOUR SACRED HEART: HEART INTELLIGENCE AND THE PRACTICE OF LOVE

THE MIND AND THE HEART

T he brain and heart both generate electromagnetic fields which transmit and transform physiologic bits of thought energy into emotions and physical events. An example of this mind-body connection is when a person blushes from embarrassment, the heart can indeed drive emotions. The heart is connected to our source of divine intelligence. Many sages have said, "The heart is an access point to the wisdom of our soul," which is neither bound by the limits of space nor time.

When we harmonize the heart and the brain,
that is the doorway to spontaneous intuition.
~ Gregg Braden

The heart communicates with the brain in ways that greatly affect how you perceive and react to the world around you. In 1991, pioneer neuro-cardiologist Dr. J. Andrew introduced the term "heart brain." He found that the heart possesses its own complex intrinsic nervous system that acts as a brain and functions independently from your mind. Indeed, heart intelligence precedes brain intelligence. It's a well-known fact that the heart of an unborn fetus starts beating before its brain has been formed. At the physical level, the heart not only possesses an innate intelligence, it's also involved in how we think, feel, and respond to the world.

Even if you lived to be one hundred years old, it's really a very short time.
So why not spend it on undergoing this process of evolution of
opening your mind and heart, connecting with your true nature— rather than
getting better and better at fixing, grasping, freezing, and closing down?
~ Pena Chodron

OPEN YOUR HEART

The heart is the human organ that feels your emotions. Open your heart each day a little bit more by making more meaningful connections with those you encounter. In order to achieve a pure heart, the first step is to cleanse and purify your mind. An open heart is not a possibility without an open mind. Detox your mind with meditation and positive thinking. Stay out of judgement and practice being in alignment with your heart. You are here to love and be loved. Feel your way into joy and happiness. When in doubt, remember to follow your intuition. Try to forgive, forget, and let go of the past. Stay in the dimension of the Now. Your attachments and inner resistance are keeping you from your personal freedom. Attempt to bring peace and a calm presence to any difficult situation that you are called to face. Where compassion lives, fear dissolves and pure love resides. Approach your spiritual journey with the intention of reaching your sacred heart. May you deliver to the world all the love that you hold inside.

EXERCISE #68
The Three Minute Heart Meditation by Dr. Judith Orloff

**"Close your eyes. Take a few deep breaths and
relax. Then place your palm over your
heart chakra in the middle of your chest. Focus
on a beautiful image that you love such as
a sunset, a rose, the ocean, or a child's face. Feel the love building
in your heart and body. Let this loving feeling soothe you. Toxic
energy leaves your body as you become purified with love. For just
three minutes, meditate on the loving kindness in your heart and
feel that energy clear away any and all negativity.**

*The truth of this path of the heart is that there is no path.
There is only the heart and the love that consumes the lover
who becomes the beloved. Love is a state of being,
not a trip from here to there.*
~ Ram Dass

HEART AND INTUITION

Most people live their whole lives only seeing and believing in something outside of themselves. Your sacred heart is your access point for intuitive guidance. Intuition is a heightened, refined sense outside of our five senses. Intuition is an internal signal that is always flowing, but we seldom embrace. Intuition is not easily recognized because it's difficult to access unless we are in touch with who we are on the inside. Accessing your intuition is not a quick trick, you have to practice opening and connecting with your heart center in order to grow it. Intuition is a process that gives us the ability to know something innately without analytic reasoning, thus bridging the gap between the conscious and subconscious part of our minds. It is also the space between human instinct and reason. The heart is really our superior brain. If you continue to look inside your sacred heart, you will find where your power of intuition lies and you can learn how to use it.

The intuitive mind is a sacred gift and the rational mind is a faithful servant.
We have created a society that honors the servant and has forgotten the gift.
~ Albert Einstein

EXERCISE #69
Heart Breathing

- **Focus your attention on the area of your heart.**
- **Put your right hand over your heart.**
- **State strong affirmations of love with your hand placed over your heart.**
- **Close your eyes and imagine your breath flowing in and out of your heart.**
- **Take three deep breaths, try to breathe a little slower and deeper than usual.**
- **Activate and sustain a restorative feeling in your inner being such as: gratitude, appreciation, kindness, compassion, or love.**

- For enhanced results, rose quartz crystal or pink tourmaline may be used in your heart healing meditation. Simply place and hold the energetic stone firmly in the palm of your free hand.
- When you begin to consciously control where your attention and energy flows, you become a master of your life.
- Radiate and transmit your renewed energy to yourself and onto others.

THE ANATOMY OF A PURE HEART

A "pure heart" or "sacred heart" are terms which describe our heart center— a subtle center of emotional and energetic sensitivity, relational intimacy, profound inner-knowing, and unconditional love. When a person consciously "centers" or focuses on their heart, the heart begins to run as their superior brain. You "hear" what you've been programmed to "hear." If fear, greed, or hate resides in you, then your heart will access negativity. If positivity resides in your heart, it will attune to love. Love is variously cultivated, given, received, and experienced through your mind, body, heart and soul. Many sages believe that the heart is the center of love and empathy. In fact, scientific studies have proven that empathy manifests in the heart's electromagnetic field in amounts greater than anywhere else in the body.

You are precisely as big as what you love
and precisely as small as what you allow to annoy you.
~ Robert Anton Wilson

THE HEART CHAKRA

As humans, we have an ionized energy field flowing in, out, and around our physical bodies connected by a network of vital power points called chakras. At the center of your chest lies your heart chakra, this energy center is all about your capacity to give and receive. It's about love, generosity, and being able to share your loving experiences. Author Kyle Gray says, "The heart chakra is the space within you that represents kindness and altruism. It's the part of you that wants to share with those who are in need." Whenever you give graciously, your heart chakra opens up and you shine brightly for all to see. Conversely, your heart chakra can become drained when you've given away too much. Whenever your energy is drained, you'll begin to experience lower level emotions like fatigue, frustration, and anger. That's because your stored energy has been depleted and you have no further capacity to give anymore. In order to achieve and maintain energetic balance in your life, it's important to learn how to become a better receiver. Learn to accept and channel positive energy and assistance from others when offered. Whenever you feel depleted, try to intake more positive vibrations. Avoid negative thinking and negative people. Your intake of energy should always be more than your outflow. Keep yourself in company with good friends, smile and laugh more, listen to your favorite music, and read inspiring books. Keep a positive attitude in relation to any problems present in your life. Take care of your body-mind, it's the only one you have. Remember to exercise daily, eat healthy, and drink plenty of water. These simple actions can revive you and keep you in a high frequency energy state.

The heart chakra is also your enlightenment chakra. Are you ready for a whole new definition of love? The opening of your sacred heart saturates all of your experiences with love. In time, you will become a divine instrument that touches everyone. That's when you'll truly blossom from the inside-out.

I am willing to receive. I recognize that
I am deserving of health, love, and support.
It feels good to give, and it feels great to receive.
Today I welcome the energy of balance into my life.
My heart is open to receive.
~ Kyle Gray

HOW TO RELIEVE BLOCKED CHAKRAS

First, you need to ask yourself, "What is blocking me?" Blocked chakras come from blocked emotions and false beliefs stemming from painful experiences in your life. You have to release all of your negative emotions and any false beliefs that you've accumulated and stored. Meditate, feel, and observe deep within your soul. Address what you may be doing today that isn't serving you, even if it's something you've been holding onto since your childhood. Get ready to face it and be prepared to release it as well. Beware of what information you take in from other people. You are responsible for your energetic amplitude at all times, there is no point in the day when you are not responsible for your mood or your vibration.

*Love needs an entry point. If our emotional body
is all blocked up with material, there's no way in.
The more we empty the vessel before
it comes, the more space love has to flourish.
Healing our hearts, gives love a place to land.*
~ Jeff Brown

YOUR HEALING ALLOWS HAPPINESS TO BLOOM INSIDE YOUR HEART

Your feelings are a key aspect to unlocking your heart intelligence. When you have an emotion within your heart, that emotion sends a signal to your brain. The quality of that signal determines what your brain does in response to that emotion. Healing your suffering brings light to your negativity and opens an opportunity to address it. Healing creates expansion of your inner space and allows love to bloom inside of your heart. At the deeper levels of your spiritual journey, you will experience your heart as the pure heart—full of love, compassion, joy, and all of the qualities of your divine essence.

SACRED HEART HEALING

The heart has long been known as the center of the body, as well as the home of the soul. The convergence of your psychological healing and spiritual awakening happens most clearly and powerfully in the depths of your heart. It's been said that what you see in the world is what you carry in your heart. The way you awaken your sacred heart energy is by healing the source of your unworthiness within. Indeed, suffering is what you heal in order to shift your unworthiness to worthiness. Your full healing takes place once you are finally fully loving yourself and also after you've accepted and forgiven yourself for your past transgressions. All is forgiven in the realm of your sacred heart. You were born to experience love at the highest level. You must awaken your sacred heart energy to complete your healing. Do not take love lightly. Love asks that we open ourselves to its beautiful and profound mystery and at the same time, to its potential loss. Get in and stay in alignment with love. The space between you and that alignment is the distance from where you are standing to your sacred heart.

When you reside in your sacred heart, you are in alignment with the universe and God. Shifting your awareness to your heart space opens the door to the powers of healing and pure presence. It is within your sacred heart that the treasures of life can be found. The further you get away from your sacred heart, the deeper you fall under the spell of your mind. If you get trapped in the realm of your ego-mind you can spend your whole life jumping from thought to thought, tree to tree, and idea to idea, without ever experiencing the freedom and power to create out of love.

EXERCISE #70
The Heart Ceremony

Press your heart against your partner's heart.
Feel the beat of their heart against your chest.
Synchronize your breathing with theirs.
Close your eyes and press them into your very being.
Imagine your heart melting into theirs.
In your mind's eye, see the convergence of two hearts into one.
A heart bond is like superglue, once bonded, you can't pull apart from it.
Tell your partner: "I love you forevermore."
Now that you share one heart and one love, let nothing ever divide you.

YOUR DIVINE GIFT IS LOCKED INSIDE YOUR SACRED HEART

What separates you from others is your divine gift. You came into this world with a unique purpose locked inside your sacred heart. Many people get lost in the world and struggle to find their direction. In order to discover your divine gift, look for a need that exists in the world and fill it. Find the one thing inside of you that you can do better than most. Believe in yourself and then set out to do it. The higher your purpose, the higher your elevation and reward.

YOUR ALIGNMENT WITH LOVE

Your number one concern in your life should be your relationship with love. Does love have a strong presence in your life? Are you aiming for more love in your life? Are you cultivating love? Are you showing love to others? You learn to love deeper by loving everyone. You raise your consciousness by practicing kindness and unconditional love. Love without consciousness is merely possession.

Love is misunderstood to be an emotion,
but is actually an awareness; a way of being in the world
and a way of seeing oneself and others.
~ David Hawkins

THE LANGUAGE OF LIFE IS LOVE

All love starts with self-love, the art of loving yourself. Love is here to be learned, practiced, and lived, until there is no separation between unconditional love and yourself. Love will sustain you over time. Live your life from the inside-out and love yourself into forever. If you are lost and don't know what to do, start with a single loving thought about yourself and build on it. Place one loving idea on top of another. It's similar to building a house, the most important thing is a strong foundation and a sound frame. Let love occupy the ground floor in your home, your relationship, and in your life.

Love is a vibrant, ever-changing, joyful state of being. You find love by simply believing in its existence. Love never stands still. Love is an action word, always moving forward like beautiful poetry in motion. Love evolves you. Real love is inspiring, liberating, and stimulates you to bloom. Love is capable of carrying you through your toughest times and supporting you at the depths of your despair. Love allows you to sail on the roughest seas and skate on the thinnest ice. Lean in on love and have the courage to stand by love. Your highest energy state is love. The vibration of love has no equal. An environment where love thrives is a space of unlimited energy and potential.

Reflection Mantra (say aloud)
"I have developed an understanding through meditation,
that my soul has agreed to every choice that I've ever made
knowing it would all come together to strengthen my
deep desire to feel, know, give, and reflect only love."

THE HEALING POWER OF LOVE

The steady practice of love brings more passion and purpose into your life. See each day as a canvas upon which you paint and practice love. Love is a powerful medicine that cures all headaches and heartaches. You are incapable of fully loving another until you are loving yourself. You learn how to love by loving more. When you are being loving, you evolve. Love transcends all experiences and emotions. You are love personified, and you are supported by many angels and powerful unseen forces. Love is the most powerful force in the universe and it can be used to change energy fields and change lives. Glory is found in the healing power of love. You are more than capable of accessing and processing your deepest feelings. Learn to love whatever emotion that arises in you and share your realizations with others.

Heart intelligence is the flow of awareness, understanding, and
intuition guidance that we experience when the mind and emotions
are brought into coherent alignment with the heart.
~ Rollin McCaraty

At the center of your being is your divine essence. Listen and feel with your sacred heart, your heart can feel what your mind can't see. Through the practice of love, you are more than capable of healing yourself. Healing replaces any existing fear with courage, doubt with certainty, anger with forgiveness, sadness with joy, and hatred with unconditional love. You are so deserving of the inner peace that accompanies deep and meaningful emotional healing.

When you find yourself in chaos, always respond from your heart.
Whenever you remain focused on love, the love within you expands
and elevates you. This is how you can find joy and peace within.
In this universal alignment, you have direct access to your higher self
for superior perspective and inner guidance. Then the people and
circumstances in your life will no longer control your mood.

The End

Made in the USA
Las Vegas, NV
03 September 2021